1

DISCLAIMER

The material presented in this book is for informational purposes only. Nothing in this book constitutes an offer or solicitation of financial advice and is not intended to provide investment, legal, tax, or other financial advice.

Nothing in this book is to be understood as a give or a suggestion to trade a security. Also, the material in this book doesn't establish a portrayal that the speculations depicted thus are reasonable or suitable for any person.

Such happy ought to subsequently not be depended upon for the creation of any private, monetary, or venture choices. People getting to this data are unequivocally urged to get proper expert counsel prior to making any venture or monetary decision.

Before contributing, kindly keep these straightforward rules: 1.Never put resources into something that you don't have the foggiest idea. 2.Never contribute in light of any other person's opinion.

3.Ask for assist when you with requiring it.

"I'M ALWAYS DOING THINGS I CAN'T DO. THAT'S HOW I GET TO DO THEM."

- PICASSO

For my father My
mother Warren
Jamie
Eric Seth
Sam Jay Pia
Lisa Mira
Mark Chris
Steve Kevin
Eddie
Shantii
Maximus
Khunploy
And my readers

ACKNOWLEDGMENTS

Special much gratitude goes out to a couple of individuals who ventured into my contributing life and gave a few direction and thoughts with flawless timing. Seth Boorstein, who was my optometrist back when I was in secondary school, asked me not long after I moved on from school assuming I'd at any point considered putting the cash I saved into a speculation that would give me more than the bank. He gave me one article to find out about contributing, and the rest is history. On account of Seth for moving me to figure out how to invest.

This book is significantly improved in light of the fine work of my manager, Eric Wyman. His inquiries and ideas subsequent to perusing the composition assisted me with fixing the book's concentration and make things more understood. In particular, he empowered more detail on how perusers could look through a yearly report and use it to acquire a contributing advantage.

Eric additionally urged me to "walk the walk" when it came to utilizing Robinhood, which I know is a famous application among financial backers who are simply beginning. I knew about the application, however I had not really utilized it enough to perceive how it functions so I can share what seems OK - and what could not - for my readers.

Finally, Eric posed extraordinary inquiries in the edges as he altered the composition, and he scrutinized the idea that one ought to hold stocks until the end of time. You can't consider to the grave, all things considered, so how might a financial backer contemplate that multitude of stocks in their record? He squeezed me to clear up the purposes behind contribute. I value the manner in which Eric's immediate inquiries assisted me with working on this book so it instructs with more noteworthy clearness and carries greater delight to the reader.

I would to say thanks to Edwin Chavez, whose drawings embellish the pages of this book. I value his ability and creative mind in drawing animals enormous and little, and they fulfill us when we check them out. Much obliged to you, Edwin, for your glorious commitments to this book.

Finally, I might want to thank the early perusers of the book on Amazon, individuals like Gordon Moore, Liqun Chen, and Michael Gohring, every one of whom read the book and shared their criticism. Their help of the things they preferred and inquiries regarding things that were indistinct assisted me with making this new release such a great deal better. Much thanks to you all.

PART I

GETTING STARTED

1

YOU GOT THIS

Don't be scared.

Everyone can do well in the financial exchange. You have the right stuff, the smarts, and you needn't bother with an extravagant advanced education to effective at contribute. All you want is tolerance, an opportunity to do a little research, and you're well en route to monetary wellbeing. Try not to stretch, don't overreact. You got this.

You can't learn everything about picking stocks in a single book. But you have better stock-picking skills than you might realize. You additionally enjoy benefits that nobody on Wall Street has, and I'm here to assist you with finding them.

Before you begin to contribute, pose yourself one inquiry: When will I want to utilize this cash? You ought to just put cash in the financial exchange that you won't require for quite a while. Temporarily, the financial exchange is unpredictable and individual stocks are unstable. A stock can go half between its high and its low in only one year. Stocks go up, stocks go down, so assuming you have a couple of year time skyline you shouldn't put resources into stocks since it's impossible to tell what will occur temporarily. Be that as it may, the securities exchange is an incredible long haul speculation for any cash you're willing to place on the lookout and leave there for five, 10, 20, or 30 years.

If you want to utilize the cash at any point in the near future, you shouldn't put resources into stocks. Assuming you need to pay for vehicle fixes, in the event that you have Visa obligation, assuming that you want the cash for lease, or to pay educational cost for a youngster went to school one year from now, you shouldn't place that cash in the stock market.

If you're overreacting about putting resources into the financial exchange, don't make it happen. Achievement isn't ensured, and certain individuals feel really awkward losing

cash assuming the market declines. You don't need to contribute in light of the fact that everybody and their neighbor is making it happen. I have a companion who prefers contributing, however at whatever point he purchases stocks he struggles at the market's gyrations; contributing makes him restless and it's not really for him. Not every person is removed to be a financial backer. Contributing requires persistence and the capacity to stay cool under tension. Assuming you think you'll frenzy and sell your speculations when the market goes down, you shouldn't put resources into stocks.

Don't be threatened you simply need the right disposition and a valuable situation to assist you with picking what stocks to contribute in.

2

ACCELERATE YOUR LEARNING

The book you're reading right now is a powerful tool.

If you're getting everything rolling, or on the other hand assuming you've been grinding away some time and your outcomes haven't been just about as great as you trusted, this book will give you a framework that will get you up and running.

Accelerate your learning

The framework I show will assist you with focusing on a couple of extraordinary organizations. It will speed up your learning and assist you with sifting through the commotion so you can zero in just on what matters.

A five-step filtering system

This straightforward methodology gives you five inquiries to pose prior to purchasing stock, and every one is not difficult to recollect on the grounds that it starts with the letters in the abbreviation "PALMS," which represents Profitable, Adaptable, Loyal, Moat, and Sensible.

I want to show you how to utilize this framework rapidly and effectively, a framework you can learn in 15 minutes.

When you begin to ask the five PALMS inquiries you will start to comprehend the insider facts held simply by the best investors.

Here are the five questions:

- **P**rofitable - Is the company profitable?
- **A**daptable - Is the company adapting to changing technology?
- **L**oyal – Does the company have loyal customers?
- **M**oat - Does the company possess a durable competitive advantage?
- **S**ensible - Is the stock selling at a price that makes sense?

How would I realize the best financial backers utilize these inquiries? Since they say so.[1] But in the event that they say as much, for what reason doesn't everybody utilize them? Since they're too simple.[2]

With this framework, you will see exactly how effectively you can make a rundown of incredible organizations and foster a feeling of certainty that accompanies getting these organizations. Assuming you go through around 15 minutes realizing this framework you will acquire a huge benefit over different financial backers and have a stock separating framework you can utilize at whatever point you really want it.

The best issue for most financial backers is that they don't have a trustworthy arrangement of apparatuses they can rely on. Without knowing how to pick the best and ignore the rest you might get yourself untied in an ocean of ticker images and graphs, defenseless against the tides of others' viewpoints or your own feelings. This book furnishes you with devices to utilize what you definitely know to assist you with making brilliant contributing decisions.

3

WHAT DO YOU UNDERSTAND?

Before you can apply the PALMS filter you will need a list of companies that you understand. It's okay if you don't know everything about each company, but if you want to have an edge over other investors you will need to understand a company's most important product or service, how that helps their customers, and whether this company possesses a clearly defined serious advantage.

What I mean by getting to comprehend an organization is to acquire direct insight as a client or sharp eyewitness. In the event that you play X-Box or use Microsoft Word, you get Microsoft's items in a more profound manner than an easygoing onlooker. In the event that you revamp or rebuild your home, you might shop at Home Depot or Lowe's, and you are familiar these stores through experience. An iPhone or MacBook Pro client comprehends their advantages more than somebody who's never claimed an Apple product.

Many easygoing financial backers put resources into loads of organizations they don't have any idea. They catch wind of stocks from companions, they see a TikTok video promoting the following hot stock, or see it recorded as probably the most sultry stock in the market today and believe it's going to the moon like Tesla. Purchasing a stock since you see it continues onward up is more betting than contributing. *Assuming you purchase a stock and trust it goes up you are guessing on cost development without getting the organization.* You will likely have improved outcomes assuming that you purchase loads of organizations you comprehend. As a financial backer, you should understand that when you purchase stock you become a section proprietor of a business.

To provide you with an individual instance of putting just in what you comprehend, science was one of my number one subjects in secondary school. I preferred doing

tests in the lab such a lot of that I studied science in school. After school, when I began contributing, I ended up attracted to organizations the clinical, life sciences, logical estimation, and innovation areas. I find out about these areas than a great many people since I invest a ton of energy finding out about them, and I consider these all inside my circle of competence1. A circle of ability is the branch of knowledge which matches an individual's abilities or expertise.

One of the principal stocks I purchased was Waters Corporation, which assembles very good quality logical estimation gadgets. I'm attracted to logical organizations in light of my advantage in science. This doesn't mean I just put resources into logical organizations, however that is the place where I have an edge. I like the term circle of skill to portray an obvious specialized topic in light of the fact that the visual part of a circle assists you with zeroing in on organizations inside its limits and disregard those outside.

You should characterize your own circle of ability and stick to it. Assuming that you attempt to see an excessive number of organizations or stocks, you will end up not knowing any of them very well.

All incredible financial backers know some region profoundly and they stick to what they know. They become learning machines equipped for retaining data and fostering a profound comprehension of the organizations they are centered around. They need to realize which organizations are superior to other people, and why. Essentially, you ought to have the option to state plainly why one organization is prevailing in its industry and another is second-best. This will help you on the grounds that in difficult stretches the solid organizations proceed to develop and advance while others struggle.

Sitting on your butt and centering for extensive stretches will be a resource in such manner; being occupied and performing various tasks is your enemy.

Your first assignment is to make a rundown of organizations you comprehend. In the event that you don't have extremely profound information in any space simply show restraint toward yourself; you can take as much time as is needed and learn more from now on. Record the names of 10 companies.

COMPANIES YOU UNDERSTAND:

If you don't really want to make a rundown, you can draw a circle and compose the names of organizations inside the circle. The circle doesn't need to be huge, nor does it need to contain many names. The thought is to characterize the regions where you have

better possibilities at progress in light of what you know.

Warren Buffett alludes to the area where you have profound information as your "circle of capability" and recommends you cautiously assess chosen organizations inside this circle2.

> *What a financial backer necessities is the capacity to assess chosen organizations accurately. Note that word 'chose': You don't need to be a specialist on each organization, or even a large number. You just must have the option to assess organizations inside your circle of ability. The size of that circle isn't vital; knowing its limits, notwithstanding, is vital.*

- WARREN BUFFETT

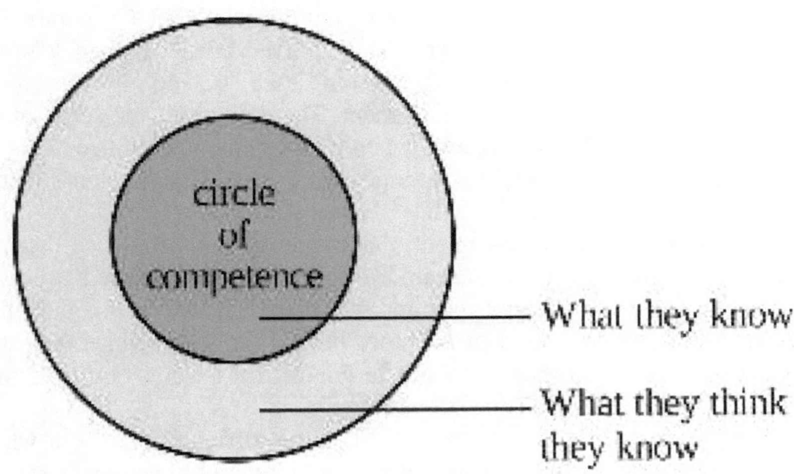

An Euler chart showing the genuine circle of skill contrasted with the apparent circle, for somebody who misjudges their degree of capability. Source: Wikipedia.

An Euler diagram3 gives a visual portrayal of a circle of skill. For a financial backer, it is significant to just choose stocks inside their genuine circle of ability and not meander past its limits. It's easy

to commit errors on the off chance that you don't get a business, and once in a while you can end up losing money.

I'll share a couple of stocks past my circle of capability. Occupied with waste disposal and reusing I have found out about Waste Management and Waste Connections. I've heard they're great organizations, yet I don't know anything about this sort of business, so I stay away. Essentially, I have no benefit with regards to energy organizations: I was unable to let you know the distinction between Schlumberger, Halliburton, Hess Corp, Occidental Petroleum or Concho Resources. I would enjoy no upper hand over the normal financial backer assuming it came to one of those organizations, and I'd most likely get average results.

It doesn't make any difference the number of organizations you know, the only thing that is in any way important is that you know about what you know and can distinguish the edges of your circle of skill. Consider yourself an insightful correspondent, an inquisitive individual who needs to find out about the business. Keep in mind, you're purchasing a piece of the business, and you intend to claim it for quite a while; you must ensure you know what's going on.

For instance, I just read an official statement from Waters Corporation, an organization whose stock I own. The delivery was named "Waters Corporation Announces CEO Succession Plan,"4 and it reported a progression plan yet named no replacement. The delivery made sense of that the ongoing CEO will venture down when a replacement is named. This is a genuine head-scratcher on the grounds that the organization's public statement needed substance.

This uncertain public statement made me uncomfortable. I had put resources into the organization around a decade sooner founded following right after its record of advancement and wide canal. However this indecisive declaration didn't make sense of the story behind the story. Since they were supplanting a CEO who had just been in control for a very long time there more likely than not been a squeezing reason.

As an external financial backer it tends to be difficult to sort out what's truly happening in the background, yet you really want to keep on top of any new improvements in your shareholdings. I'm not saying you need to keep up on the everyday news, except an adjustment of CEO is no joking matter, and you ought to figure the reason why the organization is making a change.

Back to my interest in Waters: I needed to know why the CEO is leaving. Did he get terminated for lackluster showing? Is it safe to say that he was employed somewhere else? Is the organization battling with deals, advertising, or losing ground to contenders? I would say, the unexpected reasons for a CEO's takeoff are

seldom a decent sign for a company.

In my work to sort out the thing was occurring I went to the Water's site, observed the telephone number for financial backer relations, and called to figure out why the organization was going to change the CEO. Why wait around for the evening bombshell CNBC report when it's your money on the line? If you want to be a great investor you have to act like an investigative reporter and get the news firsthand; You can't wait around to catch it on the five o'clock news because by then it will be too late. You can, obviously, wait around like an ostrich with its head in the sand and trust things improve, however that never works.

Nobody picked up the telephone when I called Water's financial backer relations, and my call went to voice message, so I got back to and the secretary let me know that a great many people were out of the workplace working remotely in light of the pandemic. I won't badger the financial backer relations individuals at home, so all things considered I chose to look out for any news that would assist me with understanding the reason why the organization was changing CEOs.

A couple of months after the fact I at last sorted out the reason for the administration change at Waters. The organization held its third quarter 2020 profit phone call and it was driven by the new CEO, Udit Batra. There were not large declarations on the call - it was standard toll with Batra saying he was "respected and grateful for the valuable chance to lead Waters," and he shared his underlying feelings of the organization and plans for the work ahead.

The income call uncovered no justifiable excuse for the change, so I began Googling lastly ran over a Morningstar Analyst Report5 by Julie Utterback that made sense of, "Following quite a while of slips up and disappointing development comparative with peers, we figure Batra will handle a few simpler issues first prior to moving onto additional difficult drives, around advancement for instance, to completely right the ship."

That investigator report responded to my inquiry: Utterback's report explained the difficulties that prompted the CEO change: Waters had followed its friends (Agilent Technologies and Thermo Fisher, to name two) in its fortresses of fluid chromatography, mass spectrometry, and warm examination. The organization was losing business to rivalry, and its stock cost was not staying aware of industry peers. At the point when organizations hit a difficult time, it's difficult to be aware in the event that the issue is with the business or the pioneer. Since it's difficult to change the business and simple to fault the pioneer, the CEO is in many cases the first to go when the organization is attempting to turn things around.

Jack Byrne was a legend in the protection business, and a dear companion of Warren Buffett, who referred to him as "The Babe Ruth of Insurance." Byrne was one of the most amazing circle back craftsmen in the business, and he saved GEICO as it wavered on the edge of bankruptcy6.

Following Byrne's passing in 2013, his companions at White Mountains Insurance Group, where he once filled in as CEO, incorporated this joke that Byrne jumped at the chance to tell.

Jack loved jokes:

When I initially came to GEICO, there were three envelopes in the cabinet with a note: 'when you get in a tight spot, open an envelope.'

So, sufficiently certain, I had an emergency in the principal week, and opened the main envelope. It said 'Fault your ancestor.' I did, and it had exactly the intended effect. In one more month, I had another emergency and opened the subsequent envelope. It said, 'Fault the framework.' Again it worked. In the long run, I was in a difficult spot and I opened the third envelope. It said, 'Plan three envelopes'

- JACK BYRNE

If you heard him make that wisecrack multiple times, you would in any case stand by in calm expectation as you anticipated the response of those consultation it for the first time.[7]

I share Byrne's joke since it's an ideal delineation of how issues lead to fault, which thus can bring about administration changes. In some cases issues at organizations are little and fixable, and at different times they are not. As a financial backer, your ideal circumstance is a stock where you can simply get it and hold it everlastingly; you don't need to stress over the organizations or the executives. This is an intriguing and extraordinary sort of organization, and in the event that you're fortunate you don't need to observe that many stocks like that in your life.

Your principle work as a financial backer is to observe a couple of incredible organizations like that, and for different organizations you should be on guard to vulnerability or issues at the organizations where you own stock. At the point when you read about CEO changes, or on the other hand assuming that you notice the stock is down for a considerable length of time or even a few

years straight, a decent inquiry to pose to yourself is, "Has the business on a very basic level changed?" Sometimes the business is strong, however the climate changes unexpectedly due to a financial event.

The 2020 pandemic decisively changed future possibilities of aircrafts, journey ships, inns, land, eateries, and numerous different region of the economy. A financial backer in these organizations would be confronted with tremendous vulnerability puzzling over whether their stocks could at any point recuperate, and how lengthy it would take.

A financial backer necessities to sort out whether an emergency will seriously disable a business (in which case they could sell), or on the other hand assuming the organization will make due and perhaps arise more grounded. Carriers and voyage ships were hit hard by the infection, yet organizations like Amazon, Apple and Zoom Video flourished as individuals telecommuted. As a financial backer, you really want to sort out whether or not you ought to sell or "hold on" and sit idle.

It ultimately depends on you to sort out whether or not the issues are intended for an organization or all things being equal assuming that they are connected with the economy, and sort out what this might mean for their stocks over the long haul. You can achieve this by perusing and posing inquiries with an end goal to obtain however much data as could reasonably be expected. Once more, consider yourself an insightful columnist doing an anecdote about an organization. Attempt to get a perfectly clear image of its future. You would rather not swiftly sell stock in an extraordinary organization just to lament the choice later.

A couple of days subsequent to finding out about the difficulties confronting Waters, I concluded that the far reaching's financial channel may fall apart. As such, the organization might be beginning to lose business to their opposition. On the off chance that this happens their upper hand may not stand the test of time, and they could lose clients. Any adjustment of the organization's canal is something I need to see as soon as possible. I would rather not stand by and trust that supplanting the CEO at Waters will immediately fix the organization's concerns. Assuming that is a case, the substitution CEO may before long need to "plan three envelopes."

As a financial backer, you should contrast any new speculation opportunity and what you currently own. Assuming the new stock is something similar or perhaps more terrible than what you as of now have it's a good idea to do nothing.

However, on the off chance that another open door guarantees new benefits with less dangers, it turns into a simpler choice. Obviously, with any change there will be vulnerability, yet when the new stock has a few up-sides and less vulnerability, the move might put the breeze at your back.

I observed an open door that I like more than Waters Corporation, so after claiming that stock for over 10 years I sold my portions and reinvested the returns in Veeva Systems, a cloud-based programming organization that gives answers for the existence sciences industry. Veeva partakes in a first-mover's benefit in this specialty, and its developing rundown of more than 950 clients incorporates drug goliaths like AstraZeneca and Merck.[8] Escalating contest among these organizations keeps them got into Veeva's administrations, and the organization faces not many direct contenders, which provides them with a ton of valuing power.

This is actually the sort of chance I search for when I offer one stock to purchase another. Waters was trapped unhappy in light of the fact that their rivals were having their lunch; Veeva Systems is the main competitor right now for a product item sought after by drug and other life sciences companies.

This is a staggering situation for Veeva in light of the fact that they have a long runway to develop their business. This is only the sort of chance I search for as a financial backer - an organization with a solid gathering of momentum clients, great development possibilities, and it's a business I comprehend as a result of my experience in biology.

Similarly, I urge you to get a strong handle of which organizations are driving the way in an industry and which ones are battling. You really want to turn into a specialist in your little corner of the world, and in the event that you don't yet realize a ton pretty much every one of the significant contenders right well that is fine. Regardless of whether you're not a specialist today, you can get familiar with somewhat more at the present time and you'll see more by dusk. *Putting away will in general move cash from individuals who comprehend a little to the people who know a lot.*

To provide you with a thought of what a limited number of organizations you want to see well, perhaps the best financial backer alive is Charlie Munger, and he possesses three stocks: Berkshire Hathaway, Costco, and interests in Himalaya Capital, run by an insightful Chinese financial backer named Li Lu. *Munger has practically all of his cash in only three speculations*, and dribs and drabs in a couple of others. I call attention to this to show that you don't have to possess many stocks as long as you comprehend them well.

The motivation behind causing your rundown of organizations you to comprehend toward the start of this part assists you with zeroing in on organizations that could make wise ventures and wipe out those external your circle of competence.

You will shift the scales in support of yourself as a financial backer by figuring out how to ponder organizations. Block out the impact of individuals who promote specific

stocks. They might be influential moderators, however they are not really gifted financial backers. Even with years of investing experience, I sometimes feel the excitement and find it hard not to be influenced by someone telling me about the next breakthrough in electric cars. Assuming you are the sort of individual who rapidly wants to purchase stocks, consider finding opportunity to comprehend an organization before you purchase its stock.

Never forget that stock is part responsibility for organization, not a ticker image that streaks red and green the entire day. Assuming you have visited "WallStreetBets" you will observer the common conviction that "stocks just go up!" and shock when the numbers become red.[9] Betting on the bearing of a stock is betting. Anybody discussing where the cost will be toward the day's end or tomorrow is conjecturing. To further develop your venture results don't zero in on stock cost development, however rather ponder the organization and how it might fill in the future.

Companies I understand

I'll share a rundown of stocks that I comprehend, or that I'm finding out about quickly. Your rundown will without a doubt be not quite the same as mine in light of the fact that our work, instruction, and encounters are different.

Seven companies I understand well:

1. Adobe
2. Amazon
3. Apple
4. Berkshire Hathaway
5. Carmax
6. Veeva Systems
7. Zoom Video Communications

In later sections I will examine different organizations that are inside my circle of ability and I need to research further. It's fantastic to find out about new organizations, particularly when it prompts another stock to consider for venture. Keep in mind, all you want is one stock to begin; it is far superior to comprehend one organization well than own 20 and not have the foggiest idea about any of them very well.

Many different organizations interest me, however they don't fall inside my circle of capability. Here are instances of 20 organizations in this category:

Abbvie, Agilent, Alibaba, Alnylam Pharmaceuticals, AstraZeneca, AutoNation, Beyond Meat, Constellation Brands, Exact Sciences, Facebook, Fanuc, Ferrari, Fiat Chrysler, Ford, Gilead Sciences, GoPro, JetBlue, L Brands, LuLulemon, Nektar Therapeutics, Novartis, Nvidia, Restoration Hardware, Ping An Insurance, Sony, Square, Tencent, Thermo Fisher Scientific, and Twitter.

I accept you will get much better returns putting resources into stocks you comprehend and skirting the others. You are purchasing portions of organizations and the better handle you have of their cutthroat assets inside their ventures and their drawn out possibilities, the almost certain you'll make savvy decisions.

Charlie Munger makes sense of that piece of being shrewd is monitoring the restrictions of your insight. "It's anything but an ability in the event that you don't have the foggiest idea about its edge," he said. "You are a calamity on the off chance that you don't have a clue about the edge of your competency."10

Buying an apartment or farm

Before we continue, I believe it's vital to recognize contributing and betting. I will give you a fast outline here, and we'll dig further in a moment.

Gamblers and momentary brokers center around the cost. They simply need to get an easy gain and attempt to stretch out beyond others. *Financial backers center around what the business produces over time.*

Short-term traders focus on price

Gamblers and transient dealers center around the value development of the stock. They are worried about whether the cost goes up or down, and they invest energy attempting to foresee its development and make conjectures. Brokers attempt to trade a stock with impeccable timing to secure in a benefit. They couldn't care less about long haul possibilities since they won't possess the stock in five years.

Investors focus on what the asset produces

Investors need to know how much cash the resource will create over numerous years. Whenever they purchase stock in an organization, they become a section proprietor of that business. The financial backer thinks often about the business pay very much like the proprietor of an apartment complex thinks often about the rental pay. How much cash will they gather from occupants in lease, what's the probability inhabitants pay lease on schedule, and how lengthy will it take for the proprietor to get done with taking care of the home loan on the building?

The equivalent goes for a homestead. In the event that you were a rancher, you'd need to sort out how much hay, milk, corn, wheat, eggs, or cheddar your homestead will create, and the amount you will procure when you sell them. A financial backer hoping to purchase the homestead will zero in on what that resource will create over numerous years.

The explanation you put resources into stocks is to get more cash back in the future than you paid when you purchased the stock. An organization can make you more affluent in three ways:

1. The organization can reinvest its benefits, which are designated "held profit" on the grounds that the organization reinvests in PCs, workers, planned operations, innovation, vehicles, stockrooms, and so forth. Held profit can make the organization considerably more important after some time assuming this cycle is completed intelligently.
2. The organization can repurchase its stock when the cost of the stock is far underneath the worth of the offers bought. Assuming an organization does buybacks at modest costs it makes an incentive for investors, yet on the off chance that it follows through on too high a cost while repurchasing it squanders cash and annihilates esteem. Organization chiefs often pay a lot for their organization's stock while completing offer buybacks. One explanation is that chief remuneration is frequently connected to expansions in profit per share. The CEO and leaders benefit from buybacks, which diminish the quantity of offers extraordinary and increment income per share.
3. The organization can disseminate profit to investors as a dividend.

I believe you should be important for the little partner of financial backers who get preferable returns over normal, however you need to remember that admission to this club

isn't free. You need to invest energy sorting out which organizations you genuinely comprehend and decide with high likelihood in the event that they won't just get by yet are probably going to create benefits for a really long time to come.

You can help rich through a couple of savvy ventures where the chiefs settle on a couple of excellent choices every year. You can simply pause for a moment or two and let the organization increment benefits, and your stock will normally increment in esteem as well. Assuming you purchase stock in an organization that makes moronic acquisitions, loses ground to contenders, or has administration issues, you'll wind up baffled as its possibilities break down prompting a decrease in the stock price.

This book urges you to say "no" while taking a gander at inadequately run organizations so you might zero in your endeavors on the really extraordinary ones.

Once you have made your rundown of organizations you will be prepared to run them through the PALMS channel that we'll inspect all the more intently in the following chapter.

PART II

THE PALMS FILTER: LEARN THE FIVE INVESTING FACTORS

4

THE PALMS FILTER

Introducing the PALMS Filtering System

The letters of the word "PALMS" stand for the five most important factors to consider for investing.

Ask yourself these five questions:

- **P**rofitable – Is the company profitable?
- **A**daptable – Is the company adapting to changing technology?
- **L**oyal – Does the company have loyal customers?
- **M**oat – Does the company possess a durable competitive advantage?
- **S**ensible – Is the stock selling at a price that makes sense?

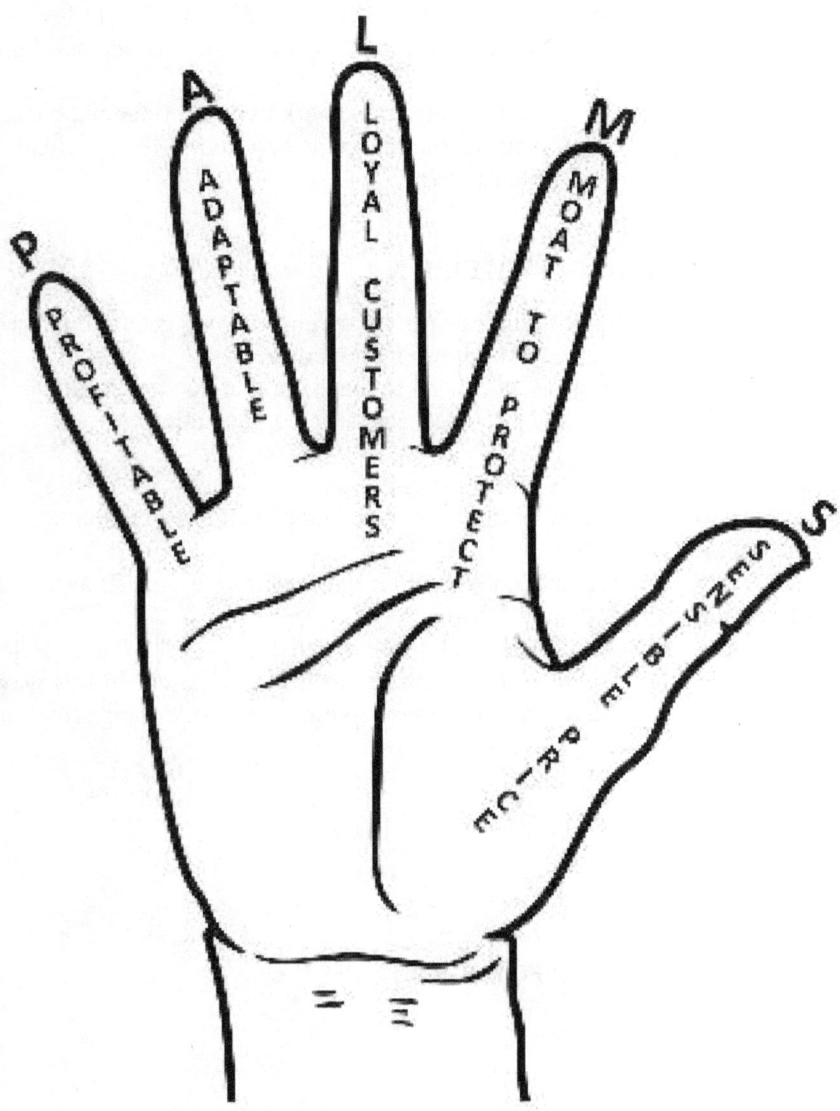

In the last section, you recorded the stocks you comprehend. Presently you want to

sort out whether or not those stocks seem OK as ventures. This strategy expects you to answer five fundamental questions.

These are not hard inquiries, yet you really want to know where to hope to track down the responses, and I'll tell you the best way to utilize the PALMS sifting framework to kill unfortunate venture thoughts and spotlight on the great ones.

I accept that the PALMS separating framework assists a financial backer with taking a judicious, efficient methodology as opposed to the speculative methodology that is more similar to gambling.

WHAT HAPPENS WHEN WE FLIP IT?

Let us test the PALMS sifting framework by seeing what we get assuming we flip the framework and upset our determination criteria.

What sort of organization do you get in the event that you transform the PALMS framework? NOT Profitable - The organization is losing money.

NOT Adaptable - The organization isn't adjusting to new innovations. NOT Loyal - Customers don't feel a solid association with the brand.

NO Moat - The organization enjoys no tough cutthroat benefit and is in this way helpless against competition.

NOT a reasonable cost - The stock is too expensive.

An organization showing these attributes would be a fiasco. In this way, we should not disregard the force of these five elements and their effect on stock selection.

5

P FOR PROFITABLE

Is the organization profitable?

Only consider buying stock in profitable companies. Yes, there are many exciting unprofitable companies that you can consider, but I want to help you pass over the "not yet profitable" ones and invest only in companies that are already successful. I want your investments to grow in value over time. I don't want you to have to wait for struggling companies to turn themselves around (unlikely to happen) or upstart companies to prove they can eventually turn a profit; those are both speculations, or bets based on the hope that things will work out. I want to steer you away from speculation and toward investing.

Yes, it's energizing to be an early financial backer in the new hot stock that everybody is discussing. You could possess Beyond Meat, Slack, Snapchat, Tesla, Uber, or some other hot stock that everybody is purchasing at madly exorbitant costs, however the issue with these "hot stocks" is that for each organization that will succeed, a few will fall flat. It is challenging to tell the champs from the washouts early. Assuming you pay an excessive amount to purchase a hot stock there is a decent opportunity it will decline quickly in cost and you may never make back the initial investment. The main rule in contributing is "don't lose money."

With contributing, fortunately you don't need to hit the ball throughout the fence without fail. You simply need to pick organizations That are now beneficial, previously developing and you get to benefit alongside them for a long time. There are less restless evenings, less pressure, and less trusting that your karma will change. That is all important for the betting or theorizing attitude. That

is the reason I urge you to skirt the not-yet-productive organizations and put resources into those that are as of now successful.

When you're initially beginning, I believe you should try not to purchase stocks that you trust will one day bring in cash yet are not yet beneficial. Stick to stocks with demonstrated track records.

Stick with big, easy decisions

Buffett made a bet that a minimal expense S&P 500 file asset would beat the profits of the best and most splendid multifaceted investments administrators north of 10 years. He won the bet by a surprising margin, and he said the last example from the bet is to "Stick with huge, 'simple' choices and shun activity."1

In portraying the bet, Buffett said, "During the 10-year-bet, the 200 or more multifaceted investments chiefs that were involved in all likelihood made huge number of trade choices. The greater part of those administrators without a doubt took significant time to consider their choices, every one of which they accepted would demonstrate favorable. During the time spent contributing, they concentrated on 10-Ks, talked with the executives, read exchange diaries, and consulted with Wall Street analysts."

Buffett's point was that awesome and most splendid with their professional educations and examinations can't beat the inactively overseen S&P 500. Luckily for you, you don't need to fulfill multifaceted investments clients, you don't need to produce returns for anybody however yourself. You enjoy benefits that Wall Street financial backers don't have, to be specific the direct information you have as a client and spectator of your loved ones and their buying propensities. You might see a few organizations better than Wall Street professionals.

For instance, I might have improved a few stock buys a decade prior assuming I had stayed with putting resources into organizations I purchased from routinely and appreciated. My first telephone (after a flip telephone) was an iPhone. I go to Starbucks frequently and my neighborhood store is stuffed all the time. I shop from Amazon. Those are three organizations not too far off that I might have put resources into from the beginning since I had a ton of direct information about them. Obviously, I didn't on the grounds that I picked another loads of organizations I knew less well.

Fortunately, I took in certain illustrations en route. Whenever you arrive at the finish of this book you'll perceive the way I utilized the PALMS separating framework to pick one of those organizations and purchase its stock.

I'm bringing up this benefit since you presumably realize three organizations well, organizations very much like Amazon, Apple, and Starbucks that I

referenced previously. As you read on in this book I trust you'll make sure to record them on your rundown so you can monitor them and comprehend if they pass the PALMS filters.

Later in this book I will show you how to peruse a 10-K. This report will show you assuming an organization has great monetary wellbeing, with more money than obligation on the monetary record, and it will likewise show you assuming the organization is profitable.

It's conceivable assuming you are simply beginning that you have never seen a 10-K. I'll just tell you now that a great deal of times individuals simply call it the yearly report, or a "report" for short. The yearly report completely is a bound booklet with a cover that has the organization's name on it and the year it's giving an account of. It additionally contains a letter to investors from the CEO and data about the yearly gathering and an intermediary articulation that is documented before a yearly gathering when an investor vote is required.

All of these things consolidated together include the "yearly report," and you can arrange it for nothing from the organization or download a duplicate as a PDF from the organization website.

I will let you in on confidential so you will not be confounded: Form 10-K is likewise alluded to by a similar name, "yearly report." To keep things straightforward to you I will simply utilize the term 10-K, and I will show you what to search for when you read one so you can become certain and familiar with the dialects of business and investing.

Find out if the company is profitable

I knew nothing about budget summaries when I purchased my first stocks, and a portion of my initial speculations have conveyed incredible returns that keep on compounding in esteem. These were simple choices to make-I just purchased shares in incredible, productive organizations with canals selling at a reasonable cost. Likewise, you can settle on savvy choices without perusing monetary reports. Notwithstanding, I really do accept that over the long haul you'll be in an ideal situation when you can foster familiarity perusing yearly reports, and assuming you're like me, you might even begin to appreciate them.

I like perusing the letter that the CEO keeps in touch with investors toward the start of each yearly report. These letters and the whole report are allowed to download and will give you a decent vibe for the organization. I like to peruse Jeff Bezos' letter to Amazon investors, and I think you'll likewise find it a good investor letter to begin with. Additionally, look at Warren Buffett's letter to Berkshire Hathaway investors and the yearly reports of any organization that intrigues you. You can simply Google the yearly report and perused it minutes after the fact. Remember that when you are beginning you will be best served by just putting resources into organizations that are beneficial. I will show you what to look for in the 10-K to ensure any potential organization is productive. You should figure out how to peruse a pay explanation, and I will show you how.

Downloading a company's annual report

You can download any public corporation's yearly report by visiting the organization's site, and afterward go to the "Financial backer Relations" segment of their site. Then download the yearly report (it's a free download, as a rule in PDF structure). Go to the "Financials" area where you will see as the "Pay Statement" and furthermore the "Total Sheet."

Screenshot of The Walt Disney Company's financial backer relations page. All public corporations have financial backer relations pages on their sites. You can arrange a yearly report, and have it sent to you, or you can download it from the site. To download the yearly report from the site, simply click the "Financial backer RELATIONS" route tab on the top row.

1. Do an Internet look for the organization name followed by the words "yearly report."
2. Click on the "Financial backer Relations" tab.
3. Locate the "Yearly Report" connection and snap that.
4. Once you have downloaded the yearly report, read the "Letter to Shareholders" to get an outline of the company.
5. Flip through the yearly report until you get to Form 10-K which contains the budget summaries. You need to see as the "Pay Statement," which gives data about the organization's profitability.

Income statements show a business's revenue, expenses, and income.

The pay proclamation shows the entirety of a business' pay and costs over the latest quarter and recent years. Search for the line at the lower part of the page that says, "Total compensation." If it has brackets around it, that is a misfortune, it is unfruitful to mean the organization. On the off chance that the number has no brackets, the organization is beneficial. See the screen captures on the following page for clear models.

The Tesla pay explanation that follows covers the period from 2013 until 2016. This monetary data was current at the hour of this book's first printing, and as you'll see, the organization had lost cash consistently. I composed in those days, "Tesla gets an opportunity to rule the electric vehicle market and become an innovator in independent driving innovation, however there is no assurance this will occur, or that it will occur as the executives trusts." Nobody knew at that point assuming Tesla would effectively increase vehicle creation and offer an adequate number of vehicles to become beneficial. No one realized the organization would join the S&P 500. At that point, That's what I composed assuming you purchased the stock you would be facing a challenge that Tesla's arrangements may not happen as expected, and in the event that you paid a lot there was a genuine opportunity you may never see the stock value return to your price tag. That surely ended up being mistaken; while the Tesla organization has continuously become productive, its stock cost has soared to more elevated levels and gave no indications of easing back down.

Tesla's development has come at a blistering speed not many might have guessed when this book was first imprinted in 2018. Elon Musk's organization at last became productive in 2020 with its unique Model S and Model X and has likewise had solid interest for the Model 3 and all frameworks are go for the send off of the Model Y in 2021. Tesla has turned into an anomaly and made a religion like following and enormous interest for its vehicles around the world. This doesn't guarantee a positive outcome for the following ten years, however it plainly shows how an unrewarding organization can make something happen. Up until this point Tesla has surpassed many financial backers' assumptions by becoming beneficial as well as acquiring Wall Street's acknowledgment into the S&P 500.

At the hour of this book's first printing back in 2018 I stated, "There isn't anything innately amiss with conjecturing in an organization like Tesla, and some theory can be solid. I simply believe you should be clear when you are contributing and when you are guessing, and assuming you're beginning, I think it appears to be legit to stay with putting resources into organizations that are now making money." That is still obvious on the grounds that you limit your gamble by putting resources into productive companies.

The problem with investing once companies are already profitable lies in the possibility that you might "miss the boat" with companies like Tesla if you require that every company achieve profitability before you invest. It seems like an inconsistency in a part about putting just in beneficial organizations, however here and there absence of quick benefits doesn't anticipate failure

- Amazon and Tesla ring a bell as organizations that were unbeneficial in their initial days.

I think it's a good idea to make a different venture represent "theory" or "wagers" in light of the fact that occasionally you will need to put resources into an organization that hasn't yet passed each PALMS channel. This gives you explore different avenues regarding your ventures access a way that keeps them in a different record, so you make these wagers with a more modest total (express 10% of your investible cash) and furthermore keep the theoretical wagers separate from your speculations. I energize trial and error in this manner as long as you make the qualification to you between these "wagers" on not-yet-productive organizations and more normal interest in organizations with beneficial track records.

Let's gander at the pay articulation for Tesla's 2017 yearly report, and afterward the 2020 yearly report so you can think about the two for yourself.

Look at the line that says, "Net gain," which is one more way of communicating "benefits." A look at Tesla's pay explanation will uncover dollar sums in enclosures, which demonstrate misfortunes. All in all, Tesla has never been profitable.

Tesla was neither productive at that point, nor was it a solid possibility to intensify venture gets back with okay of losing cash. It addressed a speculative endeavor and not a venture. Everything changed emphatically for Tesla in only a couple of years. The organization turned productive, the stock cost got so high (past $1,000 an offer) that the organization did a 5-for-1 stock split, and it effectively turned into the most smoking stock on the lookout and a consistent wellspring of interest at WallStreetBets.[2] Let's investigate Tesla's pay proclamation from Tesla's 2017 yearly report, which was highlighted in this book's first edition.

Tesla's pay explanation from 2017. See the "Overall gain" line which shows benefits. The brackets around the total compensation figures show that at the time Tesla was unrewarding at that point. Tesla became beneficial in 2020, and the pay figure is currently positive.

When perusing a pay explanation, any numbers inside brackets demonstrate misfortunes. Tesla has never been beneficial, and this is much of the time the case with organizations in "fire up" mode who presently can't seem to bring in more cash than they pay in costs. Many new businesses reinvest income into developing the organization and along these lines, it can require numerous years for another organization to show a profit.

While it's not terrible for an organization to be unfruitful, for this book I need to urge you to zero in on organizations that have exhibited the capacity to be productive. This way you don't need to gamble with putting resources into an organization that may never turn a profit.

Tesla stock might merit considering from now on, particularly in the event that the organization can deliver electric vehicles and sell them at a benefit. At the point when this occurs, Tesla stock might seem OK as a clever speculation. Simply remember for the present that if you have any desire to put resources into an organization like Tesla, you are trusting the organization will become beneficial. That is betting, and it's unique in relation to contributing, where you definitely realize the organization is profitable.

You absolutely never need to mistake betting for putting either in your reasoning or in your contributing record. To put resources into an organization that isn't beneficial, and it's a hypothesis, I suggest doing as such in a different record, so you keep theory separated from putting resources into your brain, and furthermore in your accounts.

As you will find in the 2020 Tesla 10-K (which covers the earlier year) the organization had a $775 million misfortune in 2019. The organization was not yet beneficial, however its misfortune had diminished three years straight. The following year, 2020, would be the primary year Tesla acquired a profit.

[illegible]

[illegible]	[illegible]	[illegible]	[illegible]
[illegible]	[illegible]	[illegible]	[illegible]
[illegible]			
[illegible]	—	—	[illegible]
[illegible]	[illegible]	[illegible]	[illegible]
[illegible]	[illegible]	[illegible]	[illegible]
[illegible]	[illegible]	[illegible]	[illegible]
[illegible]	[illegible]	[illegible]	[illegible]

Income explanation from 2020 Tesla 10-K (investigating the earlier year) shows a $775 million misfortune in 2019.

During the schedule year 2020 numerous things at last fit properly: the organization became productive, the stock split and was added to the S&P 500, and Musk became probably the most extravagant individual on earth. Throughout the entire existence of Tesla, 2020 was the year the world at last recognized Tesla was a genuine company.

On the accompanying pages, we should investigate Lowes and Disney as instances of beneficial organizations. While there is a great deal you can find out about budget reports from now on, all you really want to do now is center around the "Overall gain" line at the base. Assuming you see it's a positive number, the organization is beneficial. How about we investigate Lowes' pay statement.

Lowes' pay articulation. By checking out at the line that says "Overall gain" you can see that Lowes' has consistently expanded its profits.

Look at the "Total compensation" line and you will see a steady movement in total compensation (benefits) for Lowes. This pay explanation shows that Lowes has produced consistently expanding benefits. How about we investigate Disney's income

statement.

Disney's pay articulation. Assuming that you take a gander at the "Net gain" line you can see the continuous expansion in benefits from 2014 through 2017. Disney has consistently expanded benefits despite the fact that benefits for 2017 were not however incredible as the earlier year's profits.

Profitability seems to be a decent first obstacle for any organization you're thinking about for speculation. Assuming you stick to organizations that demonstrate they can bring in cash over the long haul you will be doing great to developing your speculation after some time. Purchasing stock in organizations that you trust will become productive is a hazardous bet.

I think there is a major compulsion to purchase organizations that have energizing innovation. New things are intrinsically cool and I think financial backers like possessing load of the following new thing. Individuals purchase portions of Tesla, Snapchat, and numerous different organizations that have invigorating possible prospects, however without benefits, all they need is terrible information for the organization or economy to genuinely hurt its future income potential and influence the stock cost to fall rapidly and unexpectedly.

In outline, the main things an organization can offer investors are either the guarantee of future income (benefits), share buybacks at reasonable costs, or the dispersion of profits to shareholders.

If there is a lot of uncertainty about whether a company will become profitable, then it's a gamble. In the event that an organization has proactively demonstrated productivity, vulnerability diminishes and on second thought of betting one is contributing (albeit kindly recollect that some gamble is generally present, regardless of how well you have investigated a given company).

6

A FOR ADAPTABLE

Is this organization ADAPTING to Technology?

When you consider a stock, ask yourself if the company is adapting quickly to technology in a way that helps customers. If they are, then you may be onto something. Read customer reviews, check out the organization's application in the Apple Store or Google Play, and check whether clients give it good grades. You need to get a beat of which organizations are truly "getting it" and developing with the times to work well for their clients. Assuming an organization you are thinking about is driving the way by quickly adjusting to new innovations and offering types of assistance and items that draw in clients, then its stock deserve further consideration.

Let me share the case of Progressive Insurance, a vehicle insurance agency. I as of late discovered that Progressive purposes innovation to screen its clients' driving propensities so it can offer safe driving limits. Presently, assuming you put the "Elder sibling" issue to the side I'm not completely certain I'd need my driving checked by my insurance agency the organization could really be giving something valuable to customers.

If Progressive tells a customer they can save $150 if they'll allow tracking of the speed they drive, etc., that might be a competitive advantage for the company. Suddenly they can segment their customers into those that are low risk for accidents and give them a discount. Not all customers will want this, but those that do can save more money. In this way, technology can help the company gain loyal customers.

I'm not a specialist on Progressive or vehicle protection, but rather it seems like the organization is driving the way as a guarantor by adjusting to new innovation in a manner that might possibly help clients. Assuming you search for organizations that are on the main edge like that it will assist you with sorting out quite a bit early which organizations may be acquiring an upper hand. I don't possess Progressive stock, however I've followed their stock for a really long time. It's one of the stocks I wish I had purchased when I originally found out about it quite a while back! I verged on getting it a long time prior, however there were different stocks that seemed like better open doors, so I got them all things considered. I essentially have barely any insight into vehicle protection to give me an edge on that investment.

Today's organizations need to adjust rapidly to changing innovations or they will die. Organizations in all businesses need to adjust to satisfy purchaser needs and remain in front of the opposition. I will share a couple of instances of organizations that adjust rapidly to new advances. There are many different organizations taking care of the assignment well, yet I'm simply going to specify a couple of natural ones to provide you with a thought of a few organizations on the main edge of innovation.

Amazon

Amazon CEO Jeff Bezos concluded right off the bat that his organization would constantly advance for the benefit of, and fixate on, their clients. He trusts that client must let Amazon know what they need; Amazon must develop for customers.

A culture of advancement drives all that Amazon does, and it's urgent to the "Consistently Day 1" mantra that Bezos claims is one of the keys to Amazon's prosperity. The organization holds the energy and head to advance by continuously thinking like the organization needs to concoct and adjust to client wants and needs. He said that the objective is for Amazon to never turn into a "Day 2" organization, where individuals become accustomed to doing things the manner in which they've generally been done when individuals settle in or complacent.

One of the keys to Amazon's prosperity is that the organization is continuously considering ways of making its items less expensive and convey them quicker. Bezos says that clients will constantly need quicker delivery.

"A client won't ever be miserable in light of the fact that you conveyed their request surprisingly quick," Bezos said. Adjusting to buyer needs and making new advances like Amazon's Echo is only one way that Amazon develops to get it done quicker and less expensive than its competition.

Square

Square allows independent ventures to acknowledge charge cards for retail exchanges rapidly and without any problem. The organization has adjusted well to changes in retailing, and this looks good for its future. A considerable lot of its clients utilize Square registers, and numerous others utilize a card peruser to allow them to acknowledge installments on their phones.

An illustration of Square rapidly adjusting to innovation: when Mastercards changed to chip peruser innovation from swipe innovation, Square immediately made chip-perusers accessible. This quick transformation of new innovation settled on Square a simple decision for an accomplice when Starbucks concluded it required a retail location telephone installment framework in its stores; Square was the regular fit.

By constantly improving to turn into a valuable element of the retail scene, Square guarantees that it won't effectively become unimportant. The organization has even made it feasible for independent companies to make solicitations on their cell phone and send them to clients who can then pay the receipt with a charge card. This advancement makes it simple for private ventures to get compensated rapidly and effectively, and it guarantees a solid exchange for the purchaser as well.

Square's business quickly adjusts to changes in innovation. They have reliably worked on their applications and site contributions to expect the necessities of private ventures and further develop the retail experience.

Starbucks

Starbucks has adjusted to the changing advanced world by fostering an application that is turning out to be intensely utilized by its clients. The Starbucks application allows clients to pay for espresso, food, or other store items utilizing the application, and when they make buys they acquire "stars," which are essential for a steadfastness program that rewards standard clients with free beverages or food when they arrive at a specific number of stars earned.

The organization has perceived the fast reception of the application, with more clients joining consistently since the application has been being used. Clients can arrange utilizing the portable application before they show up in a bistro and get their orders once they show up. Portable requesting has not been without its concerns, as certain stores have had issues staying aware of the quick reception and in-store clients have needed to stand by as versatile orders are filled, yet these bottlenecks have been tended to and will probably be fixed with time.

Companies that incorporate innovation and make it simple for clients to utilize their cell phones will probably well from now on, while those that are delayed to adjust are definitely going to be outcompeted by more deft rivals.

7

L FOR LOYAL

LOYAL clients drive fruitful brands

Loyalty can't be measured with math. Understanding the loyalty that customers have toward a product or service is an enormous advantage to an investor, and you can use your first-hand knowledge of customer unwaveringness as your contributing edge.

When you go to a most loved store and it's generally loaded with clients, you witness client conduct that Wall Street examiners don't have the foggiest idea. Whenever you notice that your companions generally will more often than not buy a similar sort of telephone, or all prefer to go to similar eateries, or utilize similar informal organizations, you are seeing subtleties that give you an edge. You presumably definitely know which organizations have steadfast clients and which ones don't.

Wall Street investigators might be great with regards to numbers, but since they invest such a lot of energy dissecting monetary information and perusing profit reports they pass up helpful direct data that clients like you have. Simply think, each time you purchase things on the web or visit stores you are finding out about organizations. You definitely realize a ton about a few organizations just in light of where you spend your cash. Your interesting retail encounters give you a gigantic benefit over monetary experts who come up short on sort of direct experience you have with the brands you like.

To contribute effectively, you as of now have an edge - due to your experience as a reliable client of a few brands. For instance, a companion of mine has an iPhone as well as his folks. He wouldn't buy some other brand other than an iPhone. Their entire family is faithful to Apple - their

iPhones as well as they generally own MacBook Pros. I realize numerous families like this, where they own every one of the most recent gadgets, from iPads to smartwatches. This dedication to the brand biological system guarantees the organization's prosperity for quite a long time to come.

I'm certain this story is recognizable to you. Regardless of whether you have an iPhone, you can perceive the number of individuals around you pick Apple items beyond a shadow of a doubt, and when their gadgets crush they go spirit to Apple for a substitution, never thinking about another brand. At the point when you join dependability with different variables in the PALMS framework, you'll begin tracking down productive organizations with predictable deals and a developing base of new customers.

Thinking as far as brand reliability gives you an additional an apparatus in your tool stash that numerous financial backers don't utilize. Whenever you consolidate it with different channels, you're beginning to utilize a "multi-pronged" way to deal with contributing. There is an expression, "To a man with a mallet, each issue is a nail." Well, in the event that all you use is math to assess organizations, you're in a tough spot when you go facing somebody who considers immaterial elements like loyalty.

Loyalty is a powerful tool

Understanding client reliability is an incredible asset, and it's not unexpected neglected or underestimated while checking stocks out. The people who get occupied by moving ticker images and seeing diagrams can frequently miss the fundamental, straightforward, and strong consequences of zeroing in on an organization with steadfast customers.

Loyalty is a strong, yet difficult to-characterize business trademark. An organization with faithful clients spends less cash since they don't need to find new clients continually. Faithful clients are energetic to such an extent that they become a wellspring of free promoting for the brand, and they bring an elevated degree of energy for an organization's items and administrations that cash just can't buy.

I scanned Google for "brands with most steadfast clients" and found this list.1 Brand Keys, the consultancy that directed the study, analyzed 740 brands to show up at these 20 companies:

1.Amazon (online retail)
2.Google
3.Apple (tablets)
4.Netflix
5.Apple (smartphones)
6.Amazon (video web based) 7.Samsung
8.Facebook
9.Amazon (tablets)
10.YouTube
11.Dunkin' Donuts
12.Nike
13.Trader Joe's
14.WhatsApp
15.iTunes
16.Hyundai
17.Starbucks
18.Ford
19.PayPal
20.Domino's

Loyalty is a strong benefit driver for every one of these organizations, and how clients connect with them. These brands have a spot in clients' souls. You can't learn of these "immaterial" characteristics by searching through fiscal summaries, yet in the event that you're a client of these (or other) organizations, you likely have some exceptional comprehension about client dependability that another financial backer probably won't have.

It's a good idea to join client devotion into a separating framework. It lets us know that clients feel something "enthusiastic" or a "bond" to the brand, and over the long run this can assist an organization with battling off rivalry. You can refer to it as "tenacity" or dependability or anything that you'd like, however the bring back home message here is that on the off chance that you can distinguish organizations with solid steadfastness, you are probably going to have observed an organization that will keep on having a surge of income from these clients for a long time into what's to come. As may be obvious, from the rundown above, Amazon and Apple show up two times on the rundown for unwaveringness for various products.

Many organizations have steadfast followings. I will give one model underneath that I know well in light of all of my experience as an expert picture taker. I use Adobe items (Photoshop and Lightroom) consistently and I additionally know numerous photographic artists. I can say without a second thought that each genuine picture taker utilizes Photoshop.

One method for characterizing steadfast clients is rehash purchasers who will be probably not going to change to a contender since they have a unique interaction with the

brand; they feel a practically unreasonable association with the items, and they use them reflexively. Assuming the brand name is likewise an action word, that is a decent sign that the organization has steadfast aficionados: think Google, FedEx, Photoshop, etc.

ADOBE SYSTEMS

Adobe makes the best photograph altering programming framework on the planet. There are no not kidding contenders out there. Without a doubt, there are numerous other picture altering programs accessible, however none where the name of the program has turned into an action word like "Photoshopping."

Photographers, planners, producers, visual craftsmen, and advertisers have shaped a solid bond with Adobe's items like Photoshop, Illustrator, InDesign, Lightroom, and Premiere. The steadfastness is extreme; I don't know about a solitary picture taker who doesn't utilize Photoshop, nor do I know any creators who don't utilize Illustrator or InDesign regularly.

Adobe has a large number of faithful clients for its items and appreciates almost no contest as a result of the "exchanging cost" of time that clients of programming like Photoshop, Illustrator, and Premiere would need to spend figuring out how to utilize a contender's items. This "learning obstacle" guarantees that Adobe will hold steadfast clients for a really long time to come.

I long for the days when I could purchase the CD with Photoshop on it and simply utilize that for eternity. Whenever I'd paid for it, I could involve it however much I needed, and exactly the same thing for Microsoft Office, which included Word. When you purchased the plate you could utilize that program for eternity. I recollect when Adobe changed from the CD model to the SaaS model, where you paid month to month. Numerous photographic artists were disappointed that we could never again purchase and own the plate. All things considered, we were being constrained into an interminable expense on the grounds that the expense for the circle turned out to be restrictively high.

It's been around 10 years now and I'm paying $11 per month, which works out to about $1,320 to utilize Photoshop. One advantage for clients who buy into their month to month cloud-based programming is that they don't need to pay an enormous direct front acquisition of $300 or more to purchase the product. The moderately low month to month charge (which is even lower for understudies) makes the product available to everybody. In the past it used to require investment to buy and trust that Photoshop CDs will show up via the post office, or to pay for a product download and need to go to the site and physically introduce the product and any updates when they became available.

The cloud-based membership model is charged month to month to a Mastercard, and the product is refreshed consistently and can be designed to download naturally to your PC, which is straightforward and smoothed out for the client. The common month to month charging is great for Adobe and its investors in light of the fact that their photography and video altering programming have a huge number of clients and essentially no contest. Adobe gets unsurprising income and when they need to get more cash, they can raise the month to month charge by a gradual sum and immediately increment incomes. Clients probably won't care for the expense increment, yet they are so dependent on the item and need it for their imaginative work that they won't stop utilizing the product on the grounds that the cost expanded a dollar or two.

While the present circumstance might be sub-par for the client according to an estimating point of view, as an investor it's an astounding plan of action in light of the fact that the expense of capital is low. There are no trucks, trains, extensions or apparatus expected to maintain the business. Primarily human development and inventiveness drive the business, and the organization needs to continue thinking up new items and safeguarding its licensed innovation; the expense of capital is low, and benefits go on in perpetuity.

GEICO

GEICO is a completely claimed auxiliary of Berkshire Hathaway Corp., and keeping in mind that you can't buy stock in GEICO straightforwardly, an extraordinary illustration of an organization has steadfast customers.[2] The organization's general expense structure is low, and by selling straightforwardly to the purchaser they try not to need to pay lease for retail stores, and so forth. Their administration is first rate, and that implies they hold clients, and this thusly makes for a strong plan of action since they have incessant reestablishments, which converts into less cash spent attempting to hold clients. They basically restore and this interaction makes keeping clients inexpensive.

Customer unwaveringness is a colossal piece of GEICO's prosperity. They have a huge and developing client base, and these clients spread all through the world, step by step developing the organization's market share.

As you look for organizations to put resources into, you would be all around served by searching for organizations like GEICO that have a minimal expense structure, have been developing their piece of the pie reliably over the long run, and have numerous unwavering and cheerful customers.

NIKE

Nike is one of the extraordinary unsurpassed brands and has a devoted following. There's not much to be said about the organization that individuals in everything nations don't as of now have the foggiest idea. They began with shoes and stretched out into a wide range of athletic attire. They have stayed applicable over the course of the years to more seasoned ages while speaking to the youthful. I as of late gotten the opportunity to warm up to a family in my line on a departure from San Diego to Seattle, and one of their children, who was in secondary school, let me know he has a business of purchasing new Nike shoes when they are delivered and exchanging them on eBay at a colossal markup.

I'm not conscious of the entirety of the publicity and fervor about the Nike brand, yet the organization has figured out how to engage individuals and make shoes that are worn for sports and style, yet gathered as fine art. Nike without a doubt is familiar with this fascination (they spurred the interest for it, all things considered) and they have figured out how to deliver a few tennis shoes in restricted supply so as not to flood the market.

The consistent development with their finger on the beat of style and sports and sharp attention to the significance of shortage all highlight the mental prowess of an organization that rides the universes of craftsmanship, games, and business. The manner in which they associate with their clients' hearts and psyches, as well as their bodies, guarantees that the Nike brand will stay applicable for a long time to come. As a financial backer, you need to be watching out for organizations with numerous reliable clients; they make rehash business and predictable income almost certain, and work on your chances of long haul venture success.

Loyal customers mean repeat business

Loyal clients equivalent recurrent business, and that implies an organization that has faithful clients doesn't need to continue to burn through cash to hold clients, or continually track down new clients. Repeating surges of pay are the backbone of an organization, and the organization with faithful clients has a consistent wellspring of new money streaming in each day.

Leaders

Leaders are a vital piece of any organization that you consider for venture. I have felt that the "L" in the PALMS framework could mean "Pioneers" rather than Loyalty (and a contention could be made that it ought to). To be clear, when I talk about leaders I'm talking about the CEO of a company, and in some cases, such as Berkshire Hathaway's leaders, Buffett and Munger who together have led the company for decades. Remarkable administration can be difficult to measure, however it drives an organization's prosperity. Consider Jeff Bezos' job at Amazon, Elon Musk's persistent energy and vast thoughts at Tesla, or Steve Jobs' inheritance at Apple and you can perceive how a pioneer with a strong vision for the future can give gigantic advantages to their organizations. Remove that pioneer and the organization sinks. Numerous incredible organizations have meandered erratically with normal pioneers. For instance, Microsoft appeared to have lost it contact for a long time when Steve Ballmer was CEO. Satya Nadella succeeded Steve Ballmer in 2014 and turned the company around. Before becoming CEO, Nadella was in charge of Microsoft's cloud and undertaking bunch, answerable for building and running the organization's figuring stages. When he became CEO Microsoft rose to noticeable quality in light of the progress of Microsoft Azure's cloud infrastructure that Nadella had pioneered.[3]

It is difficult to let you know how to know which pioneers are extraordinary and will keep on settling on smart choices later on, and which ones will wallow. These things are many times evident afterward, yet in the event that you're not putting resources into a huge organization with a notable CEO then it is extremely challenging to measure the ability and trustworthiness of somebody you've never met.

For this explanation, I pick "Steadfast" for the L since we as a whole have some familiarity with brands with faithful clients, and brands like Nike, Google, Apple, Starbucks, Disney and Amazon will presumably be around in 30 years (or more) and they will bring in much more cash in the future than they are presently. Pioneers will go back and forth, and some will be great and some will not, and it's an undeniably challenging errand for any financial backer to attempt to survey the ability of a CEO before investing.

I would agree that that it's a good idea to advance however much you can about the CEO, to observe some YouTube recordings, read articles, and obviously, read the organization's yearly report before you contribute. Assuming that you concur with the CEO's letter and you accept they get their industry, the organization, and get as great a thought as could be expected assuming that you think they are gifted and skilled enough to

do their arrangement. This is an exceedingly difficult assignment (to anticipate the erratic) yet to that end contributing is so difficult. Assuming you purchase stock in an organization that is controlled by individuals with high uprightness and with heaps of ability, all the other things will fall into place.

So I adhere to my recommendation of looking for organizations with faithful clients who are probably going to return and purchase over and over, yet I likewise need to urge you to keep your eyes out for the other "L" and search for pioneers with high moral principles and the capacity to settle on a couple of incredible choices each year.

8

M FOR MOAT

A moat provides a durable competitive advantage

Another method for communicating this benefit is to say that a monetary canal makes a business impervious to rivalry. An actual canal is a profound, wide trench encompassing a palace frequently loaded up with water as a guard against trespassers. Additionally, a business canal is a difficult to-copy quality that makes it challenging for contenders to duplicate or poach customers.

You need to put resources into organizations extend their monetary channels to guarantee they get by and flourish. A channel keeps contenders from taking their clients and diminishing piece of the pie. On the off chance that you put resources into an organization without a channel, any new contender that goes along can take its customers.

A monetary "channel" makes it difficult for an organization's rivals to poach their clients and remove their portion of the overall industry. Financial backers frequently consider it a "channel." Great organizations extend them to keep the intruders away!

A moat provides protection

An illustration of a wide-canal business would be Coca-Cola. Assuming I gave you $100 million and advised you to attempt to make a cola that could surpass Coke, you were unable to get it done. It's been attempted ordinarily by numerous cola organizations, however the

Coca-Cola brand is too solid in the personalities of clients, which furnishes the organization with a wide moat.

Starbucks has a wide-canal on account of the organization impact of their and worldwide brand. It would be extremely hard for a new company to make a comparative organization of bistros and a conspicuous item to take piece of the pie from Starbucks. Many have attempted, however none have succeeded.

Disney is another wide-canal organization. They have Mickey Mouse, films like Star Wars and the Marvel series, Pixar, ABC, ESPN, 12 amusement parks, 51 hotels. It would be almost difficult to take Disney out of business.

The equivalent could be said to describe Alphabet, Google's parent organization. A larger number of individuals use Google for search than some other web crawler. And more people watch YouTube videos than videos on any other platform. I would agree that Google has a wide canal since supplanting them with another internet searcher would be hard. Whenever individuals need a solution to an inquiry, they "Google" the response. I figure it would be incredibly difficult to change that way of behaving, henceforth the wide channel for Google.

McDonald's wide canal depends on a brand that is unmistakable all around the world and its size and scale would make it very difficult for any organization to go along and attempt to uproot them as the cheap food pioneer. There are different organizations whose brand names and worldwide arrive at give them wide channels: Burger King, KFC, Pizza Hut, and Taco Bell are among the best wide-canal worldwide brands.

In dress and footwear, Nike likewise has a wide canal; it would be difficult to dislodge them as the main shoe and athletic wear organization on the planet. Adidas has attempted with restricted achievement, thus has Under Armor, yet the notable Nike swoosh characterizes the brand and gives a channel that is unmatched in the athletic footwear and clothing industry.

What are the characteristics of a moat?

According to Warren Buffett, "The best canal… clearly… something that would be safeguarded from any contest. Ordinarily, profit are controlled in organizations like that. The ideal item is something that costs a penny and sells for a dollar and is propensity forming."1

Speaking of Coke, Buffett additionally said, "In 1886 some person named John Pemberton down in a drug store in Atlanta hit some unacceptable nozzle or something and it came out and consistently, basically from that point forward, deals have expanded around the world."

To accentuate the worth of a wide canal, Buffett said this solid cutthroat position assists give you certainty the business with willing bring in cash into what's to come. "Essentially, you're attempting to find something where you think you have an exceptionally high likelihood about being correct about foreseeing the procuring power out 5, 10, and 20 years… and that relies upon serious positions."

Examples of companies without moats

The cutthroat semiconductor chip market makes it difficult for organizations to have a channel. There are such countless organizations contending (frequently on cost) to sell microchip chips to organizations like Amazon, Google, and Microsoft

- and that is simply naming the tremendous organizations. There are numerous more modest PC and cell phone organizations that need chips to control their devices.

These chips are seen by quite a few people as a ware item, since they can be make inexpensively and on a huge scale, and they are fungible to the degree that one focal handling unit (CPU) can frequently be traded with one more without a change in performance.

This makes it exceptionally hard for chip producers to separate themselves. Intel has been the biggest and most prevailing chip producer, yet they are battling of late with extreme contest from organizations like Nvidia, AMD, and Micron Technology who are on the whole nipping at Intel's heels. To additional important point Intel's canal, a few organizations like Microsoft have chosen to make in-house chips to supplant Intel processors on Surface laptops.[2]

At one time, chip vendors went after the best ergonomics, programming, and a few selective elements. Presently, everything is changing on the grounds that immense organizations like Apple, Huawei, and Samsung have begun to foster their own framework on-chips (SoC) to separate at all levels. Google is currently fostering its own chips for Pixel cell phones and Chromebooks.[3]

If you're a financial backer reasoning of putting resources into a chip organization you ought to at minimum kPresently about this new circumstance. Now, not exclusively is contest among chip creators themselves warming up, yet the colossal tech organizations who purchase from them are choosing to tweak chips to their own particulars and lower costs by getting fabricating house.

An article in the Wall Street Journal distributed as the refreshed release of this book went to press declared that Intel and Nvidia currently face new dangers from their previous clients. Organizations like Amazon, Google, and Apple - who used to be their clients. *It is really a no-channel business when your clients abruptly become your competitors!*

Back in the day the clients were more modest and the chip organizations like Intel were the tremendous beasts. Presently the innovation organizations are commonly bigger than their little chip suppliers.[4]

The article made sense of how Amazon has decided to tweak contributes a work to speed up and bring down costs."Amazon this month uncovered another chip that, it expresses, vows to accelerate how calculations that utilization man-made reasoning gain from information." Amazon has proactively planned processors for its distributed computing arm, called Amazon Web Services (AWS), including the cerebrums of PCs known as focal handling units.

If you're considering putting resources into a chip maker remember that right now the opposition is warming up from different producers around the world, however from their clients too.

For total honesty - as you will find later in this book - I own load of NVIDIA Corporation, which is known for its strong and sought-after illustrations handling units (GPUs). I'm mindful of the cutthroat idea of the chip business, and I know that building a moat is so difficult. In any case, I chose to contribute in light of the fact that the organization has exceptional administration and I accept the nature of Nvidia's GPUs places them in a class of their own.

What are a few different instances of organizations without canals? The Gap makes clothing, yet so do many different retailers, and clients can undoubtedly switch between retailers. Likewise for Urban Outfitters and their Anthropologie image. They need more of a specialty, a solitary excellent item, or estimating that gives them a serious advantage.

The camera producer GoPro is one more illustration of an organization with no canal: they make a little activity camera, yet there are numerous little camera makers, and with more individuals having a cell phone camera with them consistently, it's getting harder for GoPro to persuade clients to purchase their specialty camera. GoPro as of late left the robot business yet needed to exit in view of steep contest from DJI and other robot producers. This is on the grounds that GoPro had no channel; there was nothing about their robot that made it unique and held the opposition back from taking their customers.

Within the eatery and inexpensive food industry, many organizations have no canal since clients can undoubtedly go to another café at whatever point they need. Gold country Airlines, Chipotle, Delta Airlines, Dunkin Donuts, Fiat Chrysler, Ford, General Motors, Lululemon, Subway, Tesla and United Airlines, Volkswagen, and Wendy's are only a couple of models. There is no reliability, no exchanging costs, serious industry rivalry, and low hindrances to section that make it trying for eatery administrators to assemble a monetary moat.

Moats on moats on moats

The inquiry you might have right currently is "How can I say whether an organization has no channel, a limited canal, or a wide canal?" and that is an incredible inquiry. No "one" answer exists for each organization. All things being equal, channels change over the long haul contingent upon how well the organization develops its upper hands. The following are three inquiries to decide whether a canal exists:

1. *Could contest at any point go along and drive them bankrupt? For instance, it could be truly difficult to design a cola that could beat Coca-Cola; many have attempted and failed.*
2. *Is there any other person who sells this item or administration? For instance*, with Adobe Photoshop - there could be no other photograph altering programming like it. With regards to the huge outlet center, Costco has a wide channel as a result of their seriously faithful clients, organization of stores and low costs. Those things make it incredibly difficult for a contender to attempt to open a contending chain of rebate warehouses.
3. *Does the organization have elusive resources, exchanging expenses, or organization impacts that make a canal? For instance*, Costar Group constructed its business giving business land information to institutional clients and acquired the matter of numerous business intermediaries. After Costar turned out to be deep rooted, it gained LoopNet and Apartments.com; these two significant arrangements established the organization as the prevailing web-based business land commercial center and information business. Costar Group has four primary business lines: CoStar Suite, Commercial Property and Land, Multifamily, and Information Services. No other business land organization even verges on giving CoStar's commercial center access and information, and these resources make a network impact that adds to the broad's channel. Representatives are

> anxious to pay the membership based income for admittance to CoStar's information and postings since they are a vital piece of their work, and this reliance makes a tenacity that keeps merchants faithful and makes exchanging costs high. This lollapalooza of variables, joined with the absence of contest, give Costar Group a wide moat.

LaCroix carbonated water, a result of the National Beverage Corporation (FIZZ), has been famous for the beyond quite a long while, surpassing most other water brands. Does LaCroix have a canal? I have to strongly disagree, it's simply water and despite the fact that it has a pleasant assortment of flavors, I figure any organization could make bubbly water and put it in a pretty package.

Most organizations don't have canals when they're getting everything rolling since they haven't had sufficient opportunity to fabricate one. At last, assuming that they do their best and execute immaculately, they might get a channel. Tesla is an illustration of an organization with no canal yet. This is basically on the grounds that they don't sell the main electric vehicles, and there's a great deal of contest liable to show up in the following couple of years. It is conceivable that Tesla could turn out to be so prevailing in the business that individuals who need an electric vehicle naturally purchase a vehicle from them. If that happens then we can say they have a wide moat. However we are currently at the beginning phases in Telsa's day to day existence cycle, and the organization doesn't enjoy a getting through cutthroat benefit yet.

Apple doesn't have a wide canal, yet they truly do have a thin channel as I would like to think. The explanation it's not wide is that there's no changing expense for a client to purchase a Samsung or Google cell phone or a PC from some other organization. The iPhone has appreciated solid purchaser devotion, yet there's nothing that would keep clients from purchasing their telephones somewhere else assuming Apple had a few issues improving and a contender concocted the following extraordinary smartphone.

The iPhone is by all accounts a remarkable superficial point of interest nowadays, and the steadfastness got from their swarms of faithful clients give them this restricted channel. Assuming they some way or another turned out to be prevailing to the point that Google, Samsung, or Amazon could never poach its clients, then Apple would partake in a wide channel. While I would attribute a thin canal to Apple, I don't consider it possessing the wide channels that Amazon, Costco, Disney, Nike and Starbucks have in their industries.

If you stick to considering organizations that have wide channels you won't need to stress as a lot over that organization being driven bankrupt by a canny contender. The presence of a channel gives certainty the organization will persevere and stay impervious to competition.

9

S FOR SENSIBLE

"Never purchase a stock following a significant ascent or sell one following a significant drop."

- BENJAMIN GRAHAM

Everybody wants to buy stocks when they're cheap. For every buyer, there is a seller, and one of those people wind up on the better side of each trade.

Buy a stock at a sensible price

You want to move the chances in support of yourself, and one way you can do this is by not overpaying when you purchase stock. In the event that you follow through on something over the top and the stock cost drops a ton it might never recuperate to the cost you paid.

One great method for holding this back from happening is to be focused with regards to choosing the amount to pay. As such, *don't overpay.* Presently, this letter of the PALMS framework is one of the hard ones to decide with full confidence on the grounds that nobody knows the specific cost. You're in an ideal situation attempting to think of a scope of costs that check out instead of pick one cost as it tends to be difficult to know the exact thing a stock is worth. You need to observe a reach inside which you believe you're addressing a reasonable cost. Assuming the organization is superb, you'll really do fine and dandy after some time regardless of whether you get it soil cheap.

There is nothing off about purchasing stock when it's modest, however these mispricings are not normal. You want a tolerance and best of luck to purchase the portions of an extraordinary organization at a major markdown, yet these open doors show up each so often.

If you can purchase underneath the reasonable, or fair cost, you're getting what Benjamin Graham called a "edge of wellbeing." It is by and large the thing it seems like-a cost you pay that is less expensive than what you consider a stock is work. Graham encouraged investors to buy at a discount, so if you decide that a stock is worth $100 and you seek a 25% margin of safety — to make up for bad luck or bad math — then you should aim to pay $75 or less. The contrast between those two figures is your edge of safety.

You need to abstain from paying excessively. Try not to climb into a stock since every other person is getting it. In the event that you're purchasing at an untouched high, you're in many cases paying excessively. Once in a while you must be patient and trust that the market will serve you a reasonable price.

Waiting for a sensible price

Sometimes you can mess up assuming you stand by excessively lengthy at your reasonable cost. You can commit the error of not accepting a stock since you lounged around trusting that the cost will get extremely low and that never happened.

My greatest mix-ups have been mistakes of "oversight" instead of blunders of "commission." I have lived in Seattle for quite a long time, and I've seen organizations like Amazon, Microsoft, and Starbucks ascend to noticeable quality directly in front of me. Microsoft had proactively turned into an enormous and effective organization when I showed up in Seattle, yet Amazon was only a gleam in Jeff Bezos' expression at that point. It turns out he and I went on street outings from the east coast (he drove from New York, and I drove from Boston) in 1994. I was moving to Seattle to begin my vocation as an expert picture taker, and Amazon had not yet sold its first book.

So, I got to see the Amazon story unfurl before my eyes. It was not generally clear that Amazon would overwhelm such countless enterprises and have such a lot of outcome in both retailing and cloud computing.

Many individuals who worked at Amazon could see that something unique was going on at the organization, however numerous external spectators saw another Internet organization battling to make money. Even in the early 2000s, many people thought Amazon might never turn a profit. However a ton changed in the following ten years or two. Perhaps the most key change was the small

examination of Amazon Web Services (AWS),1 which has ended up finding actual success for Amazon.

AWS got a huge early advantage on its opposition while building its distributed computing stage on display while contenders like Google, Microsoft, and Oracle lounged around and sat idle. However, by 2015 it was becoming evident that something noteworthy was going on as Amazon was overwhelming web-based retail as well as turning into a strong power in distributed computing as well.

I saw that more individuals had become individuals from its "Prime" dependability program that offers facilitated delivery, and they purchased things from Amazon constantly. I had been a Prime part for a really long time, and I saw that I was depending on Amazon for a ton of purchases.

Amazon was exchanging the $500 territory in 2015 and around then the stock appeared to be costly to me. You need to understand that it had been in the $200 territory a few years sooner, so paying $500 an offer was over two times that and appeared to be costly. I sat around idly for a lower "passage point" that won't ever appear. Amazon's stock kept on moving to $600, $700, $800, and afterward $900 en route to $1,000. The stock never appeared to be modest, however with the progression of time this is on the grounds that undeniable that those would have all been great section focuses for a long haul investor.

If you comprehend an organization well, and you're a dependable client, and you see that large numbers of your companions or family like purchasing from the organization don't stand by too lengthy to even consider purchasing the stock.

Amazon is an uncommon illustration of strong, supported achievement that pushes its stock cost higher over the long haul while never getting modest. Supplies of incredible organizations decrease in value at regular intervals, and these amazing open doors allow the patient financial backer an opportunity to purchase shares at a discount.

These purchasing open doors in some cases happen during brief periods, from half a month to a year or more, during which the stock cost might decline by 30%-half. These are important open doors for the pre-arranged financial backer who has cash prepared to invest.

Sometimes lounging around sucking your thumb and hanging tight at a lower cost can leave you with lament. I have tracked down a methodology that works for me. I like to get some stock - not my whole situation without a moment's delay, however a set number of offers or dollar sum - so I don't pass up a major opportunity through and through. It's an approach to settling on the choice to put resources into another stock, and dunking my toes in the pool rather than simply plunging right in. It assists me with turning into a proprietor and furthermore keep my

choices open to purchase more offers assuming the cost declines not long after that first purchase.

In 2020 I chose to purchase portions of Veeva frameworks, a supplier of cloud-based programming answers for controlled enterprises that incorporate biotech, life sciences, and drug organizations. Veeva's industry-explicit applications for these organizations grabbed my attention on the grounds that as a previous science major with an interest in science, I know about organizations like GlaxoSmithKline, AstraZeneca, Bayer, Biogen, Eli Lilly, Merck, Moderna, and Novartis, all Veeva Systems clients. At the point when I understood these organizations rely on Veeva's cloud-based programming to maintain their organizations, oversee deals and client records, and meet administrative necessities, I chose to put resources into Veeva.

The more I read about the organization I understood there was almost no contest for programming planned explicitly for these organizations, which flagged that the organization has a wide canal. I definitely realized the organization was beneficial, *versatile*, and had faithful clients, so when I saw a canal existed the main thing left was to sort out a reasonable cost. I read Veeva's Value Line Survey, Morningstar exploration, and whatever else I could find about Veeva prior to concluding that cost was $275.

I'd settled on this choice over the course of the end of the week, and on Monday morning I was prepared to purchase my first piece of stock. I saw the cost floating around

$277 an offer, well inside what I considered a reasonable cost, so I began building my position.

I will probably purchase more Veeva shares, however until further notice I'm fulfilled in light of the fact that I purchased stock as opposed to sticking around watching it take off. I could be able to purchase more offers at lower costs by pausing. Once in a while tolerance pays off and you understand you bring in cash sitting tight at modest costs. Assuming Veeva drops to $230 that would be a 16% edge of wellbeing in light of my gauge of a reasonable cost. There's an opportunity the stock cost won't climb and ever get that modest, which is the reason I like purchasing that first lump. Another advantage is that when you have a dog in the fight, you're bound to see the cost decline. In the event that you're not a proprietor, you could not notice.

Patience pays off

I purchased my first portions of Berkshire Hathaway around 15 quite a while back. After that underlying buy, I generally needed to purchase more offers, yet the organization had performed well, and the cost generally appeared to climb. By 2015 the stock was selling for $140 an offer, not entirely set in stone to be a reasonable cost. I had cash saved to put resources into the organization, and I needed to check whether I could get it at a discount.

After hanging tight for seemingly an unfathomable length of time, in January 2016 I at long last got my opportunity since financial exchanges cratered in view of monetary feelings of dread. On one occasion I saw that the offer cost for Berkshire "B" shares tumbled to $125 an offer so I felt free to purchase more offers. Watching out for a stock you like and showing restraint can work for you as well. The market's gyrations are not there to show you anything, and occasionally they serve you a fabulous bargain.

Benjamin Graham's recommendation to never purchase after a significant ascent by and large appears to be legit. Be that as it may, with loads of developing organizations like Amazon, which has been developing at an arid speed for quite a long time, sitting around idly at a reasonable cost can keep you from truly purchasing the stock.

You can avoid the error of paying a lot by taking note of Graham's advance notice not to purchase a stock just after a significant ascent in cost. Once in a while you should be patient and sit tight for a reasonable price.

The second piece of Graham's recommendation not selling after a significant drop - is a lot more straightforward to do, as I would see it. It doesn't expect you to do anything. You should simply fight the temptation to sell when the market declines. This is simple for me since I fight the temptation to sell, yet I'm holding on to purchase more offers when they get modest. As Buffett says, "Be unfortunate when others are insatiable, and eager when others are fearful."

How to determine a sensible price

I might want to show you a basic approach to deciding the reasonable cost to pay for a stock.

There are a couple of steps included on the grounds that I needed to separate this into little noteworthy things. There is some math included too, yet don't be frightened away by it. It's not confounded, there are no equations to memorize.

For this model, how about we utilize the Disney Corporation. Through my underlying exploration, I discovered that Disney owns:

- 21st Century Fox
- Mickey Mouse
- Star Wars
- Marvel
- Pixar
- ABC
- ESPN

Also, Disney possesses 12 amusement parks, 51 retreats, 387 stores, has more than 195,000 representatives, and $55 billion in revenue.[2]

1. You want to decide a "reasonable cost" per share for the organization you're thinking about for speculation. To do this you really want to make a stride back and structure an assessment on what the entire organization is worth-you were a private purchaser and purchasing the organization in its entirely.[3] This next recommendation is significant: *Do not take a gander at the organization's stock cost prior to doing this computation; it might add a predisposition to your choice*. My own valuation of the organization if I somehow happened to purchase the whole organization inside and out is $275 billion.
2. Next, you really want to decide the quantity of exceptional offers, which are the offers accessible to exchange. Finding this number: simply do a web-based search utilizing the organization's name and the words "remarkable offers." You can likewise take a gander at the organization's yearly report on Form 10-K and the all out number of offers extraordinary are on the cover page's simple. I recently Googled "Disney Corporation remarkable offers" and observed the absolute recorded as 1,810,000,000 shares.
3. Divide the dollar sum you would pay for the whole organization (from step #1) by the exceptional offers from step #2. The

numerical resembles this: $275,000,000,000 ÷ 1,810,000,000 = $151.93 dollars for every offer. That is the sum you consider a "reasonable cost" to purchase the organization on a "per share" basis.

4. Now that you've settled all alone (fair by the provided cost estimate) you can investigate the ongoing cost statement for Disney stock, which, as of December 18, 2020 is $172.89. Disney is selling at a cost about $21 above, on a "per share" premise, what I would pay for the whole business. This is more than I consider a "reasonable value," the S in the PALMS filter.
5. In the model above, assuming that you paused and had the chance to purchase Disney stock at a cost in the neighborhood of $121.55 you would get a 20% rebate on a "per share" premise from your assessed "per share" worth of $151.93 . You can allude to this markdown as a "edge of wellbeing," and we will talk about this idea below.

What if your math is inaccurate?

It might appear to be quite difficult for you to shape an exact assessment on the worth of an organization. There are Wall Street experts who burn through 50 hours seven days zeroed in on only one organization, or a couple of organizations, and their examination is definite. That doesn't imply that they have a more profound comprehension of an organization than you, however I maintain that you should see that certain individuals commit a great deal of time to learning.

It's difficult to pinpoint a precise dollar sum that an organization is worth, yet I accept it's more practical to think of a scope of dollar sums that you gauge an organization to be worth. For the valuation of Disney displayed above I began with the all out esteem that I showed up at for the organization, which was $275 billion. I can't say with accuracy that the figure is exact, however there is a scope of values that would inexact the worth of the whole business.

Margin of safety

Margin of safety4 is a designing term that can be applied to venture. A financial backer attempts to purchase stock just when the provided cost estimate is far beneath the worth of the offers. This is to compensate for human blunder in assessing the worth of the stock or more terrible than normal karma. Consider driving a weighty vehicle over a scaffold. Assuming you're driving not too far off in a 9,500 pound truck and need to cross a scaffold with a sign that says, "Weight Limit 10,000 Pounds," why risk it? You're barely making it and the outcomes can be deadly. All things considered, continue to drive not too far off until you get an extension worked to securely endure 20,000 pounds-which provides you with an edge of safety.

With stocks, assuming you attempt to purchase shares when the cost addresses a rebate to a reasonable cost (esteem financial backers frequently call this inherent worth) on a "per share" premise. The contrast between the cost you pay and the worth of what you get (your gauge of the inborn worth) gives the edge of safety.

Ideally all stocks would be bought with an edge of wellbeing, however all things considered, smart financial backers are content to buy loads of brilliant organizations at reasonable prices.

Margin of safety for Disney

We can carve out a time of security by deciding a stock value that gives a 20% rebate to our gauge of the "per share" esteem. The cost of $121.55 per share for Disney stock gives a pad to shield us cost us from botches in our math or more awful than normal luck.

Note: The costs above for Disney, beneath for Costco, and all through this book are absolutely utilized as illustrative models, and they don't propose an assessment on engaging quality of Disney, Costco, nor some other organization referenced in this book.

Let's run Costco through the PALMS filter

Profitable: Yes. Costco is beneficial. It creates a gain prior to selling a thing as a result of participation duty. It brings in a minimal expenditure selling merchandise, and huge amount of cash selling memberships.[5]

Adaptable: Yes. Costco's model endures the strongly serious retail climate through cost authority. This technique involves keeping up with the most minimal costs conceivable. Walmart additionally utilizes this system, however Costco's model is more versatile in light of the fact that its participation base is stepped back to go through their enrollment benefits which guarantees rehash business.

Loyal: Yes. Costco has an unwavering client base with solid traffic and 90% US participation restoration rates. Costco's enrollment program permits it to undersell the opposition and guarantee client unwaveringness, and its it is zero to publicize financial plan. Costco's clients return to outfit the full benefit of their enrollment dues6.

Moat: Yes. Costco has a wide channel that permits Costco to develop portion of the overall industry regardless of extreme contest.

Reasonable: Yes. Costco's stock is selling at a reasonable cost. *Without taking a gander at the stock cost first,* I would gauge the incentive for the whole organization (what I'd pay assuming I were a private purchaser buying the entire business) at $164 billion. On the off chance that we partition this number by the 441,520,000 offers exceptional [$164,000,000,000 ÷ 441,520,000] we show up at a "per share" worth of $371.44.

As of December 18, 2020, Costco's stock is right now 367.00/share. It is selling for somewhat short of what I esteem it on a "per share" basis.

If we take the ongoing stock cost: $367.007 x 441,520,000 (shares exceptional) = $162,037,840,000 - which is the market cap of the organization. This implies on a "per share" premise the market esteems all portions of Costco at a worth that is not exactly the $164,000,000,000 we showed up at for the whole organization. It is absolutely impossible to show up at an exact incentive for a whole organization with a serious level of sureness, however our gauge above is very near the market esteem in view of the "per share" price.

Therefore, the stock cost is selling somewhat under a reasonable cost in light of my $164 billion valuation of the whole Disney company.

Obviously, I would like to purchase shares assuming the open door went along to get a lofty rebate - at a cost around $330 we'd get a 10% markdown, and at $294 we'd get a 20% discount.

Three tips to avoid buying after the price has gone up a lot

1.Remind yourself that you are putting resources into an organization. You would rather not overpay for the organization. As Ben Graham said, "A stock isn't simply a ticker image or an electronic blip; it is a possession interest in a real business, with a basic worth that doesn't rely upon its portion price."

2.Ask yourself "Would I be blissful claiming this organization for the following 5 to 10 years?" Only purchase assuming your response is "yes."

3.Look up the right now provided cost estimate for the stock. Is it at or almost a 52-week high? In the event that the response is "yes," trust that the cost will fall. Make an effort not to purchase at the untouched high.

This approach will guarantee you don't pay the "most exorbitant cost" ever for the stock. The issue with this approach is that assuming the stock cost never declines, you may never purchase the stock.

Seth Klarman, a regarded esteem financial backer, made sense of the advantages of purchasing a stock at a low cost. "We as a whole realize that the proof shows that when you enter at a low value, you will have great returns, and when you enter at a high valuation, you will have unfortunate returns," Klarman said. "Keeping away from full circle trips and transient destruction empowers you to be around for the long term."8

It's good to have stock prices do nothing

Warren Buffett mentioned this observable fact back in 1963:

"... Our business is one requiring tolerance. It shares little for all intents and purpose with an arrangement of high-flying fabulousness stocks...It is for our potential benefit to have protections do nothing pricewise for quite a long time, or maybe years, while we are getting them. This focuses up the need to gauge our outcomes throughout a satisfactory timeframe. We propose three years as a base... "

Final thoughts about paying a sensible price

Investing is a craftsmanship that requires inventive reasoning and imagination.

If math abilities guaranteed contributing achievement, then, at that point, every one of the mathematicians on the planet would be more extravagant than Bezos.

Having great numerical abilities and applying them to perusing monetary reports won't make you a decent financial backer. Math and numbers are just a single device and a little one at that with regards to contributing. Probably the best ventures are made with only a basic comprehension and a story you can tell about an organization in a couple sentences.

This is the reason the PALMS separating framework is a helpful device; it gives a multidisciplinary system that requires some subjective dynamic that you essentially can't do with math alone. At the point when you join a few unique elements benefit, versatility, reliability, channel, and reasonable price - you get a more hearty mosaic of the organization that loans to you "seeing" a considerably more complete picture.

Each of the PALMS channels requires exploration and reflection, and your capacity to monitor various things in your mind and mindfully gather them to recount the organization will turn into an innovative flow. No two individuals comprehend an organization in the equivalent way.

At the day's end, an organization might pass each channel aside from the reasonable cost. Assuming you accept the organization checks out on any remaining models aside from cost, considering "settling up" for quality. You might pay more than you need at first, however assuming it's an incredible organization and you hold as long as possible, your venture could appreciate 100 percent, 300%, 500%, or more.

If you feel positive about each and every piece of your thinking, you might need to feel free to purchase a stock that appears to be costly. You can continuously begin by purchasing a limited quantity and add all the more later. This way you will keep away from errors of oversight (you hang tight for quite a long time and never purchase as the organization develops and the stock cost goes up). You can limit your lament by purchasing stock in an organization, regardless of whether it appears to be a piece costly. Extraordinary organizations are only sometimes modest in light of the fact that different financial backers perceive their true capacity, and, similar to you, are willing to

pay a premium for them.

Stocks won't be costly constantly. Assuming you pause, there are market separations at regular intervals or something like that. To the patient financial backer, this can give open doors. In a forthcoming section, "Buffett on Edge," we will see a picture that shows how Ted Williams realized which pitches he could hit for a high normal. Likewise, a financial backer sits tight for the perfect stock at the ideal cost, with the benefit over a baseball player since you can't get called out on strikes. As Warren Buffett said:

"What's great about contributing is you don't need to swing at each pitch. You can watch contributes come one inch above or one inch beneath your navel, and you don't need to swing. No umpire will get down on you." You cause problems, Buffett says, when you pay attention to the group reciting "Swing, hitter, swing!"9

- WARREN BUFFETT

Finally, you should genuinely believe in your realities and thinking. As Benjamin Graham said:

"You're neither right nor wrong in light of the fact that others concur with you. You're correct on the grounds that your realities are correct and your thinking is right - and that is the main thing that makes you right. Also, assuming that your realities and thinking are correct, you don't need to stress over anyone else."

- BENJAMIN GRAHAM

A last pondered addressing a reasonable cost. You should show restraint; since you need to contribute right currently doesn't imply that costs are reasonable (or modest). At the hour of this composition, stocks have been getting more expensive for the beyond 10 years without a genuine drop in costs. I would say that it's highly likely that while prices are not entirely overpriced, they are not cheapeither.

Keep as a main priority that effective financial backers like Warren Buffett and Charlie Munger, and numerous others, became rich since they were contributing on occasion when stocks sold at outrageous limits. Stock costs went no place during

unstable times somewhere in the range of 1966 and 1982. Savvy financial backers exploited these exceptionally low costs for stocks and purchased intensely then. Those low buy costs added to their wonderful returns in the many years that followed.

At the hour of this composition, stocks are not selling at low costs in any way shape or form. There are not very many pieces of the market, maybe with a couple of special cases, that anybody could say are reasonably valued. Notwithstanding, for the patient financial backer, there will be chances to purchase stocks when markets become silly and financial backers are fearful.

10

USE YOUR OWN PALMS FILTER

In earlier chapters, you've already written down a list of companies you understand. We've gone through the process of asking the five questions about each company, but I want to make sure it's easy for you to put this to work.

Now that you restricted the rundown to organizations you see well, for every one of them pose yourself these inquiries about the company:

- Is it **P**rofitable?
- Does it **A**dapt to change?
-

Does it have **L**oyal customers? Does it possess a **M**oat?

- Is the stock selling at a **S**ensible price?

If you want an update on concluding if an organization meets these rules, simply flip back to the beginning of this section. Go through and ask yourself inquiries. Get inquisitive. Try not to be baffled on the off chance that you don't have a response, it simply implies you should be patient and learn more.

If anything is too challenging to even think about getting it or any inquiry is too hard to even think about replying, go ahead and throw it into the "Excessively Hard" heap and continue on toward something simpler. Keep in mind, you don't get additional focuses for putting resources into tough spots. You get compensated when the organization performs well, and every one of these means in the PALMS sifting framework stacks the chances in your favor.

PART III

STICK TO WHAT YOU KNOW

11

A NEW WAY

INVESTING IN THE TECH AGE

Today's tech stocks are developing a lot quicker with less unsurprising possibilities than the organizations that were famous back when The Intelligent Investor1 was composed - before the age of the Internet. You can glean some significant knowledge from that book, yet assuming you depend on it you will be in a difficult situation with regards to surveying organizations like Amazon, Alphabet, Apple, Tesla, and Nvidia, among others. I gained some useful knowledge from Benjamin Graham and enthusiastically suggest his book, however you should refresh your acquiring with another ability set to put resources into present day times.

Companies like tech goliaths Google (Alphabet), Amazon, Apple, Facebook, Microsoft, Netflix, Tesla, and Zoom overwhelm the economy today. Be that as it may, in the earlier century it was significantly more straightforward to take a gander at an organization's resources, liabilities, pay articulations, and incomes and make a sensible conjecture about what benefits could resemble from now on. I'm not saying it was simple, yet things didn't change as fast in business then as they do today.

I have perused a significant number of the best books about contributing, and I have watched endless meetings including the best financial backers alive. The more I read, the more I realized that investing books from the 1940s, 50s and 60s used examples of companies that were current then, but are less dominant or no longer in business today. The stock models were of organizations associated with the railroad, oil, farming, power, phone, and tobacco industries.

The stocks referenced didn't have anything to do with PC equipment, programming, the Internet, distributed computing, web based video, electric vehicle or

innovation stocks on the grounds that a considerable lot of these advances didn't even exist.

The old contributing books show numerous helpful illustrations contributing, yet numerous models are presently not important in the flow mechanical age. The present financial backers merit a book that shows them how to apply the insight of the past to stocks in the present current age.

Since no book like this right now exists, I chose to keep in touch with one myself. This book is not the same as large numbers of the books you'll find about the securities exchange that show transient exchanging, specialized examination, portfolio hypothesis, how to peruse stock diagrams, and how to anticipate momentary stock cost developments. These exceptionally speculative instruments are not liable to work with any consistency, and they are incredibly challenging for financial backers to master.

Combining great ideas with flexibility

I composed this book for you, the advanced financial backer, who needs to purchase stocks in the present quickly developing business sector. This book combines the fundamental wisdom of "old school" investors with a forward-thinking approach that helps an investor make high-velocity decisions to keep pace with rapidly changing companies in the stock market today.

My point recorded as a hard copy this book is to show a better approach to contribute; one that holds the smartest thoughts of financial backers like Warren Buffett, Benjamin Graham, Peter Lynch, and Charlie Munger, and gives new standards to assist financial backers with making quick, top notch choices about quickly developing organizations. Graham lived before the Internet existed, and Buffett has conceded that he doesn't have a comprehension of innovation that he would expect to put resources into tech stocks.

The initial architects of contributing never had some awareness of the Internet. Assuming you just gain from individuals who turned out to be great financial backers during a prior age you will not have the instruments important to assess the present quickly developing distributed computing, Internet, and innovation companies.

Consider index funds or ETFs

There is something I really want to impart to you before you make a plunge and find out about the subtleties of the framework that I frame in this book. It's exceptionally difficult to beat the market and a great many people will not. The people who in all actuality do beat the market struggle with outflanking it over lengthy periods.

Anyone can beat the market with a couple of hot stocks for quite a long time or a year, however proceeding to beat the market is troublesome. I'm well aware that for many people, picking stocks provides a sense of excitement similar to gambling. Nothing bad can be said about feeling those feelings, yet you

ought to ensure they don't make you make awful decisions.

Index assets and list trade exchanged reserves (ETFs) seem OK for financial backers who would rather not invest energy exploring stocks. While this book teaches dynamic financial backers, perusers ought to know that record assets and ETFs are compelling ways of catching the market's return.

One methodology is to fabricate a strong contributing establishment with enhanced list assets or ETFs. For instance, an absolute financial exchange list reserve or a S&P 500 record store furnishes financial backers with a differentiated portfolio. Whenever you have put resources into the file reserve for some time, you can continuously add corporate securities later.

I began with common subsidizes when I began contributing. I was in my 20s and I realized nothing about putting resources into stocks at that point. As

I learned more I made a couple of corporate shares, and this was not difficult to help realizing I previously had out contributing establishment whereupon to build.

12

HOW TO INVEST TODAY

Tech Companies Dominate

Companies like Adobe, Alphabet, Amazon, Apple, Facebook, Google, Microsoft, Netflix, Nvidia, Tesla, and other quick producers are the huge thing in the present business sectors. The contributing environment is unexpected now in comparison to it was only a couple of years ago.

Some of the incredible contributing books I grew up perusing The Intelligent Investor, *Margin of Safety, Common Stocks for Uncommon Profits,* and One Up on Wall Street1 were generally extraordinary books in their time. However on the off chance that you read them today you won't track down notice of the Internet, sites, electric vehicles, the gig economy, or distributed computing. These books were composed by financial backers who presently couldn't seem to learn of the innovative powers that shape our advanced world. I composed this book since in no way like it exists. There are old books that instruct about putting resources into old-school retail stocks, modern stocks, and other "blocks and concrete" organizations, and there are new books that evidently show you how to bring in cash effectively with day exchanging, swing exchanging, and different plans that cause it to appear like anybody can contribute effectively with little comprehension of stocks.

Yes, this book intends to take the contributing ideas of the past and apply them to our new tech-overwhelmed world. Financial backers need to know how to evaluate loads of organizations occupied with selling electric vehicles, cell phones, streaming motion pictures, PCs, pet food, practice bicycles, meatless meat, Internet deals stages, and cloud computing.

We live during a time of quick advancement, and keeping in mind that organizations have changed in the previous century, the books about how to put resources into organizations have not. Ben Graham's fundamental book, *The Intelligent Investor*,[2] was written in 1949 when a protective way to deal with contributing checked out to financial backers, a large number of whom actually had the 1929 securities exchange crash consumed newly to them. While it was helpful for now is the right time, the cutting edge financial backer gives themselves a raw deal in the event that they stress over discouragements or the following monetary crisis.

Because of the idea of the tech-overwhelmed economy, and changes to the manner in which the Federal Reserve mediates during a market emergency, it is absurd to incline too intensely on the more established ways to deal with surveying organizations. Doing so implies a financial backer might pass up inventive organizations like Amazon, Google, Salesforce, Shopify, Tesla, or Zoom. I'm not saying each new tech organization that goes along will appear to be legit, however I am saying that a financial backer requirements new instruments that are valuable in the ongoing environment. Perusers merit a wise way to deal with stock picking in the time of technology.

I realize you're most likely saying, "Sure, I realize you think you know a ton about contributing, however for what reason would it be a good idea for me I pay attention to you when Warren Buffett and different creators have heaps of cash and long haul records?"

The response is basic: they created ranges of abilities that worked during a previous age. These standards might in any case work today, however fundamentally just with "old economy" organizations in light of the fact that the ancestors of putting didn't have ability in distributed computing, electric vehicles, illustrations handling units, online business, and man-made consciousness. The underpinnings of our economy have changed tremendously, and an astute stock financial backer today needs devices intended for current times.

This book clarifies how for put resources into our tech-filled world. It shows you the main variables to search for while purchasing a stock, and it shows you a sifting framework you can use to rapidly and effectively assess organizations and choose if they "seem OK" as investments.

Warren Buffett himself perceived the need to adjust, yet rather than finding out about new innovations himself he employed two brilliant and lively financial backers who both have phenomenal records overseeing cash and continually read about momentum organizations, a significant number of which are tech-based.

To address the need to comprehend interests in innovation and other current organizations, Buffett recruited Todd Combs as a venture director in 2010, and the following year he employed Ted Weschler. At that point, Buffett gave every supervisor between $1 billion and $3 billion to put resources into Berkshire Hathaway's portfolio. With each ensuing year, Buffett has expanded how much cash that each contributes, and in the 2017 Berkshire Hathaway

Annual Report, Buffett made sense of that Combs and Weschler, "Each, autonomously of me, oversees more than $12 billion; I as a rule find out about choices they have made by taking a gander at month to month portfolio summaries."

A couple of years after Combs and Weschler joined Berkshire, the organization made its first interest in Apple Computer. By employing two new speculation chiefs Buffett successfully extended Berkshire Hathaway's contributing circle of competence3 on the grounds that Buffett himself didn't know to the point of putting resources into innovation and PCs. Buffett might have had a go at moving past his circle of ability to find out about Amazon, Apple, or Alphabet, yet he didn't have to in light of the fact that his fresh recruits comprehended these organizations better than he did.

This book is intended for the financial backer who needs to put resources into this advanced age. However you can't employ your very own Todd Combs or Ted Weschler, *you can utilize what you definitely know to go with canny choices*. To begin, how about we investigate Google and Amazon, two tech organizations that frustrate conventional investors.

Google earns $10 a click

You really want to turn out to be great at perceiving plans of action and settling on choices when you just have 70% of the data you wish they had. We'll go into additional profundity on this later in the book, however the bring back home illustration is that assuming you have a profound comprehension of the organization, particularly as a client, then you are in a superior situation to pursue an educated speculation choice than somebody who is not.

For instance, in the event that you take a gander at an organization like Alphabet (which possesses Google), you'll see that they bring in cash for each advertisement clicked. Google is certifiably not a capital-serious business, meaning it doesn't need to persistently purchase new trucks, keep up with planes, or railroad tracks. They have low capital expenses, they employ splendid individuals, and they update their servers and registering gear. However they bring in cash each time somebody clicks an advertisement. Their business resembles a cost for the advanced parkway; a high-benefit business that costs essentially nothing to work and produces cash 24 hours per day.

Letters in order likewise claims YouTube, which is a huge benefit creating motor. A greater number of individuals watch recordings on YouTube than some other video stage. The organization benefits each time a watcher watches the promotions that play during its recordings, and they additionally benefit when individuals purchase its top notch "YouTube Red" administration to observe advertisement free recordings. Individuals are watching

YouTube recordings 24 hours every day overall around the world.

A financial backer who sees this nonstop stream of money that Google and YouTube produce can pursue an educated choice on purchasing Google stock. The prior a financial backer can see the worth, the good they'll be contrasted with different financial backers who don't see the worth or are delayed to act. A few financial backers don't buy tech-related stocks since they don't comprehend them alright. The decision today is straightforward: learn to the point of making superior grade, fast choices in light of restricted data, or sit idle and lament not settling on a choice when you had an unmistakable image of what was occurring however didn't buy stock.

For instance, Warren Buffett has never purchased Google stock for his organization's stock portfolio, and that is something he regrets.[4] At the 2017 Berkshire Hathaway yearly investors meeting, he told financial backers he committed an error by not buying partakes in the tech monster quite a while back when Google was procuring $10 per click from GEICO-an entirely claimed auxiliary of Berkshire.

Buffett said he ought to have understood Google's huge benefit potential in light of the fact that GEICO paid such a great amount for Google Ads. This is not a weakness of Buffett's—he recognizes that Google is beyond the realm of what he understands well—but an investor who does understand some of today's immensely successful companies (many of which are tech-based) will likely do well if they can be decisive a few times in their lifetimes and hold onto the stocks they buy for the long haul.

Don't miss big time

You can pass up an extraordinary stock on the off chance that you're not adequately adaptable. You need to have a strong system for pursuing venture choices, however understand that organizations change quicker today than they did 10 or 20 a long time back. I'm not proposing that you put resources into an organization you don't have the foggiest idea, or address a ridiculously significant expense for the supply of an organization you do comprehend, however in some cases you need to act with deficient information.

Amazon organizer and CEO Jeff Bezos said, "Most choices ought to likely be made with somewhere near 70% of the data you wish you had.[5] If you hang tight for 90%, as a rule, you're presumably being slow. In addition, in any case, you should be great at rapidly perceiving and correcting awful choices. Assuming you're great at course rectifying, being off-base might be less exorbitant than you suspect, though being slow will be costly for sure."

One key to Warren Buffett's venture achievement is that his first rule of contributing is to never lose cash, and one way he does this is by being mindful so as not to overpay. His methodology functions admirably for him, and to execute on that plan he restricts himself to a little gathering of speculations where he has expertise.

Buffett says he passed up a major opportunity by not it Amazon's stock to purchase. "Clearly, I ought to have gotten it Along these linesme time in the past," he said, "in light of the fact that I respected it some time in the past. But I didn't understand the power of the model as I went along. And the price always seemed to more than reflect the power of the model at that time. So, it's one I missed enormous time."6

Be adaptable in your reasoning, not affected by contributing authoritative opinion. Do however much perusing and advancing as could reasonably be expected this moment and pursue choices rapidly when you have sufficient data. You can constantly course-address later assuming that you make a terrible decision.

High-velocity decision making

Leaders like Bezos make top caliber, high-speed choices inside their organizations. I accept that financial backers in these creative organizations should apply a similar way to deal with evaluating their stocks.

As such, you need to foster a great assessment of an organization's stock and pursue a choice rapidly. How rapidly depends on you, yet assuming that you stand by three to five years to purchase a quickly developing organization you could pass up this great opportunity. In this way, you need to embrace a similar conclusive demeanor and capacity to choose with "barely enough data" similarly that the organizations where you contribute make decisions.

Who might have known only a couple of a long time back that Amazon could be all around as fruitful as it has with its voice-enacted aide Alexa? It looked like Apple's Siri or Google's Home would lead around here, however instantly, Amazon took huge steps with man-made consciousness. It's difficult to anticipate which organizations will be victors and failures, and assuming you hold on until you understand the situation completely create before your eyes, it very well may be too late.

Bezos said that the chief initiative group at Amazon is great at settling on top notch choices, and they keep dynamic speed high. They realize that occasionally they'll pursue awful choices, yet numerous decisions

are reversible, two-way doors.[7] Buying stock is a reversible decision, because if you make a mistake you can always sell. On the off chance that you improve at course revising, being off-base about purchasing stock won't be exorbitant, though being slow will be costly for sure.

13

WHAT IS A STOCK?

Think like an owner

Simply put, a stock is a piece of ownership of a company. When you buy stock, you don't just own a little number that blinks green and red and jumps up and down on the screen—you become a *partial owner* of a business.

You'll run over the words "offers" and "values" in your perusing, and the two of them allude to stocks. Despite the fact that they address exactly the same thing-halfway responsibility for organization they really do have somewhat unique connotations.

Shares get their name since when you purchase stock, you in fact "share" in the responsibility for organization. Financial backers are alluded to as shareholders.

Equities get their name since each of the offers in the organization have equivalent worth; none are more important than others, henceforth there is "value" among shares.

How do stock owners benefit?

A stock proprietor can benefit in a few ways:

- The company reinvests its profits. For example, Amazon has been reinvesting profits for years to build out its logistics, warehouses, cloud-computing business, etc. Those investments, if made wisely, can increase the company's revenue, which can, in turn, increase the worth of its shares.
- The company distributes dividends to shareholders. For example, Disney, Starbucks, and Nike all pay a portion of their earnings to shareholders in the form of dividends. This is money that you can save, spend, or reinvest to buy more shares of a stock.
- The company can "buy back" shares, which means it spends some of its cash to purchase shares, which reduces the number of outstanding shares. The company's earnings are then spread across fewer shares, which increases the earnings per share. The purchase price matters; companies create value when they buy back their stock when it's cheap, and they can destroy value when they overpay.
- Investors benefit from buying their shares and having the share price rise so they can sell their shares at a higher price for a gain.
- An investor can lose some or all of the value of their stock if the underlying company does not turn a profit, can no longer compete, or if it is in a struggling sector of the economy. There is no guarantee that when you buy stocks that their value will go up, and many companies go out of business every year. For this reason, it is crucial to do your research before investing. You want to increase your chances of success and limit any events that cause a permanent loss of value.
- I offer this definition of "stocks" because I've noticed that many beginning investors in stocks know little about them. Because of the relentless stock market ascent of recent years many new investors take the gambler's view when it comes to stocks, and they seem to think, "*They only go up, right!?*" Grasping the idea that stocks represent partial ownership of a company is the investor's mindset.

A useful investing mindset

Here's a statement by Warren Buffett that communicates what I accept to be the right viewpoint on stock ownership:1

> *"Charlie and I view the attractive normal stocks that Berkshire possesses as interests in organizations, not as ticker images to be purchased or*
>
> *sold in light of other 'diagram' designs, the 'target' costs of investigators or the assessments of media savants. All things being equal, we essentially trust that assuming the organizations of the financial backers are effective (as we accept most will be) our speculations will find success too. In some cases the settlements to us will be unassuming; sometimes the sales register will ring uproariously. And sometimes I will make expensive mistakes. In general - and after some time - we ought to obtain respectable outcomes. In America, value financial backers have the breeze at their back."*

- WARREN BUFFETT'S BERKSHIRE HATHAWAY 2017 ANNUAL

LETTER TO SHAREHOLDERS

You, as well, will have the breeze at your back when you contribute like you are a proprietor of an organization like you were purchasing an apartment complex or a homestead that produces pay each year.

When you consider purchasing stock turning into a proprietor in a business you will be patient and advance however much as could reasonably be expected, and you'll go with choices in view of your conviction on where the organization is going in the long haul and not in light of what could occur one week from now or next month.

"Your financial backer's edge isn't something you get from Wall Street specialists. It's something you as of now have."

- PETER LYNCH

Peter Lynch captures the essence of investment success: "You can outperform the experts if you use your edge by investing in companies or industries you already understand."

You as of now have an extraordinary comprehension in light of your work, your schooling, or your side interests that provide you with a profound comprehension of business or the economy, whether you have aptitude with vehicles, clothing, PCs, design, telephones, photography, science, and innovation, or some other piece of the economy. We should go through a rundown of businesses so you can find out about those where you have master knowledge.

Here are seven areas where you may as of now have a contributing edge.

1. Retail/Fashion/Clothing - You know something about: Lululemon, Nike, Louis Vuitton, Ralph Lauren, Kenneth Cole, Gap, Coach, Chanel, Banana Republic
2. Computer Hardware/Software/Internet Services - You get Apple, Microsoft, Samsung, Amazon, Netflix, NVIDIA, Google, Alibaba, Salesforce
3. Healthcare/Pharmaceutical - You get Pfizer, Gilead Sciences, AstraZeneca, Express Scripts, CVS, Sanofi, Glaxo Smith-Kline, Novartis, Roche
4. Photography/Digital Imaging/Animation - You get Canon, Nikon, Adobe Systems, Panasonic, Sony, Fuji, Pixar, Disney
5. Scientific/Measurement/Lab Equipment - You get Agilent Technologies, Thermo Fisher Scientific, Waters, Mettler Toledo, Illumina
6. Cars/Trucks/Hybrid Vehicles/Electric Cars - You get Tesla, Toyota, Fiat-Chrysler, Hyundai, Audi, BMW, General Motors, Mercedes, Volkswagen, Subaru, Chevrolet, Ferrari, Honda, Ford

7. Aircraft/Transportation/Logistics - You get Airbus, United Airlines, Delta, American Airlines, Alaska Airlines, JetBlue, Southwest, Boeing, Embraer, Lockheed, Honeywell, UPS, FedEx

Even in the event that you don't know a large number of the areas or organizations recorded over, that is good as a financial backer you are compensated for the profundity of your insight around a couple of things as opposed to a shallow comprehension of many.

No one has a profound comprehension of all organizations; it's difficult to have the opportunity expected to go top to bottom on each public company.

Warren Buffett says you don't need to know it all; you simply must be clear about what you know. He discusses the idea of a circle of skill, and he recommends drawing a circle around organizations you comprehend and leaving all the other things out.

"You don't need to be a specialist on each organization or even a large number. You just must have the option to assess organizations inside your circle of capability. The size of that circle isn't vital; knowing its limits, in any case, is vital."1

- WARREN BUFFETT

Tom Watson, the organizer of IBM, put it thusly: "I'm no virtuoso. I'm brilliant in spots-however I stay around those spots."

There is no disgrace to pass on things that don't squeeze into your circle of skill. On the off chance that something's past what you can undoubtedly get a handle on, simply say no thanks to it. Warren Buffett has a metal recording box around his work area with the words "TOO HARD" composed on it. He says around close to 100% of the speculation thoughts he audits end up there.

Develop the certainty to pass on venture thoughts you don't have the foggiest idea. You need to be sure about what you comprehend in light of the fact that that is your actual edge. Charlie Munger communicated this obviously when he said, "It's anything but a capability in the event that you don't have a clue about its edge. You are a calamity in the event that you don't have a clue about the edge of your competency."2

Your job provides your edge

My edge comes from my experience as a photographic artist. I have utilized Adobe's product programs like Photoshop and Lightroom for around 20 years. Adobe likewise sells Illustrator, InDesign, Premiere, and numerous different projects that fashioners, artists, picture takers, producers, and advertisers utilize each day all around the world.

Because I use Adobe programming consistently, I realize they make extraordinary picture altering programming. I have likewise seen the organization's smooth movement from CD-ROM and DVDs to a "cloud-based" membership model. Adobe's cloud-based application refreshes save time and guarantee that clients are generally "cutting-edge." Adobe charges month to month or yearly for utilization of their product, which is an awesome way for the organization to guarantee steady incomes. As a Photoshop and Lightroom power client, I was stung when they basically eliminated my capacity to "pay once" for the product and not consistently. In any case, they made it simple to keep my PC refreshed and the membership model deters the need to purchase another form like clockwork. As a client, you are allowed to go somewhere else, yet as I have encountered with Adobe's channel, there's no place else to go. As is commonly said, *"in the event that you can't beat them, join 'em!"*

Based on my own experience as a loyal customer for about 20 years I have insights into the quality of Adobe's products and services and a belief (which could be wrong) that the company will likely produce the dominant image-editing software for many years into the future.

Think about what you know on account of your school, where you work, individuals you know, or where you live. Which organizations are getting along admirably? Which organizations do you appreciate and accept will fill in the future?

A simple exercise you can do now

I'd like you to do an activity right now to assist you with tracking down your edge. Find a

pen and a piece of paper (or use your phone or computer if it's closer) and write down your investing edge—something you already have. For example, if you love Nike sneakers and clothing and you are kind of an expert when it comes to understanding demand for their products, how well they're keeping up with current styles, etc., make a note about Nike. If you worked at Victoria's Secret and know a lot about their customers, stores, how much demand there is for their products, write that down too. If you shop at Amazon, are a member of Amazon Prime, and stream music with their app, then you have an edge.

This activity of recording your edge will help you in the impending chapters.

This is your test. In your regular routine, you will catch wind of hot stocks from companions, online articles, papers, and stock pamphlets that show up in your inbox. You'll most likely become amped up for a portion of these stocks. Regardless of whether you believe you're safe, there is an inclination an intrinsic predisposition in us-that drives us to think we know more than we do.

Before you submit any cash to a speculation, simply inquire as to whether you get the business and assuming your insight gives you a benefit over others. The entirety of your reasoning and energy ought to be centered around finding out about organizations where you have an edge.

15

BUFFETT ON EDGE

"The main thing is to have the option to characterize which ones you can come to a savvy choice on and which ones are impossible for you to assess. You don't need to be correct around a great many and large number of organizations, you just must be correct about a couple."

- WARREN BUFFETT

Buffett's best advice for investors is to invest only in stocks of companies they understand.

There's an incredible narrative I observed as of late, "Becoming Warren Buffett."1 What stayed with me subsequent to watching that film is the means by which specific Buffett is with regards to purchasing stocks. He is mindful so as not to overpay for a stock, and he says "no" to organizations that are excessively difficult for him to understand.

At one section in the narrative, Buffett said,

"There's [sic] a wide range of organizations I don't have any idea. I'm ready to see some given rate. Ted Williams composed a book called 'The Science of Hitting,' and it has a chart, he's remaining at the plate, and he has the strike zone isolated into 77 squares, each the size of a baseball. And he says, "If I only swing at pitches in my sweet zone, which he shows there, and he has what his batting average would be, which is .400. Assuming that he needed to swing at low external contributes - yet the strike zone - his normal would be .230. He said the main thing in hitting is sitting tight for the right pitch."

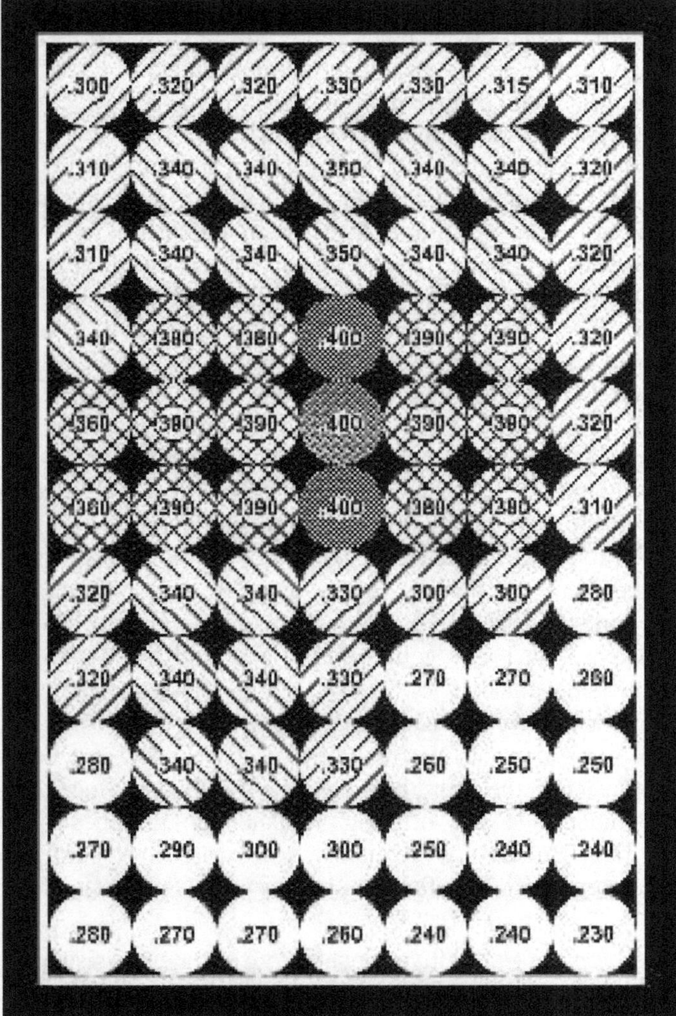

A baseball strike zone separated into 77 circles. Ted Williams realized he could hit with a great .400 batting normal assuming he just swung at balls in his "perfect balance." All

different circles address below midpoints from swinging at less helpful pitches. In baseball you should swing at any throw in the "strike zone" or you can get called out on strikes. In contributing, you can allow many pitches to cruise by, and you never get called out.

Buffett proceeded to say that assuming you partition the strike zone into 77 circles,

there were a couple of pitches Ted Williams was certain he could hit for a .400 normal. In the event that he swung at different pitches he realized he wouldn't hit too. Presently, in baseball you actually need to swing at throws in the strike zone-regardless of whether you need to-or you risk being called out on strikes. But you have an advantage with investing because there is no umpire to call a strike. You can simply hold on until you see the organization you need to put resources into selling at a cost that checks out to you.

Ted Williams was at a huge disadvantage because if the count is 0-2 or 1-2, even if that ball was down where he was going to bat .230 he actually needed to swing at it. In contributing, there are no called strikes. Individuals can toss Microsoft at you, Nike, Disney, and so on, any stock, and you don't need to swing, and no one will call you out on called strikes.

Buffett said, "The stunt in contributing is simply to stay there and watch a large number of pitches go by, and hang tight for the one in your perfect balance, and when individuals are shouting 'swing you bum'... disregard them," he said. "There's an allurement for individuals to act excessively much of the time in stocks essentially on the grounds that they're so liquid."

The Ted Williams model is a visual portrayal of a sort of channel that shows his probability of accomplishment in light of the area of a pitch. This is like the possibility of just purchasing stocks where you have an edge.

Buffett makes sense of this selectivity when he said, "Throughout the long term, you foster a great deal of channels. And I do know what I call my circle of competence, so I stay within that circle. And I don't worry about things that are outside that circle. Characterizing what your game is-in the same place as you will have that edge hugely important."

This idea is something that Warren Buffett rehashes and it doesn't get a great deal of inclusion in the press, however it is significant. Since the 1990s, while visiting undergrads and offering guidance on the most proficient method to get rich, Buffett has frequently accentuated the significance of understanding an organization before you invest.

> "I could work on your definitive monetary government assistance by giving you a ticket with just twenty openings in it so you had twenty punches - addressing every one of the ventures that you got to make in a lifetime. And once you'd punched through the card, you couldn't

make any more investments at all. Under those guidelines, you'd truly consider cautiously about what you did, and you'd be compelled to stack up on you'd's thought process about. So you'd accomplish such a great deal better."

- WARREN BUFFETT

A punch card with 20 punches on it. Warren Buffett said that assuming understudies got a punch card with 20 punches on it when they move on from school, and that is all the speculation choices they get to make in all their years, they would get exceptionally rich since they would take time to consider each one.

"as a matter of fact," Buffett said, "I've told understudies assuming when they escaped school, they got a punch card with 20 punches on it, and that is all the venture choices they got to make in all their years, they would get extremely rich since they would really mull over every one. And you don't need 20 right decisions to get very rich. You know, 4 or 5 will likely do it over time."

This punch-card strategy might sound basic, however that is on the grounds that it is. It can change your venture results as well. Lou Simpson used to contribute all of GEICO's value portfolio. He was probably the best financial backer on the planet, and Warren Buffett said that his stocks frequently performed better compared to Buffett's own selections.

Simpson said that this specific "punch card" procedure helped him gigantically in his record of devastating the market more than a few decades.

16

A RELIABLE SYSTEM

You need a reliable investing system composed of a few simple factors. Those stocks that pass are candidates for investment, and those that fail can be easily eliminated.

The following part will acquaint you with a framework that comes as a basic agenda of five significant variables you can go through to ensure a stock you're considering putting resources into meets specific models. You can consider this agenda a sort of channel. Most stocks won't endure the channel since it's so specific, yet those that pass through it are nice possibility for contributing. You will get better the more you read, plan, and learn.

You need to put resources into a judicious, efficient way and embrace an attitude where you keep cool-headed and don't get too invigorated when the market goes up, nor too furious when it goes down. Your methodology ought to be that of a cool commander, not influenced by feelings at some crucial time. You will be a particularly shrewd, strong financial backer once you embrace this framework and get the hang of utilizing it each time you consider a new investment.

Investing in stocks resembles learning another dialect. It requires investment, and right away, everything appears to be previously unheard-of. Here and there you will have an unsure outlook on the thing you're doing, and that is ordinary. Try not to surrender, and don't get baffled. Simply mean to hit the sack undeniably savvier than when you awakened. Peruse a ton, partake all the while, request help assuming you want it, and you will turn out to be more familiar with the language of investing.

People get some information about stocks constantly. They say, "What is your take on Nvidia?" or "Do you think Tesla is a wise speculation?" They maintain that me should give them tips to assist them with settling on which stocks to purchase, however they don't know how to sort these things out themselves. They request exhortation the same way they would request a café proposal. I never let individuals know what stocks are ideal. It is vastly improved to tell individuals the best way to utilize the apparatuses themselves so they can partake during the time spent learning. The best financial backers need to disregard the exhortation of others who are frequently dumbfounded. On the off chance that you pay attention to others you will unquestionably get befuddled, as most financial backers get cleared up by emotion.

I'm composing this book to show you a decent framework in which you pose a progression of five inquiries about an organization. You will figure out how to address these inquiries yourself so you can go with savvy choices about stocks. One intriguing truth I will share is that the world's best financial backers use channels constantly. It helps them rapidly conclude what stocks merit more consideration and which have a place in the heap checked "excessively hard" to understand.

My ability comes from direct experience contributing for over 20 years and gaining from the huge loads of slip-ups I have made. I planned a "sifting" framework that you can use to choose if a stock seems OK for you. This framework depends on five significant inquiries, and when you answer them you will actually want to choose if a stock checks out as an investment.

I fostered this sifting framework through of need since I needed a bunch of apparatuses I could use to pursue top notch choices rapidly. I'm great at making sense of complicated things in straightforward ways, and I've applied this expertise to making sense of stock putting resources into a way that anybody can understand.

Five obstacles make investing difficult for beginners:

1. Most starting financial backers have just seen the market go up. They accept that contributing is simple, and everything you need to do is placed cash into stocks and you will get rich. Difficult to rapidly accomplish something straightforward takes little knowledge and become rich. It's difficult to get rich rapidly with stocks and remain rich. That is the delusion of a buyer market when stocks appear to possibly go up.
2. When individuals are beginning to contribute they will more often than not depend on others for stock counsel. Despite the fact that it's enticing to request exhortation, rather they will be ideally serviced by perusing a ton and finding out about organizations themselves and afterward framing their own opinions.

   Good contributing requires autonomous thought.
3. Beginning financial backers may not as yet know about the benefit of perusing yearly reports before they contribute. In the following section, "How to Read a 10-K," I will show you the principle parts of this structure that I center around to get an image of the organization's monetary wellbeing. Whenever you wrap up perusing a 10-K you will have an unmistakable thought assuming an organization's wellbeing is improving or weakening. *Whenever you've perused a few yearly reports you will begin to see organizations that create cash through advancement and serving clients well.* All organizations give yearly reports to free, and anybody can demand a free duplicate sent to them or can download them quickly from the "Financial backer Relations" part of the site. Most youthful financial backers I realize purchase stock while never perusing the yearly report, which I accept is a not kidding botch. I will show you precisely what areas to really focus on when you read the 10-K.
4. Buying stocks is more straightforward than any time in recent memory, however accomplishing something rapidly doesn't liken to doing it competently. New applications make it simple to trade stocks utilizing your cell phone, and the simplicity of fast execution can make a starting financial backer detour the perusing and learning important to make insightful stock decisions.
5. The securities exchange has been hitting new highs consistently for over 10 years. This is extraordinary for venture returns, yet I genuinely think starting financial backers may (dishonestly) accept that stocks just go up. At the point when the securities exchange ultimately declines or crashes (and it generally does) these new

> financial backers may be gotten unsuspecting, that things can rapidly get ugly. Numerous financial backers not barely getting started, this happens constantly to experienced financial backers lose huge measures of cash stealthily, anguishing encounters that they never talk or expound on the grounds that they were doing things they never ought to have done.

I might want to include that the positive side, many starting financial backers today have found how to purchase stocks on the web or by utilizing cell phone applications like Robinhood to purchase stock. I see this as a positive in light of the fact that by purchasing only a couple of offers, new financial backers are learning through the active experience of dunking their toes in the speculation waters. Advancing by doing is a decent methodology, as long as you just contribute limited quantities so your awful decisions won't cost too much.

The main thing I need to share is that it's not likely that you will get rich rapidly in the financial exchange. It can require quite a while for your stocks to get along nicely. The hot stocks won't increase 100% of the time. It's critical to have the legitimate mental system to contribute, and that implies you ought to be patient and not be deterred by the securities exchange's present moment actions.

Someone as of late asked me, "What site do you use to get contributing data?" I don't depend on one monetary site or even a couple of them. I attempt to get news from a wide range of sources including The Wall Street Journal, *The New York Times*, and the Financial Times. I watch numerous YouTube recordings to find out about organizations, and I like to watch interviews with the CEO to measure their ability and integrity.

I don't think it seems OK to depend on any site or market observer for exhortation or direction on what could occur with the market. I don't completely accept that most talking heads on finance channels know however much they guarantee, and in the event that they did I don't think they'd share their significant data for nothing with viewers.

"In the event that the explanation individuals put away is to bring in cash, in looking for counsel they are requesting that others let them know how to bring in cash. That thought has some component of naïveté."

- BENJAMIN GRAHAM, "THE INTELLIGENT INVESTOR"

It checks out to begin perusing the yearly reports of the organizations that premium you. You can likewise understand papers, books, magazines, and read articles online about the organizations who make and sell you the things you purchase. The more you read and find out about an organization, the better educated you will become.

It is fine to keep current by perusing the monetary press and visit monetary sites, yet don't depend on them as the sole wellspring of monetary data. But if you're reading the same articles as other people then your results will be the same as theirs—average. If you want to become more intelligent than the crowd, then you will need to expose yourself to different sources of information.

I like to peruse an organization's 10-K (more on that soon), Value Line Surveys,

and I like watching YouTube interviews with the CEO. I additionally like paying attention to digital broadcasts with business pioneers. I want to watch a video or paying attention to a digital broadcast interview resembles eating with somebody. You can acquire bits of knowledge into their character and vision for the organization's future. The energy in their voice, their humor, and their excitement comes through when you hear somebody's voice in manners that probably won't be clear while perusing an article or investor letter.

I have a hardcover diary with a dark cover, and it's split into various segments in view of what I like to expound on. At the point when I see a YouTube video about an advantageous venture thought I will record it. Assuming I read about an imaginative organization, I will take a few notes and compose what grabbed my eye. I like to make arrangements of organizations and take notes to see what I see as of now and where I really want to find out additional. I like to follow my reasoning over the long haul, and I have many piles of yearly reports, old and new, that I'll flip through to help myself to remember an organization and attempt to check whether they're prevailing on that plans they set out in earlier years' reports.

If you think of every company as having a story, then as an investor you are watching attentively to see if the company is executing to make that story unfold as planned. This is hard to do looking at the situation at one point in time, and that's why I like to take notes and keep the annuals in piles so I can flip through them now and then. It's over the long stretch of time that you start to see the story playing out, and if you can see it happening successfully as in Amazon, Google, Tesla, etc., then you're in a good position to decide to buy the stock if you've been reading and taking notes for a while.

Even great investors make mistakes

Warren Buffett purchased a lot of IBM stock for Berkshire Hathaway's portfolio in 2011. He had found out about the organization for a long time however never gotten it. In the end, he put resources into that organization, writing in the yearly report "not what you see matters, it's what you see," and years after the fact he conceded that IBM was an awful speculation and he made sense of, "I was off-base… IBM is a major solid organization… yet they have enormous solid contenders too."1

I accept Amazon, Apple, Google were the innovation organizations that appeared to be legit at the time Buffett made the huge acquisition of IBM stock. Then, at that point, a couple of years after the fact Satya Nadella succeeded Steve Ballmer as CEO

of Microsoft, and the organization fostered the Azure foundation and turned into a powerful forerunner in distributed computing. You probably won't have followed the huge changes at the organization except if you were perusing the yearly report every year and seeing the organization's changes.

Microsoft income age changed under Nadella's authority. At the point when he assumed control over the principle income sources from individual buyers through Office Consumer, Devices, Gaming, and non-volume authorizing of Windows working framework. The organization additionally procured income through offer of first party computer games and outsider computer game sovereignties. The organization additionally served associations of various sizes by permitting Office Commercial, Microsoft Dynamics business arrangements, Server items and administrations, and Advertising on MSN Display and Bing (recollect Bing?)

Okay, so you're saying, "The typical programming organization stuff, authorizing, servers, and a little publicizing and internet searcher stuff tossed in!" What's will you find in the yearly report?

Well, you could find a gem waiting to be discovered. One explicit piece of the yearly report, called the 10-K, has a thing called "The board's Discussion and Analysis," otherwise called MD&A, and that is the place where you will find what the executives thinks about the organization's most prominent victories (and disappointments) of the past year.

If you read the 2020 Microsoft yearly 10-K you will see another storyline that didn't exist five years sooner, in the 2015 report. Notwithstanding the items and authorizing, you would see that Microsoft gives an exhaustive arrangement of cloud administrations called Microsoft Azure. Microsoft produces a ton of income from clients who buy into this service.

Eventually, Buffett has constructed a sensational history. Each financial backer commits an error at times, and the IBM speculation was one foul ball that is not really observable contrasted with his many homers. If back in 2011 when he made the IBM venture Ted Weschler or Todd Combs had been working at Berkshire, Amazon, Apple or Google could have been picked rather than IBM, yet Ted and Todd in the end joined Berkshire, and they ultimately put resources into both Amazon and Apple.

When we purchase stocks we do this is on the grounds that we comprehend or like an organization and its items or administrations. There's an anecdote about an organization and why we figure it will be a wise speculation. We are anticipating that a tale about this organization should work out, yet at times things change. Saying a corporate share as a mistake's likely incorrect. You settle on the most ideal choice you can at a specific moment with the data accessible. It's more exact to say the organization changed, or unexpected contest posed a potential threat, or the interest for the item lessened. At the point when the organization's circumstance changes, our assessment of its stock might change also. At times things improve likewise with Amazon and Microsoft with their exceptional accomplishments in distributed computing with Amazon Web Services (AWS) and Azure.

In the following part you will figure out how to peruse a yearly report, *and in then how to peruse Form 10-K.* Understanding how to peruse these monetary records will give you a benefit over the relaxed financial backer who doesn't take the time or stand out enough to be noticed range to really comprehend a company.

In the following section I will show you precisely what sorts of data I effectively look for when I read a 10-K. You will witness firsthand the way things are coordinated, and which parts of it to zero in on to all the more likely see any company.

17

DOWNLOAD AN ANNUAL REPORT

In an earlier chapter you identified your area of expertise, or circle of competence based on your education, interests, or work experience. Now it's time to use your understanding to identify some companies.

Just to recap the activity toward the beginning of the book, you ought to cause a rundown of the organizations that you to see well. You can pick as many as you'd like, however I think you'll be best off on the off chance that you start with 10 or less organizations. You can continuously add more to your rundown later.

Make a list of companies you understand

Download the Annual Report

- Now you have your list. It should be on a piece of paper, your laptop, or your phone. Just write it down somewhere.
- Once you've written down the names of a few companies, you are going to start learning more about each of them by reading their annual report.
- Go to the website of each company. Find the "Investor Relations" section.

Screenshot from the Walt Disney Company's financial backer relations page

found on the organization's website.

Click on "REPORTS" to see the yearly report.

REPORTS

Annual Reports

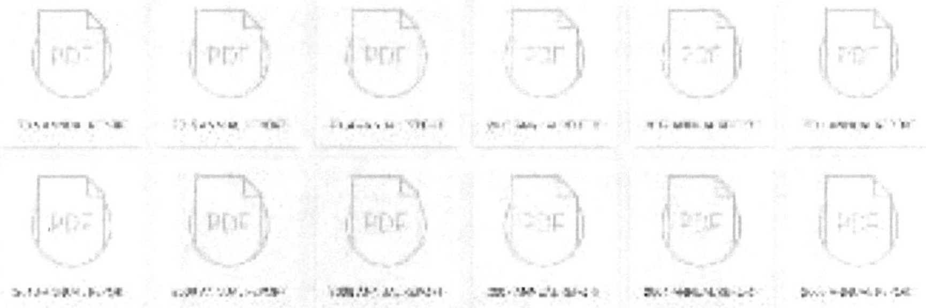

Screenshot from the Disney site. Click on the "Financial backer Relations" route button.

- Download an annual report for each company on your list. It takes less than a minute per report. You can download the report easily by clicking the link, such as those pictured below on the Walt Disney Company's website.
- Read the annual report for the current year. It's the single most important document you can read to gain a solid understanding of the company. I recommend reading several annual reports from the same company over a number of years to get an idea of what the

company has been doing in recent years, and whether they are making progress in accomplishing what they set out to do.
- Wonderful companies tend to have one new development after another; deteriorating companies don't have the same positive surprises. Once you study several annual reports you will begin to get a good sense of which companies are continuing to grow and innovate, and which have their best years behind them. The "Letter to Shareholders," written by the CEO, is packed with useful information about past accomplishments and plans for the future.

The following part will show you a nitty gritty methodology for perusing the yearly report on Form 10-K. Whenever you've perused the yearly report you will acquire a superior comprehension of the company.

18

HOW TO READ A 10-K

I have discussed the importance of the information annual reports offer the intelligent investor, and now I will help readers to truly see how these publications serve as incredibly useful investing tools.

To go after the test of analyzing a yearly report appropriately one could compose a whole book. There is such a lot of detail, both subjective and quantitative that should be unloaded and inspected to acquire a full-variety perspective on an organization's monetary position and future potential.

It is stupid to attempt to catch everything about the examination of fiscal summaries in once section, yet my objective isn't to introduce an extensive aide, yet rather to show the peruser what a 10-K is and how to concentrate their perusing to best further develop their venture prospects.

I will show you the main regions where I put my energy so you can see with your own eyes the sorts of data that I view as most important.

As you will see, the expressions "yearly report" and 10-K are frequently utilized conversely and this can be a piece befuddling to another financial backer. The expression "yearly report" is a more broad term that is frequently used to portray a once shiny distribution shipped off financial backers (or likely financial backers). To save things basic for you, this section plunges into what's formally known as the Annual Report on Form 10-K.

I know when somebody specifies a yearly report, the initial thing that jumps into my head is that softcover distribution that organizations ship off investors (the vast majority throw them in the waste without reading).

A similar material is accessible as a computerized download from the corporate site. I will let you in on confidential so you will not be befuddled: Form 10-K

itself is additionally alluded to as the "yearly report." To keep things basic, I will utilize the term yearly report to allude to the whole distribution (or its computerized variant) which incorporates an investor letter, yearly gathering date and intermediary proclamation, and 10-K to allude to the structure we won't dissect.

Even assuming you have ever taken a bookkeeping or business class, you will realize what to search for in the 10-K so you will turn out to be more certain and familiar with the language of business and contributing. *Show restraint toward yourself*, simply attempt to learn each or two things in turn, and with a long capacity to focus you will slowly find the data you want in the 10-K to improve as an investor.

How to get Form 10-K

In the past part you could see the specific strides to download the yearly report. To rapidly audit, you visit the organization's site to arrange a printed duplicate from the financial backer relations page.

If you don't really want to sit around idly for snail mail you will see a connection to download a duplicate of the 10-K as a PDF. It's extremely basic as you can see to pick precisely the archive you need to read.

[2019 Annual Report (PDF file)]

[2019 SEC Form 10-K (PDF file)]

Download joins for the Annual Report and Form 10-K. These two connections show up on the Berkshire Hathaway site. Downloads are free and one of the most outstanding speculation values you will at any point find. Where else could you at any point acquire owl-like insight for nothing? Your main expense is the time you spend reading.

I like perusing paper duplicates since I can undoubtedly flip to and fro between pages that I can't do with a computerized record, however recently I have been perusing numerous yearly reports and it's such a great deal quicker to download a duplicate that I haven't requested a paper duplicate in a long time.

The yearly report and Form 10-K give the organization a chance to convey everything about the business with investors (and possible investors) during the year. There are additionally quarterly reports submitted and a few organizations have income calls, however these are not as complete.

The year imprinted on the front of the Annual Report talks about the earlier business year. For instance, the 2020 Salesforce Annual Report covers business during the earlier year (2019).

The 2020 Salesforce Annual Report. You can arrange the paper distribution and have it sent to you, or you can download it from the organization's website.

The annual report often contains four parts:

1. A letter from the CEO
2. Notice of a yearly meeting
3. Proxy proclamation, which is an archive containing the data the Securities and Exchange Commission (SEC) expects organizations to give to investors so they can pursue informed choices about issues that will be raised at the annual meeting.1 Specifically, an intermediary articulation is expected of a firm while requesting investor votes, and the organization should record the assertion ahead of the yearly meeting2 .4
4. Form 10-K iS a yearly report expected by the U.S. Protections

and Exchange Commission, that gives an extensive synopsis of an organization's monetary performance3.

I generally prefer to peruse the letter from the CEO since it gives a thought of what occurred from the organization's chief. It's a prologue to the business data and budget summaries that follow, and it's significant reading.

The "basics" of the yearly report is called Form 10-K. This particular structure is frequently alluded to as the yearly report as these terms are utilized conversely; the 10-K is the most significant piece of the yearly report and contains all of the monetary statements.

What is a 10-K?

A 10-K iS an extensive report recorded yearly by a public corporation about its monetary execution and is expected by the U.S. Protections and Exchange Commission (SEC).

Some of the data an organization is expected to record in the 10-K incorporates its set of experiences, authoritative construction, budget summaries, income per share, auxiliaries, chief pay, and some other significant information.

The SEC requires this report to stay with financial backers mindful of a's monetary condition and to permit them to have sufficient data before they trade partakes in the organization, or prior to putting resources into the association's corporate bonds4.

In the past you could have needed to stand by seven days between requesting a paper duplicate of the 10-K from the organization and getting it via the post office, yet presently it takes under a moment to download it from the organization's site and beginning perusing it.

I will lead you through the Salesforce 10-K to provide you with a thought of what I see as most valuable in the archive. There are a couple of huge benefits you can find assuming you know where to look, and furthermore a few significant warnings that you should be aware of before you contribute. I picked this stock to show you because

it's another stock in my portfolio and I needed to dig somewhat more profound into the financials and share the experience with you. This way you can track and find the exact thing I search for in a stock before I invest.

Let me first give you a little foundation about the organization. Salesforce presented the product as-a-administration (Saas) model to the world. Assuming you've bought into Microsoft Word, Dropbox, or Adobe Photoshop in the beyond quite a long while you definitely have some familiarity with SaaS. Salesforce offers its membership to organizations as opposed to people, and this is known as big business software.

Marc Benioff established Salesforce in March 1999 in a leased San Francisco condo and characterized its central goal in a showcasing explanation as "The End of Software."5 This was a trademark he utilized habitually to teach about programming on the Web

Instead of organizations expecting to have rooms loaded up with administrations in their workplaces and IT staffs committed to keeping up with them, Salesforce.com gave Sales Cloud, which turned into the first salesforce robotization item, which smoothed out process the board for deals leads and valuable open doors, contact and record information, process following, endorsements, and region tracking.[6]

Salesforce.com's basic differentiator is programming got to through an internet browser and conveyed over the Internet; they imagined the SaaS programming conveyance model.

Now that I've downloaded the Salesforce 10-K I'll depict my strategy for taking apart the report. To track with simply Google "Salesforce Annual Report" or go to salesforce.com and afterward select "Financials" from the menu and afterward "Monetary Report" and afterward look down to "Yearly report" and select the latest release. Presently that is FY (Fiscal Year) 2020.

You can likewise download the 10-K of your decision and track. All yearly reports follow a comparable design on account of the principles in regards to administrative filings. While the subtleties will differ as per the business, the essential construction and monetary data are universal.

Entire books have been devoted to the examination of fiscal reports; this isn't one of those books. All things being equal, I will show you the parts I center around when I read the 10-K and explain to you why I find these areas and figures most useful.

How to Read a 10-K

If you have any deSire to follow or put resources into a U.S. public organization, you can track down an abundance of data in the organization's yearly report on Form 10-K. In addition to other things, the 10-K offers a point by point image of an organization's business, the dangers it faces, and the working and monetary outcomes for the financial year. Organization the executives additionally talks about its point of view on the business results and what is driving them.[7]

I will frame areas of the 10-K that I see as generally helpful and explain to you why I read them and what I search for when I read. Before you contribute you should find out about judicial actions that could influence the organization, expected dangers to the business, and the executives' viewpoint about the monetary state of the company.

The Balance Sheet

I like to take a gander at the asset report when I first air out the 10-K. This resembles the principal thing a specialist does during an actual test: a couple of quick inquiries and a concise gander at the patient, examining, looking, touching, perceiving how everything shows up initially. With the 10-K we are attempting to learn by and large soundness of the organization. Is the organization looking great and developing, or is it debilitated and decaying? What are the central grumblings we really want to address?

I look to page 68 which is the place where Form 10-K starts. To keep things straightforward and conversational I will allude to the yearly report basically as the "report" and the Form 10-K as the "K" as it's frequently alluded to in monetary circles.

I scroll rapidly to the "Solidified Balance Sheets" which is on page 68. The accounting report records the resources and liabilities, and those are the two most significant numbers to me. In the upper left section, under the heading "Resources" you'll see the words "Current resources" and afterward another heading marked "Endlessly cash counterparts." If you glance over to the right side the figures for the years finishing January 31, 2020 and January 31, 2019. Pointing out our the segment for 2020, I see the Salesforce had $4,145 million in endlessly cash reciprocals in addition to $3,802 million in attractive protections and adding these two things together I get the organization's ongoing by and large cash

position, which I round to $7,947 million. That's what the facts confirm "attractive protections" are not cash, yet they are fluid resources that could without much of a stretch be changed over to cash, so I put them in a similar can for straightforwardness. Taking a gander at the 2019 segment, I see the organization had $2,669 million in endlessly cash reciprocals in addition to $1,673 million in attractive protections and adding these together I get the general money position of $4,342 billion. This is an excellent sign that the organization expanded its money position somewhere in the range of 2019 and 2020; you will not frequently see such a great addition over time. *I like to see the money position expanding*, or possibly continuing as before. As often as not, it turns out that long-term debt exceeds cash, the cash has been shrinking and debt has been growing, and the company is in weak financial shape. That is an organization you would rather not own. This exercise will

let you know as to whether the organization is solid or weak.

You need to keep an eye out for an organization where the money heap is incredibly diminished except if there is a valid justification for it (for instance, in the event that the organization paid money to purchase one more business at a sensible price).

I then scroll down to the bottom half of the balance sheet and look for the "Liabilities and stockholders' equity" section and look for the companies "Long-term debt" entry. Salesforce utilizes a somewhat unique name, they refer to it as "Noncurrent obligation" which incorporate long haul credits, securities payable, conceded charge liabilities, long haul rent commitments, and annuity benefit commitments. The part of an obligation that is not due inside the forthcoming year is delegated noncurrent[8].

Looking at the obligation, I see the 2020 long haul obligation was $2,673 billion and in 2019 the figure was $3,173 billion, and that implies that the organization paid off $500 million of obligation. I like to see the long haul, or noncurrent obligation paid off in light of the fact that obligation decrease on the monetary record is an indication of flourishing, very much like taking care of your Visa implies you owe less money.

When money builds comparative with obligation it's a further developing surplus sheet.

When obligation expands comparative with cash it's a falling apart total sheet.

Subtracting the long haul (noncurrent) obligation from cash for 2020 I show up at $5,275 million as Salesforce's "net money" position. At the point when money surpasses obligation it's a good circumstance and it shows the organization isn't going to hit a financial dead end on account of its solid and developing heap. While you're maintaining an enormous business it's great not to need to depend "on the generosity of strangers."[9]

How much cash per share?

Now I need to realize how much money the organization has per share exceptional. At the end of the day, there's really a specific measure of money per share that would be assigned to you assuming every one of the offers were dispersed and you got to keep a portion of the cash. We need to know how much cash.

At this point I like to flip back to the principal page of the K to perceive the number of portions of Salesforce stock are remarkable. This is one more approach to saying the number of offers "exist" that every one of the investors own in total. It states obviously, "As of February 29, 2020, there were around 895 million portions of the Registrant's Common Stock outstanding."

Now everything we do is partition the aggregate sum of the "net money" position we determined prior by the offers exceptional: $5,275,000,000/895,000,000 =
$5.89. By doing this basic numerical statement I presume that there is $5.89 in net money to oblige each portion of Salesforce. Experiencing the same thing, Salesforce stock shut at $220.1510 and the money position is $5.89 which implies the money position is just 2.7% of the offer cost. This is anything but a huge money position in relation to share cost, but there are cases where the share price is $80 and the cash per share is $10 and when that's the case you need to be aware that if you "back out the cash" (financial speak for subtract it from the equation) you're really getting each share for $70 and you can make a more accurate assessment of the company's value when you remove the cash portion from the calculation of the share price.

Although there is certainly not a lot of money for every offer this is plainly not a decaying accounting report with more obligation than cash. While assessing accounting reports make a point to take away obligation from the money position and ensure there is cash left finished. This is a superb method for passing judgment on an organization's monetary health.

Item 1. Business Description

The initial segment of the 10-K gives a business outline, or depiction of the business. It doesn't make any difference the amount I think I am familiar with the business toward the beginning, I generally approach it like an absolute novice since I need new eyes so I can imagine I know nothing about the organization yet. This way I'm bound to find new things.

Here's the outline of Salesforce:

"Salesforce is a worldwide innovator in client relationship the executives ("CRM") innovation that brings organizations and clients together."

Ok, so right out of the entryway we know what the organization does...

"Established in 1999, Salesforce empowers organizations of each size and industry to interface with their clients in new ways through existing and arising advancements, including cloud, versatile, social, blockchain, voice and man-made reasoning ("AI"), to change their businesses.

This additional data gives us some set of experiences about the organization, and it shows that this product organization utilizes new instruments (notice of blockchain and AI stick out) as a component of their contribution. This right away separates them from other programming organizations who might never manage blockchain or AI. I also note the phrase "enable companies of every size and industry" because it suggests that this is a horizontally integrated company (they have a broad range of addressable customers) compared to a vertically integrated company like Veeva Systems that focuses their efforts (for now, at any rate) on organizations in the existence sciences and drug niche.

I see that "Salesforce's Customer 360" has all the earmarks of being the organization's "crown gem," the core of the organization whereupon all the other things rotates. It appears to be "an integrated platform that unites sales, service, marketing, commerce, integration, analytics and more to give companies a single source of truth about their customers." Ok, all in all, the organization is giving all that from start to finish, from A-Z that an organization might actually have to keep in contact and deal with all client interactions.

The center arrangement of values ("trust, client achievement, advancement and equity") are made sense of, and the organization's road and web address are additionally provided.

Okay, so presently I have a decent outline of the historical backdrop of the organization, what it does, and its fundamental beliefs. That is a beginning and gets me into outline mode, yet I want to dig further. This is the very thing I need to find out about the company:

What is the crown jewel?

What is the organization's fundamental money generator, *the core of its business? I really want to know this immediately*. Generally assuming that I surmise I realize it I'll be off-base. For instance, yesterday I thought I realize that the crown gem for Adobe was

Photoshop and it turns out I was off-base. I imagined that due to my own insight as a photographic artist, however this shows why you need to peruse the depiction, on the grounds that your bias could be off-base. For the individuals who are interested about Adobe, Digital Media portion income was $7.71 billion, with Creative and Document Cloud accomplishing record yearly income of $6.48 billion and $1.22 billion, respectively.[11]

The crown gem for Adobe is plainly Digital Media, which incorporates Creative Cloud (counting Photoshop) and Document Cloud.

Most of the time the crown gem won't be the very fragment that I'm searching for in the following segment (the significant development generator). The crown gem is the organization's fundamental money generator and heart of its business - an organization can't get by without it, and it gives the soundness important to the organization to foster high-development regions. An organization needs to examination to develop, and the crown gem gives the income expected to help proceeded growth.

Salesforce's Crown Jewel

The crown gem is uncovered through this heading:

Our Service Offerings

Salesforce Customer 360 incorporates applications and stage administrations for each touchpoint in a client's excursion. It incorporates the accompanying offerings:

- Sales Cloud
- Service Cloud
- Marketing and Commerce Cloud
- Salesforce Platform and Other.

So that's it: Salesforce's crown gem is Salesforce 360.

For any business you need to comprehend, ensure you recognize the crown gem, also known as the core of the business, and it's significant income generator.

There are itemized portrayals for every one of the things above, however I won't get into them on the grounds that the place of this part is to assist you with distinguishing the royal gems. As you keep on perusing the 10-K you will observe that all of the significant income generators will fall inside those segments.

I momentarily referenced over that more often than not the crown gem isn't going to be the significant development generator. You can imagine it along these lines: the crown gem is bringing in cash today, and the significant development generator will (the organization trusts) be driving development in the future.

The growth generator

The Salesforce 10-K presently makes sense of their development generator.

Our Business and Growth Strategy

This segment makes sense of, "We situate our business procedure and contribute for future development by zeroing in on the accompanying key priorities:"

- Expanding relationships with existing customers
- International expansion.
- Extending go-to-market capabilities
- Targeting vertical industries.
- Expanding into new categories.
- Expanding and strengthening our partner ecosystem.
- Promoting strong customer adoption and reducing customer attrition.

Mergers and Acquisitions and Strategic Investments: Under this part, the organization clears up that from time for time, the organization will "assess amazing chances to get or put resources into corresponding organizations, administrations, advances and protected innovation freedoms to supplement our natural development and advance the improvement of our Customer 360 Platform. In 2019 Salesforce consented to purchase Tableau, an information examination organization, which had been the biggest procurement in its set of experiences, for $15.3 billion. Then, in 2020 Salesforce bought the messaging platform Slack for $27.7 billion. Salesforce has been on a securing spree.

The risks associated with growth

I believe it merits expressing a portion of the dangers to development by procurement. There is a ton of strain on an organization like Salesforce to develop. Some of it comes inside from the supervisory crew and CEO, and some might come from investors who believe that the stock cost should continue to go up.

Regardless of the explanation, an organization can develop naturally (from inside by working out new advancements or sections "in house") or by obtaining. Obviously, for Salesforce's situation it showed up more worthwhile to purchase different organizations that "supplement our natural development and advance the improvement of our 360 Platform" (their crown jewel).

But what if Slack never really takes off as a part of Salesforce's 360 Platform? What if Salesforce overpaid for Slack? What if integrating the new company takes time and attention away from working on things that would be a better use of time and money?

Well, these are generally the sorts of inquiries you really want to consider. Luckily for you, as a likely financial backer, the dangers are summed up as we will see below.

I strongly prescribe perusing the segment titled:

Item 1a. Risk Factors

To keep you engaged as you read through this segment, you want to ask yourself "What are the significant dangers to the crown jewel?"

Here is the way Salesforce clarifies the primary gamble for their business:

> *If our safety efforts or those of our outsider server farm facilitating offices, distributed computing stage suppliers or outsider assistance accomplices, or the hidden framework of the Internet are penetrated, and unapproved access is acquired to a client's information, our information or our IT frameworks, or approved admittance is hindered or impaired, our administrations might be seen as not being secure, clients might shorten or quit utilizing our administrations, and we might cause huge reputational hurt, lawful openness and liabilities, or a negative monetary impact.*

These are for the most part definitely worth considering before you put resources into an organization. It's an approach to guaranteeing you are going into a venture with "eyes totally open." There will undoubtedly be dangers to any business, as we have all become mindful of during the 2020 pandemic. Many individuals who put resources into aircrafts, voyage lines, inn stocks, oil organizations, eateries or travel organizations - among numerous others - learned about the genuine dangers implied in those industries.

Often we don't consider takes a chance until it's past the point of no return. Assuming we contemplated them doing anything may be hard. I feel like astute speculation is tied in with being completely mindful of dangers and concluding which ones you can live with. I observe the 10-K is an astounding method for familiarizing yourself with a large number of the particular dangers implied in one specific company.

The selection beneath showed up in the 10-K distributed before Salesforce obtained Slack, yet it covers the sorts of dangers I just started to specify. I observe this segment especially intriguing in light of the fact that the $27.7 billion that Salesforce paid for Slack made it the organization's biggest procurement yet12.

I observe it interesting to perceive how a colossal securing like this turns out. Salesforce frames a significant number of the things that can turn out badly while securing and putting resources into organizations in this extract from the organization's 10-K.

As we gain and put resources into organizations or advancements, we may not understand the normal business or monetary advantages and the acquisitions could demonstrate hard to incorporate, upset our business, weaken investor esteem and unfavorably influence our working outcomes and the market worth of our normal stock.

As a component of our business system, we occasionally make interests in, or acquisitions of, correlative organizations, joint endeavors, administrations and innovations and licensed innovation privileges, and we anticipate that that we will proceed should make such speculations and acquisitions in the future.

Acquisitions and different exchanges, plans, and ventures imply various dangers and could make unexpected working challenges and uses, including:

- potential failure to achieve the expected benefits on a timely basis or at all;
- potential identified or unknown security vulnerabilities in acquired products that expose us to additional security risks or delay our ability to integrate the product into our service offerings or recognize the benefits of our investment;
- difficulties in increasing or maintaining the security standards for acquired technology consistent with our other services, and related costs;
- difficulty of transitioning the acquired technology onto our existing platforms and customer acceptance of multiple platforms on a temporary or permanent basis;
- augmenting the acquired technologies and platforms to the levels that are consistent with our brand and reputation;

Those are just the main five things referenced, to provide you with a thought of the detail and assortment of all hazard factors you will find listed.

The risks section will discuss a number of other factors that are well worth your considering, such as disruptions in services, efforts to expand beyond the CRM market, industry-specific regulation, intense market competition, privacy concerns and laws, risks related to the business or industry.

Some business gambles are no different for each organization, so you can simply skim over many parts that don't appear to be well defined for the current organization. You can consider yourself an insightful correspondent doing investigate for a story. Turn over however many stones as you can about this specific story, follow each lead, and advance however much you can.

Item 2. Properties

You can skim through this part as there's nothing special going on in this section. There are no big surprises, it's just a list of offices, warehouses, distribution centers, administrative offices, etc. It's funny, for Salesforce I've recently heard about a skyscraper in San Francisco called Salesforce Tower. Now I'm reading about it in the 10-K. "As of January 31, 2020, our executive and principal offices for sales, marketing, professional and administrative services and development consist of approximately 2.1 million square feet of leased and owned property in San Francisco. " Each of the three main buildings that comprise Salesforce's "Urban Campus" occupy one of the four corners of a major intersection in downtown San Francisco. Again, this section of the 10-K is not going to be that consequential in terms of business performance, but it's interesting to know about, and I'll look out for that intersection on Google Maps or the next time I'm in San Francisco.

Item 3. Legal Proceedings

This is where you'll find out if the company is involved in any litigation. This is not particularly important for many companies, but sometimes it's linked with the business risks section. If you're looking at an oil company then management might highlight a certain lawsuit related to a spill or if it's a tobacco company, they may discuss litigation related to smoking. Your main purpose for skimming this is to make sure there are no major lawsuits that could devastate the company.

Item 4. Mine Safety Disclosures

Not applicable to most companies.

Item 4a. Information About Executive Officers

This presents the names, ages, and positions of each company executive along with a biographical sketch.

Item 5. Market for Equity

This is really basic stuff, and if you're looking into the stock you already know the range that the stock has been trading within recently. If the company pays a dividend it's listed in this section, and if the company has been buying back its shares it will be listed here as well. This section often notes the number of stockholders and can provide a graph comparing the company's cumulative total return relative to indexes like the S&P 500 or Nasdaq.

Item 6. Selected Financial Data

This is the first time you'll see the actual financial number that describe the performance of the business. We already looked at the balance sheet earlier in this chapter, and now we can look at the other financial highlights. Look for the consolidated statements of operations to see if the revenues are increasing or decreasing. I don't spend a lot of time on this section, but I think it makes sense to look it over to make sure nothing particularly horrible jumps out at you. For example, below revenues on the consolidated statement of operations are lines for gross profit, income from operations, and net income. These numbers should be positive, and ideally, they should be increasing over time. If the profit numbers are within parentheses, that signifies a loss. If the company lost money during a given time period you'll want to investigate further and find out why.

Item 7. Management's Discussion and Analysis

Management's discussion, along with the footnotes to the financial statements themselves, are where the rubber meets the road when it comes to figuring out what's really happening with a business. I'll read this over and take notes and I recommend you do too.

The earlier sections of the 10-K were merely a warm up for this part, which is often referred to as MD&A. Get a nice cup, mug, or carafe of coffee and some chocolate chip cookies or peanut brittle to accompany you as you take your time reading through this section. This is where the CEO and their management team discuss in plain terms what happened during the fiscal year. This is where they talk about successes, failures, and any big and / or cool projects they have in the works.

Try to figure out what the important data is that the management team used to assess performance. For example, with Salesforce they point to the Acquisitions of Tableau Software and two other smaller purchases. They also point out that total fiscal 2020 revenue was $17.1 billion, an increase of 29 percent year-over-year. They also point out the amounts of earnings per share, and the total cash and cash equivalents. Acquisitions, revenue, and earnings, in that order, seem to be the data that matter most to management. Knowing this gives you a metric to track from year to year when charting company progress.

As part of your job as investigative reporter researching this company you will want to jot down notes on any items that management explains that aren't clear to you. The point of this is to ask "follow-up" questions to get clarification. This section of the report will either leave you feeling unsettled and scared to invest in the company, or confident that you understand the company's current trajectory and have confidence in their future. Trust the little hairs on the back of your neck; if you feel something's not quite right, keep asking yourself why. Verify any details that seem sketchy or incomplete because this is the work that leads you to understand the truth about a company. It's your reading, learning and understanding at this detailed level that gives you an advantage and sets you apart – whether you decide to invest in the stock or say "no" and pass – that provide your edge over someone who buys stock without ever having read the 10-K all the way to the MD&A.

Item 8. Financial Statements and Notes to Financial Statements

If you're just starting out as an investor, then you've done really well to make it this far into a description of a 10-K. As you've figured out, this is high-level fluent discussion of all aspects of the business. I don't expect you to immediately have the skills of an accountant or financial analyst; to merely put in the hard work of finding useful information in the 10-K is an admirable pursuit and you deserve the benefits you will derive. I have noticed (especially in our era of smartphones and screens everywhere) that people are getting short attention spans. It's getting harder than ever before to avoid distractions. You will have an enormous advantage if you possess a long attention span.

Summary:

You will greatly benefit from learning about companies before you invest, and the annual report is a great starting place. For years I tried to read annual reports, but I never really got beyond the shareholder letter from the CEO on the first few pages. I truly wanted to understand the financial statements and the 10-K, but I had taken no accounting or business classes. I wanted to know more, but I didn't know how to learn it on my own (in the days just before YouTube).

You can still invest without reading these documents — I flipped through them without understanding them for years. I'm here to let you know that even if you are not great at math you need not fear – you can still do well in stocks.

For example, I really like watching video interviews with CEOs and I can get a strong sense about them through the ideas they express and my interpretation of their personality. I realize that I can be fooled, so I don't rely on this, but I find it a useful tool. I watched a few interviews with Jeff Bezos and was impressed by his deep understanding of many things, and also his sense of humor. I learned how important it is to experiment to innovate, and how sometimes you fail — which is going to happen because by definition, you don't know how an experiment will turn out. My favorite interview with Bezos was a funny and informative video in which his brother Mark Bezos interviewed him.[13]

I also admired the clear way that Zoom Communications CEO Eric Yuan talked about how he wanted to simplify video communications. He said he wants his customers and employees to be happy. "Our culture is to deliver happiness; everything centers around that. If the team can deliver happiness, we double down on that."[14]

Yuan undoubtedly knows a ton about business and technology, but he doesn't focus on revenues. I instantly knew that I would invest in Zoom in 2019 before the pandemic started.[15] It was that rare blend of wanting customers to be happy and ability to innovate that sold me on him and his company. I remember calling a friend in the summer of 2019 after watching the interview with Yuan on YouTube. I asked him if I could call him on his smartphone so we could try out this new app called Zoom. He asked me "what's Zoom?" Looking back, it's hard to believe there was a time when some people had never heard of Zoom.

Most recently I watched an interview with Peter Gassner, the CEO of Veeva Systems, and I was equally impressed with the way he spoke of his company in an honest and unrehearsed way. I particularly liked the way he admitted to not having the answers to every question. He admitted to not knowing all the answers when he started the business, and said he crafted the software one step at a time.

I bring up these examples to just point out that I didn't know how to read a 10-K when I started out. Instead of calculating with numbers in financial statements, I relied on my perceptions which led me to invest in Amazon, Zoom and Veeva because intuition told me that Jeff Bezos, Eric Yuan, and Peter Gassner deeply understand their customers and how to use technology to make them happy.

Finally, after several years of wanting to understand 10-Ks, they finally make sense to me. Don't worry if you don't know anything about them yet, and remember that you can learn about them one step at a time. Keep in mind that an investor's job is to get a complete picture of a company before making an investment. 10-Ks and financial statements are just one piece of the investment puzzle. Charlie Munger knows there's a lot more to investing than math when he said, "Most people calculate too much and think too little."

The 10-K is a new tool to help you invest. Each bit of wisdom you collect is like a new arrow to add to your investing quiver. With practice you will improve your aim and put more wood behind your shots.

PART IV

USE YOUR IMAGINATION

19

WHY INVEST WITH ROBINHOOD?

Most readers will most likely have heard of the company, but for those who have not, Robinhood is a financial services company founded in 2013[1]. The company operates a website and mobile apps for iPhone and Android.

Robinhood revolutionized stock trades

Investors used to have to pay to trade stocks. In the early days the fees were quite high. An investor had to call a broker on the phone and place an order to buy or sell stock. Each of these orders could typically cost $100 a trade.

Then, the Internet let investors place their own trades, and suddenly the prices paid to these "discount brokers" became really cheap. Now for $29.99 you could buy or sell stock, and that was super cheap at the time. This trend continued, with all of the online brokers duking it out for market share. Before Robinhood, anyone who wanted to invest in stocks, ETFs or options would be charged between $5 to $10 a trade. They also needed to invest a minimum of $500 to open an account.[2]

As you could guess from the name, the company's mission is to "provide everyone with access to the financial markets, not just the wealthy."3

Suddenly there were no fees to trade. The Robinhood app made it free to buy or sell stock. You could do this all day long, and they didn't charge you a dime. In fact, Robinhood gave people a free share of a random stock just for signing up.

Robinhood started an investing revolution because it opened the door to an enormous group of young people. As of January 2015, 80% of the firm's customers belonged to the Millennial demographic and the average customer age was 26, Fifty percent of users who have made a trade use the app daily and 90% use the app weekly. By November 2020, Robinhood had 13 million user accounts, and this number has been growing rapidly, having more than doubled from just 6 million users in just two years.[4]

Why Consider Robinhood?

The Robinhood mobile phone app makes it easy for beginning investors to learn about stocks and investing. Robinhood's mobile phone app is head and shoulders above the rest and makes it very easy to learn about stocks and sectors of the economy with its intuitive and thoughtfully designed display. There are some unnecessary features (like confetti raining on the screen after buying stock) that are distracting and gamify investing, but the minimalist design, creative visualizations, and capacity to educate new investors offer many benefits to beginning investors.

I am going to share a story about my own Robinhood experience. The Robinhood app helped me to develop a new and experimental way to invest in the spirit of Benjamin Graham, who was innovative, and for whom "Everything was experimental. Everything was new. Everything was exciting."5

The Robinhood app categorizes stocks in a simple and minimalist way, and this makes it easy for a user to quickly compare companies in a similar sector. The interactive charts that adjust dynamically help you see returns over different time frames.

There is an ease with which you can absorb information on the Robinhood app because of the user interface that makes it easy to absorb new data. I have never actually traded using the app, so I'm not talking about trading at the speed of a whirling dervish. I'm talking about an intuitive way to comparing several companies and getting a feel for the differences among them. The Robinhood app needs to be experienced to be understood.

Through using Robinhood to uncover new stock ideas, and I found new investments I likely never would have found without the experimental research the app facilitates.

I used the app to develop investment ideas, but in the end I made my stock purchases on a different brokerage platform.

There is love and hate for Robinhood among people who are familiar with the app.

Here are the pros and cons of using the Robinhood app:

Pros:

- Robinhood charges you nothing to use it
- The user interface is intuitive
- The visualizations are unequaled by any trading app
- You can trade easily with a few gestures on a smartphone
- It is easy to learn how to trade with the app
- You get a free stock for setting up an account

Cons:

- Though Robinhood is a "free" app, the company profits from your trades by receiving payment for order flow
- There is no customer service phone number
- The trading platform has experienced several glitches

- These service outages seem to occur most often during the morning, especially during times of busy trading
- The stock research information is limited compared to research information offered by other brokers

I believe you will find as many opinions about Robinhood as people you speak with about the app. As with any revolution, there are people who feel it opened up the gates and opportunities that did not exist before, and there are those who feel the new reality is horrible.

So, let's crack this open and I'll explain what I personally detest about the app and what I (now) love about it. There, I said, it, I have a love/hate relationship with the app. I have been watching videos by a lot of investing YouTubers over the years and I envy the amount of fun they have with Robinhood. Here I am, taking my time, learning about stocks, and maybe, after three years of research I would finally have enough information gathered to buy a new stock.

Then I watch these YouTube videos and people are just scrolling through their smartphones, tapping and swiping up and whoosh, they just bought a new stock. They were having all this fun, experimenting with stocks, having fun, and buying new stocks like it was nothing. I wished I had that kind of freedom to just experiment and try new things. That's one great way to learn: to try lots of different things, see what works and what does not, and then adapt and keep going. I saw everyone else having fun with the Robinhood app...everyone but me!

I actually downloaded the app when it first came out, but I didn't follow the steps to give them your social security number and bank information. I heard a few stories about Robinhood that made me hesitant to give them my financial information. Some people don't think twice about online security and how safe your social security number or bank account info are when you hand it over to a startup, but I'm not in that camp. So the app just sort of sat there on my phone, unused.

My thinking changed

I wanted to write about Robinhood because I imagine that many readers are just starting out with investing, and it's likely that they will make their first stock trades with Robinhood or another similar app if they aren't already.

I really wanted to write about Robinhood, but I can't describe it with any credibility unless I've used the app myself. I'm sure you can see the problem. So, what I did was downloaded the app to my phone and started using it.

Why didn't I use this earlier? I asked myself. I know why: I got stuck thinking I had to hand over my social security number and bank account info to use the app. This was incorrect. You can use the app all you want, look at the cool charts and read the research without ever handing over that info. I thought I'd just take Robinhood for a test drive so I could report back to my readers on these pages. I was not prepared for how much Robinhood would rock my world.

Wow.

Right out of the gate I will say that Robinhood is head and shoulders above every other app out there when it comes providing an outstanding user experience. There's an entire field called UX design (short for user experience) that focuses on the interaction between human users and everyday products and services, such as websites, and apps. It is an extremely varied discipline, combining aspects of psychology, branding, business, market research, design, and technology.[6]

If you're going to buy or sell stocks, then you're most likely going to place trades yourself using a website or mobile phone app, and you're going to enjoy the process if the design is simple and makes your experience smooth, and painless.

The job of the UX designer is to make technology usable, enjoyable, and accessible for humans.[7] Robinhood has totally nailed it with fantastic UX design. Other brokerage firms run the gamut between having websites and apps that make tech usable and accessible to those that make you dread having to use them.

I have brokerage accounts with Fidelity, Schwab, TD Ameritrade, and Vanguard, and I have experimented a lot with their mobile apps. I can say without hesitation that all of these large brokerage firms can learn an enormous amount from Robinhood about designing an immersive and intuitive user experience.

Let me summarize how I use Robinhood. I log on to the app on my phone and tap the big magnifying glass "search" icon. From there I arrive at a page where I can instantly see all of these useful lists of stocks and market sectors.

Robinhood makes it easy to research stocks:

- 100 Most
- Popular Top
- Movers

Technology
- Food &
- Drink
Finance
- ETFs
- Energy
- Entertainment

- Real Estate
- Apparel & Accessories
- Upcoming Earnings
- Crypto
- Index ETFs
- Consumer Goods
- Tech, Media, & Telecom
- Consumer Services & Retail
- Business
- Healthcare Services
- Banking
- Cannabis
- Healthcare
- Supplies China
- Pharma
- Energy & Water
- Healthcare
- Hospitality
- Manufacturing & Materials
- Agriculture
- Automotive

I can either click on one of those topics above to see the entire set of stocks in each category. It's laid out to make it easy to see all of the stocks in a given sector. You can skip the lists above and search for the stock you want to learn about.

This is helpful because of the way the stocks are organized. It helps an investor see all companies in a given sector. Another thoughtful feature is you can type in any state and see a comprehensive list of the publicly traded companies domiciled in that state.

Robinhood's stock analysis alone will not give you a deep understanding of a company. I consider it a point of departure, and a source of new stocks that you might not have considered otherwise. In a future chapter I will tell you about several stocks I bought after originally coming across them on Robinhood.

I would consider Robinhood's app a great point of departure for more learning about stocks. I will often Google a few articles about a company, watch a YouTube video, or check out a Value Line Survey to gain a deeper understanding. I don't trade on the app, and I don't think it's the beginning and end for an investor.

What Makes Robinhood So Special?

Robinhood's app is designed to make the user's experience smooth, easy and immersive. The layout is optimized for diving in and swimming around. It is not great for a deep dive.You won't leave the app with any in-depth business understanding, but you may get some new ideas. I think that as long as you're not expecting too much you might find some investing ideas and useful data.

I don't use Robinhood to trade stocks. As much as I appreciate the user experience, the graphs and the way you can flow effortlessly through the app and learn about new sectors, I don't trust the brokerage part of the app with my money. I have a few basic requirements which I'll discuss below.

My brokerage requirements

- Any broker I use to buy or sell stocks must be reliable and ensure that when I place a trade it executes right away.
- I want to know that I am getting the best buy or sell price (known as the execution price) when I place a trade. I don't want my broker to earn a profit by selling my trade information to another firm, a process known as "payment for order flow."
- I want to be able to call customer service if there's a problem.

Robinhood misses the mark regarding meeting these necessities. During my exploration for this book I read numerous Robinhood audits on the Apple App Store. I read both positive and negative audits. The positive audits raved that exchanging is sans commission and how the application makes it simple for starting investors.

The negative surveys that examine issues clients experience while attempting to put exchanges that prevented me from utilizing the app.

I utilize other solid stages from representatives that proposition phone client care when needed.

Brokerage Firms I Have Used

I set up a record with Charles Schwab to use for corporate securities. I have involved different firms before, however right now the company's unwavering quality, phenomenal telephone support, and further developing cell phone application client experience make them my financier firm of choice.

Opening my Charles Schwab account was simple, and I did everything on my cell phone. Schwab's application is phenomenal and the couple of times I have called client assistance the delegates were caring and effective.

I likewise have a record with Vanguard, and their firm is great as well. They offer a dependable stage, and cordial and fit telephone support.

Here's a speedy once-over of cell phone applications since I have accounts with a few financier firms and have attempted all of their apps.

- **Fidelity:** Fidelity offers decent phone support, but I have found the firm is large and disorganized. For users who don't ever call phone support this may not be an issue. Fidelity offers a wide variety of mutual funds, index funds, ETFs, and brokerage services. They are well-known for managing retirement accounts. Their mobile app is basic and functions reliably, but it scores low marks for UX design; it is functional but not enjoyable.
- **Charles Schwab:** Excellent phone support. I have been impressed with the kindness and knowledge of their customer support. Full-service brokerage and wide variety of funds, ETFs and stocks. Their smartphone app is very good. They have an excellent visualization of your stocks called a "Bubble Chart" that puts your holdings in bubbles according to size and arranges them by daily return and also lifetime gain / loss. This is a step in the right direction for Schwab, which has clearly started to invest in the mobile app's user experience. Schwab also offers a product called "Schwab Slices," their brand of fractional shares. They make it very easy to buy a "slice" of one stock or several stock. You enter the amount of money you want to invest and the stocks you want to invest in and the app divides your money among the share(s). Schwab's app functioned superbly the several times I have used it, and it continues to be my "go to" app to make a stock purchase. Charles Schwab needs to continue to improve their app's user experience to

match or surpass Robinhood's and they will draw in huge number of clients who need dynamic perceptions and Charles Schwab's degree of magnificent client service.

- **TD Ameritrade:** This brokerage is functional but nothing to write home about. My experience with their systems, website, and customer service have been adequate. They are not the best, but not the worst either. After all, some online brokerage firm has to be average. I don't really like using their website or app, and calls to customer service have not been handled effectively. TD Ameritrade is currently being acquired by Charles Schwab (the acquisition began in 2020, and all TD Ameritrade customers will eventually migrate to Charles Schwab's platform, so all customers will likely transition to Schwab's website and mobile app once the merger is complete.
- **Vanguard:** Jack Bogle founded this firm, and his invention of the low-cost index fund was one of the greatest gifts to the small investor. While the Vanguard Group was originally a mutual fund company, it has grown into a full-service brokerage that offers ETFs and a full-service brokerage arm, Vanguard Brokerage Services (VBS). Vanguard gives the customer a fair deal and provides excellent phone support. Vanguard puts the customer at the center of their world with a broad range of index funds, ETFs, and stocks.

I've illustrated these business firms to give you an outline. There are numerous others clamoring to inspire you to open a record with them. The four recorded above are not be guaranteed to preferable or more regrettable over the others: they are essentially those with which I have some experience.

As you read more about Robinhood, remember that you can utilize large numbers of the incredible elements of their sublime versatile application to find out about stock contributing without utilizing the application to purchase stocks.

I figure you will be a superior financial backer assuming you comprehend you have numerous options with regards to investigating organizations and stocks, and I trust you'll recollect that the stage you learn on doesn't need to be a similar one on which you trade.

SHADE THROWN ON ROBINHOOD

Robinhood's dependability problem

Robinhood has pioneered a new concept with the commission-free trade. While their app is beautifully designed, users have experienced reliability problems that seem to occur when the market opens in the morning or during times of expanded market activity.

I will give surveys I found on the Apple App Store. I will incorporate them precisely as they were composed - kindly note that spelling blunders or contractions will be incorporated without adjustment for transparency.

"Crashes on market open frequently"

> "The application regularly crashes when the market opens making me lose cash or be trapped in an exchange. I would be aware."
>
> - AGEIS54BUT1115

"Unreliable"

> "I lament composing this given the effect this beginning up has had and the free help they offer however with business sectors moving constantly and particularly assuming you're effectively dealing with your positions this stage is amazingly temperamental be warned."
>
> - VITALITY118

"Poor platform"

"Slacks a lot during the mornings "because of high traffic." It is without commission yet remember you are playing against the market as well as rh too since you wont have the option to sell or purchase anything when they are encountering issues (as often as possible)… "

- LYOTTO

Though there are obviously numerous clients who are baffled with the Robinhood stage's absence of dependability, they are just important for the client base. A significant number of Robinhood's clients observe it makes contributing open to them and assists them with figuring out how to invest.

Massachusetts SEC officials fine Robinhood

Massachusetts controllers recorded a claim against Robinhood, and Robinhood consented to pay a $65 million fine for beguiling clients.[1] Some of the allegations appear to be genuine and others appear as though they're accusing Robinhood unfairly.

SEC authorities in Massachusetts expressed that somewhere in the range of 2015 and 2018 the organization just somewhat made sense of on its web-based FAQ page how it brings in cash, discarding insights concerning its biggest income source - exchanges. "Robinhood takes a client's stock request and offers it to a bigger exchanging firm that executes the exchange, a cycle known as "installment for request stream," the SEC request states.[2]

I experienced issues sorting out how Robinhood brought in cash while composing the primary version of this book. I realize that the organization advertised "Robinhood Gold," a top notch administration for clients who needed to do edge exchanging, yet I had no reasonable approach to knowing how they made money. It appeared to be unthinkable that they could give exchanges to free, create and great cell phone application, and give clients let loose stock for marking all without making any money.

However, in all actuality Robinhood got compensated large number of dollars from organizations that needed to buy information about which stocks Robinhood's clients purchased so they could expect their exchanges and benefit from their timing advantage. While Robinhood showcases its administrations as "bonus free," the SEC cases that clients as a general rule got sub-par exchange costs that, "in total denied clients of $34.1 million," regardless of any reserve funds they got from paying zero in commissions.[3]

The SEC said that Robinhood didn't reveal their benefitting off of client exchanges, and that by neglecting to fulfill its obligation to look for the terms to execute client orders they were deluding the client. They additionally say that Robinhood profited from finishing exchanges at costs that were not exactly ideal for its clients. In total, those charges denied clients of $34.1 million, even subsequent to considering the reserve funds from the without commission trades.[4]

Robinhood said to "Gamify" Investing

They Critics guarantee that Robinhood gamifies contributing, and a Massachusetts claim expressed that while Robinhood markets itself as twenty to thirty year olds' door to the securities exchange, the organization utilizes "gaming procedures to control clients" to exchange more request to support its fees.[5]

The suit made sense of that for persuade clients on its foundation to exchanging, Robinhood rewards clients "with beautiful confetti pouring down their screens in the wake of executing exchanges," as per court reports. I imagine that Robinhood has made contributing available to numerous youthful financial backers who might not have contributed without the stage, however I truly do feel that it does gamify contributing, which isn't good.

A Bloomberg assessment article by Adam Brown introduced a contention that Robinhood isn't gamifying markets, but instead democratizing them.[6]

The article blamed controllers in Massachusetts for going after Robinhood Financial LLC, in what they call the most recent in a long example of controllers bugging immensely helpful innovations.[7]

The article reviewed an age of high expansion when the SEC fought currency market assets when they introduced an imaginative way to deal with battling expansion. "Who can forget the mid 1980s, when expansion was running at twofold digit rates and banks were restricted from paying revenue on really taking a look at stores, yet the Securities and Exchange Commission was battling currency market funds?"

Brown concedes that the two Massachusetts complaints8 are authentic, yet they are normal. Indeed, Robinhood has had administration blackouts, and they have additionally obviously endorsed a few records for dangerous choice exchanging, yet all financiers have these kinds of problems.

What actually happened?

According to an article by Chris Valazco, which showed up in engadget, for a really long time, Robinhood situated itself as a way for beginner financial backers to figure out stock exchanging, and its without bonus exchanges made each YouTube contributing channel and their great many supporters, alongside every one of the fellas at Wall Street Bets bounce overwhelmed with passion for the free exchanges. "In the background, however, the SEC claims that the organization occupied with a training known as "installment for request stream," in which market producers (like rapid merchants) basically pay for the option to execute those exchanges. And these payments aren't handled in lump sums; instead, *think of them a stream of micro-kickbacks* delivered to the brokerage firm for each share sold.[9]

Taking installments for request stream from Wall Street firms is a questionable, however legitimate practice done by most electronic intermediaries. For Robinhood, it's the greatest income source.[10] Robinhood got $180 million in installments for exchanges the subsequent quarter, as indicated by a SEC filing.[11]

The training isn't unlawful, yet it is questionable since it has the undeniable potential to make clashes of interest.

Robinhood's concerns with the SEC basically fall into two buckets:

1. The SEC observed the organization had distributed "misdirecting explanations and oversights in client correspondences" somewhere in the range of 2015 and 2018 about how it made the vast majority of its money.
2. Robinhood financial backers who thought they were getting a reasonable arrangement with no-commission exchanges were more awful off contrasted with individuals who exchanged with Robinhood's opposition - the customary brokers.

   "To a great extent because of its abnormally high installment for request stream rates," the SEC assertion peruses, "Robinhood clients' requests were executed at costs that were mediocre compared to other representatives' prices."

Robinhood clients who thought they were getting free exchanges were really losing more cash to terrible exchange execution costs than if they had quite recently addressed a contending merchant's cost for the trade.

One charge against Robinhood recorded in the grumbling blames Robinhood for "giving records to urge clients to buy protections without thought for suitability."12

This is out of line analysis of Robinhood, as I would like to think. As I displayed over, the Robinhood application gives an assortment of records and puts together stocks into classes like innovation, energy, and medical services. As somebody who has explored stocks for quite a long time, I can say that Robinhood's show is the most clear, straightforward and straightforward of any I have experienced. Indeed, one can condemn the consideration of the "100 Most Popular" on the grounds that a few new financial backers could erroneously think those stocks are superior to other people, or that different stocks are not appropriate. Indeed, individuals could will more often than not buy what others are purchasing and this might actually send the costs of famous stock higher, yet this occurs regardless of Robinhood. Sharing a rundown of famous stocks isn't equivalent to let individuals know what they ought to purchase. I think the controllers should really try to understand that grown-up financial backers ought to be provided the capacity to pursue their own choices without being safeguarded by the state. Assuming they commit an error, they can constantly gain from it and work on from now on. It could help youngsters to urge them to pursue their own decisions through genius than to attempt to shield them from each conceivable danger.

However, these issues are not brought about by Robinhood giving records. The controllers need to get that their substantial worries (clients being ignorant about Robinhood benefitting from request stream) are reduced when the grievance further reprimands Robinhood for something all agents do.

Adam Brown, in an article in Bloomberg Opinion proposes that Robinhood isn't the only one to give arrangements of stocks.[13] "All specialists give arrangements of stocks and suggestions, and similar records to all clients. Who might believe their specialist should redact specific organizations from stock records since it believes you're inexperienced?"

Brown clears up that there's a little point for be made, specifically that, "the vast majority of Robinhood's rundowns are guidelines like the most dynamic stocks, biggest gainers and failures, least and greatest cost to-income development, or most noteworthy profit rates, the firm used to likewise list the most well known stocks on its foundation prior to suspending the training. Such a rundown has questionable speculation esteem and could urge clients to charge into the equivalent stocks."

I really look at my Robinhood App on December 18, 2020 and the "100 Most Popular" are to be sure recorded. Evidently, this rundown has not been ended, but it records Apple, Tesla, Ford, General Electric, American Airlines, Pfizer, Microsoft, and 93 different organizations. These are altogether parts of the S&P 500 and accordingly parts of the biggest file assets and ETFs in the United States. It's a horrible idea that Robinhood ought to be rebuffed for posting them. Running against the norm, I accept Robinhood's rundowns are superior to most I have seen, and they are introduced so that starting financial backers can find out about the universe of stocks accessible for speculation and assist them with zeroing in on unambiguous stocks they might want to learn more about.

21

SUNSHINE FOR ROBINHOOD

There are 13 million users and the average review on the Apple App Store is 4.8 out of 5, so they are clearly delighting their target demographic.

I might want to share a couple of positive audits since I realize I've tossed some shade Robinhood's direction, and I figure perusers ought to get a sound portion of the bright side of the app.

New member.

> "I joined Robinhood barely 3 months prior… I think it is an incredible resource for the average person who doesn't have huge number of dollars to put resources into stock at the same time. Robinhood is a way for the normal individual to study and find out about various stocks themselves and conclude where they need to put their cash. Then via the telephone application they can actually take a look at their stocks the entire day consistently. An individual can contribute however much they need, pennies or more. I've had the option to contribute north of 3,000 dollars… I never stop for cheap food or purchase everything except necessities now since I've observed that I'd prefer take the $5.00 or whatever I would spend on unhealthy food and so forth and purchase stock. With the infection dropping all sports I've observed watching my speculations on Robinhood be more

engaging particularly since I really have a stake in the game now."

- MUTTLIKEPOP

Freedom IS Actually Free!

"Time is the main benefit you have while contributing. Or on the other hand so my granddad told me. For a really long time, be that as it may, I paused and put off contributing until I had "enough" the means to make the expenses most merchants charge worth the effort. But I never seemed to have "enough" and I hated waiting (and therefore wasting the magic of compound interest) ... The design is intuitive. The monetary graphs are straightforward, without being overpowering... I'm not excessively affluent, yet, yet truly this application is one of my top choices on my telephone since watching the profits come in and the accumulated dividends develop year-by-year really fulfills me. Robinhood is essentially finished genuine serenity in a wonderfully planned application. I can't thank its makers and originators enough!"

- GRANDPATOLDME

When I read these reviews I'm genuinely happy that Robinhood is filling a need with so many new investors who may never have started investing if it were not so easy to get started and free of trading commissions.

What do I do?

So, we have seen all the shade and some daylight as well. What's this book's writer to do? I partake in the smartest possible solution: I use Robinhood to investigate stocks and market areas, and I get to partake in the astonishing visualizations.

Robinhood gives a fabulous client experience that is fun and natural, and it's the best tasteful contributing app.

Yet, when now is the ideal time to really trade stocks I depend on various financier stages. I believe that a dependable way should put an exchange, I don't need my representative creating a gain to my detriment, and I need a telephone number to bring in those uncommon circumstances when I really want to examine my record with a human.

22

EXPERIMENTAL, NEW, AND EXCITING

"He was innovative, it was a new approach. Everything was exploratory. Everything was new. Everything was exciting."

- EDWIN SCHLOSS, SPEAKING OF BEN GRAHAM

As you've learned, investing is more than just a bunch of numbers and ratios that, if you look at them enough, will magically lead you to good investments. Financial analysts and day traders focus on short-term earnings, charts, meaningless ratios, and other metrics that attempt to forecast future price movements. All of this noise does little to illuminate the basic businesses.

Traders compose books about shorting stocks, selling puts and purchasing calls. They exchange stock subordinates rather than the real stock. These methodologies are loaded with specialized drivel that is tied in with anticipating the future cost, however they should simply be perusing tea leaves or becoming crystal gazers. They become enveloped with the innovation of exchanging and encircle themselves with PC screens, attempting to divine importance from stock outlines that spread across electric Ouija sheets. An endless stream of useless numbers, measurements, and proportions are not a viable replacement for profound idea or a long ability to focus to zero in on a couple of extraordinary companies.

I think the best financial backers contemplate organizations and their upper hands in the economy in innovative ways. They see things in organizations and pioneers that others miss.

Every financial backer brings interesting abilities and points of view about the process, and every individual has an alternate personality too. Eventually, it depends on every financial backer to utilize their creative mind to track down new organizations. How you recognize them depends on you. Continuously make sure to zero in on what interests you.

23

ROBINHOOD DREAMS

Einstein once said,

"Creative mind is a higher priority than information. For information is restricted to all we currently know and comprehend, while creative mind encircles the world."

Robinhood and the imagination

Robinhood further develops contributing creative mind. It assists financial backers with seeing stocks in an outwardly vivid manner. It likewise gives a financial backer look at a few organizations access a particular sector.

One of the most amazing aspects of Robinhood's application is the expulsion of obstructions that make it burdensome and exhausting to investigate organizations and stocks. As I would like to think, Robinhood assists clients with getting into the contributing stream, and touches off their creative mind and interest to learn more.

Robinhood does not diminish knowledge; it encourages imagination.

The suddenness I felt while utilizing the application drove me to find a few new stocks that I ended up purchasing. Now that I've logged half a month on the application I'm shocked when I go to another financier application, get my finger across an outline, and nothing happens!

Most of the present portable applications are caught before. Charles Schwab, E-Trade, Fidelity, TD Ameritrade, or Vanguard - were totally evolved utilizing static UIs of application originators who took in their exchange a few years

back. Robinhood sloped everything up to another level with perceptions that exploit the present cell phone technology.

Today's huge web-based merchants would presumably acquire a huge load of starting financial backers particularly Millennials and Zoomers1-assuming they further developed the UX plan of their portable applications, with thoughtfulness regarding further developing representations and making it simple to see graphs and access research. I anticipate the primary trustworthy internet based dealer to make their application as powerful as Robinhood's will acquire tremendous portion of the overall industry of starting financial backers who need a dependable application, great client care. There is an enormous chance for any business firm that perceives the solid interest for a dependable versatile application with all around planned visualizations.

As you're seeing, smart venture doesn't need to be generally not kidding. Whenever it's done well, similar to a competitor in their prime, it tends to be energizing and fun as well. A smooth business application is a positive development. The internet based merchants (and their cumbersome, exhausting applications) that I've been utilizing for quite a long time don't assist the creative mind with tracking down groundbreaking thoughts. It's the ideal opportunity for a breath of new air.

This statement discusses things trapped in the past:

> *"Your time is restricted, so don't squander it living another person's life. Try not to be caught by authoritative opinion - which is living with the aftereffects of others' reasoning. Try not to let the clamor of other's perspectives overwhelm your own inward voice. And most important, have the courage to follow your heart and intuition."*
>
> \- STEVE JOBS

Most financier sites and applications were fabricated utilizing another person's reasoning, caught in the past with old tech and unfortunate plan. Utilizing Robinhood I felt my own internal voice, in a contributing sense, coming through. This smooth route let me take a gander at one stock and afterward with a couple of taps effectively contrast it with another. This easy experience put me in the investing flow and made me feel what they call *beginners mind,*[2]—an attitude of openness, eagerness, and lack of preconceptions when studying a subject, even when studying at an advanced level, just as a beginner would.

Experimental, new, and exciting

Prior we examined Benjamin Graham,3 one of early financial backers to present a viable way to deal with judicious stock choice. I read The Intelligent Investor year prior, and I return to it now and again, yet I didn't understand from that book how much fun he had exploring different avenues regarding contributing. One of his understudies, Edwin Schloss, said, "He was creative, it was another methodology. Everything was test. Everything was new. Everything was exciting."4

It's loads of fun while stock contributing is trial, intriguing. It's cool as a squirrel playing saxophone. Drawing by Edwin

Ben Graham's fascination with speculation

I needed to explore and have something very interesting in my venture life. However there was something missing… some guidance from Ben Graham himself on the most proficient method to go about it. And afterward I read this:

> *"Hypothesis is continuously entrancing, and it very well may be loads of fun while you are on the ball. To take a stab at it, set to the side a part the more modest the better-of your capital in a different asset for this reason. Never add more cash to this record on the grounds that the market has gone up and benefits are coming in. Never blend your speculative and venture tasks in a similar record, nor in any piece of your thinking."*
>
> - BENJAMIN GRAHAM

I knew immediately what I expected to do, which was to lay out a different record only for hypotheses; I wouldn't blend my theoretical and venture activities - in a similar record, nor in my thinking.

As I referenced beforehand, I set up a different record with Charles Schwab in light of the fact that I have viewed their organization as productive and solid while opening another record, they offer great telephone backing, and I've never disapproved of exchange execution. Schwab's cell phone application is phenomenal and the best part is their "Air pocket Charts." Schwab covers them under the rundown of stocks you own on the application. Bubble Charts are phenomenal perceptions, and I trust Schwab keeps on further developing their versatile app.

While Robinhood altered the rebate dealer model since sans commission stock exchanges behaved like a magnet to draw in Millennials and give them their first openness to stock trading.

Before Robinhood, financial backers expected to have no less than $500 and here and there as much as $1,000 or more to set up a money market fund, and afterward pay exchanging expenses in addition. Charles Schwab, E-exchange, and TD Ameritrade all mixed to match Robinhood in 2019, shamelessly pursuing Robinhood's juvenile crowd.[5] Robinhood's free exchanges for all obviously upset the industry.

Despite their prominence with financial backers, Robinhood is trapped in a difficult position: on one hand they are making it more straightforward for youthful financial backers to get everything rolling and figure out how to contribute. Then again, they are benefitting off their clients by selling request stream, and a portion of their clients probably won't deal with their recently discovered stock exchanging liabilities well.

I believe it's fabulous that Robinhood has opened up contributing to more youthful financial backers by bringing down the record least (different firms require $500 to begin, yet many starting financial backers don't have that much). I additionally accept the clients of the stage should instruct themselves about how to contribute - and that accusing the stage might be off track in light of the fact that numerous clients are figuring out how to contribute, intensifying their profits over the long haul, and watching their stock profits roll in.

I like how Robinhood energizes trial and error and "imaginative play." One of the most lively things about the application is the means by which you can get your finger across the screen and the outline immediately uncovers a stock's return for the afternoon, week, month, 90 days, year, and five-year time spans (however hopefully you will consider 10-year durations to be well). Also, assuming you have contributed through the application you can follow your record's worth throughout a wide range of time-frames. To the extent that I have seen, this powerful perception is extraordinary to Robinhood.

Here is my technique for utilizing Robinhood. I will open the application, click the amplifying glass, and afterward when I get to the "Famous Lists" and look at something like "Medical care Services" or "Tech, Media, and Telecom." Another way I like to look is to type in a state. I'm in Washington State, so by basically composing in the state name I see these stocks recorded: MSFT (Microsoft), AMZN (Amazon), TMUS (T-Mobile), COST (Costco), SBUX (Starbucks) and more than 50 other stocks.

This is for the most part a pursuit mission, and I'm simply searching for something that gets my creative mind that I need to investigate further. For instance, I went over T-Mobile and I never acknowledged it was situated in Washington. I have heard great stories from T-Mobile clients, generally about great PDA plans and inclusion in significant urban communities. That was great data, however truly I don't have the foggiest idea about a ton about T-Mobile.

So then I went to the listing on Robinhood for T-Mobile. I look at the outline, and I can see that (however beside late great returns, I don't advance anything from past execution) and I read the concise investigator reports. These are tiny passages from Morningstar investigator reports. I wouldn't depend on this examination since it is conceivable that it is old data, and there is not

sufficiently profundity to assist you with pursuing a choice. There are a million other sources for better company information: the 10-K, Value Line, a complete Morningstar Analyst Report (all three sources discussed in this book) and many articles that are one Google search away. I additionally prefer to watch YouTube recordings about the organization, and I glean some useful knowledge from interviews with the CEO.

Speaking of CEO interviews, not more than a day or two ago I watched a YouTube video that was a recording of a Zoom call with Andy Florance, the CEO of CoStar Group, the main supplier of land data, investigation, and online commercial centers. I had close to zero insight into him prior to watching the video and truly delighted in it.

What I truly like about the opportunity to explore that Robinhood gives, is that I put resources into a couple of organizations that got my creative mind, yet I could not have possibly contributed it in any case. CoStar Group is one such organization, and I purchased the offers two or three weeks prior and now that I'm an investor I'm much bound to follow each improvement about the organization since I have skin in the game.

For instance, only two days prior while Googling CoStar gathering to look into the organization (since I'm an investor now) I ran over an article declaring CoStar Group bought the houses.com URL.6 My exploration on Robinhood (and doing a few Google searches and perusing studies on Value Line and Morningstar) showed me how fruitful CoStar has been on creating and drawing membership incomes from the Loop Net site and apartments.com. Then, when I saw this news article about the purchase of houses.com I could quickly see that CoStar is possible going to assemble another wellspring of development and incomes by entering the private land data, investigation, and online marketplace.

If CoStar's prosperity with business land (it was a $6 stock in 1998 and $939.50 an offer on December 28, 2020) is any sign of its true capacity with private, I am happy I put resources into this company.

I didn't buy a solitary stock utilizing the Robinhood application. In view of my own exploration, and concerns raised in the articles examined before, I for one incline toward putting my exchanges utilizing an alternate financier application. I like Charles Schwab's application right now, however assuming perusers favor various specialists, including Robinhood itself, that is entirely satisfactory. I would simply agree that it's a good idea to sort out every one of the subtleties of how the dealer brings in cash, and assuming they're benefitting at your expense.

10 stocks using Robinhood imagination

I chose to purchase 10 stocks as trial speculations. I noticed Benjamin

Graham's advice:

> "to take a stab at it, *set to the side a piece the more modest the better- of your capital in a different asset for this reason. Never add more cash to this record on the grounds that the market has gone up and benefits are coming in. Never blend your theoretical and venture tasks in a similar record, nor in any piece of your thinking."*
>
> - BENJAMIN GRAHAM

I put the cash into these 10 stocks:

1. Alibaba (BABA)
2. Apple (AAPL)
3. CoStar (CSGP)
4. Costco (COST)
5. Nvidia (NVDA)
6. Salesforce (CRM)
7. Thermo Fisher (TMO)
8. T-Mobile (TMUS)
9. Veeva Systems (VEEV)
10. Zoom Video (ZM)

What I like about each company:

- **Alibaba:** A force in online retailing in China, analogous to Amazon's power in the US. I have always wanted to own shares in Alibaba.
- **Apple:** I have owned iPhones, iPads and MacBook Pros, and every time I need to replace a device I return to Apple. I know I'm not the only one. I've always wanted to own Apple stock.

CoStar: This company is the leader in commercial real estate data. Their niche websites including Loopnet are essential tools for brokers and real estate professionals. CEO Andy Torrance's scraped together money for pizza and beer with Jeff Bezos, his fried from physics class at Princeton. Wide moat business combined with terrific leadership.

Costco: Another wide moat company with phenomenal leadership and extremely loyal customers. Once they get that Costco membership they just keep coming back to get their money's worth! I've invested in Amazon for years because I saw the power of their model and the success of AWS, but I always thought I'd like to own shares of Costco and now I do.

Nvidia: They make the graphics processing units (GPUs) that power video games, game consoles, and autonomous driving vehicles. These powerful graphics cards will likely be essential parts of the development of artificial intelligence (AI) computers. Nvidia is the best in this class and the demand for their 3090 RTX graphics card is strong. Powerful customer demand coupled with a moat in the GPU sector make Nvidia best in class.

Salesforce: Marc Benioff has created a cloud-based computing dynamo that shows no signs of slowing down. His company was the first to sell software-as-a-service (SaaS) and through numerous acquisitions (Tableau and then Slack) he has built an enterprise software company to give Microsoft and others a run for their money. I like visionary leaders and wide moat companies.

Salesforce has both. Salesforce is simply beginning to taxi and they have a long runway.

Thermo Fisher: They make laboratory supplies and equipment, and they design high-tech measurement systems for scientific and pharmaceutical companies. Any lab researcher or scientist is familiar with their equipment and systems. It makes sense to invest in the companies that provide tools to scientists rather than pick the next biotech or pharmaceutical blockbuster. Thermo Fisher is a "pick-and-shovel" play that benefits from health care, pharmaceutical, and scientific innovation.[7]

T-Mobile: Everyone who seems to like their cell phone plan and coverage seems to have T-Mobile. The company is on the leading edge when it comes to delighting customers, and from a service perspective they appear to be eating AT&T's lunch. Valid, they are not the biggest organization in media communications, but rather their new procurement of Sprint and the way that they're developing their 5G capacities proposes that this organization will stand out in the ten years to come.

- **Veeva Systems:** Veeva's a cloud-based software company serving pharmaceutical and life sciences customers. Revenues from its subscription enterprise software have grown as more of its customers need to access their cloud-based system to run their businesses. Veeva's CEO, Peter Gassner is just the kind of innovator that leads top-notch technology businesses centered on data, right up there with Amazon's Jeff Bezos, CoStar's Andy

Florance, and Zoom's Eric Yuan. Veeva is a profitable company running an adaptable cloud-based platform, with loyal customers, a wide moat, and it was selling at a sensible price.

- **Zoom:** This company first appeared on my radar in 2019 when I was researching start-up companies that I thought had potential to rapidly grow their market share. I remember calling my friend Sam and asking him if I could try out this new video app called Zoom. He had never known about it. To think there was a day when there were individuals who had never known about Zoom. Presently I believe most would agree that pretty much every individual in the US (and numerous past) have been on a Zoom call no less than once. I could never have imagined back in 2019 when I previously investigated this stock that a year after the fact it would be a fundamental device of human correspondence in 2020. Zoom is from the get-go in its development stage and staying put. I've for a long time needed to claim offers and presently I do.

I longed for involving Robinhood for a couple of years, lastly I figured out how to involve it in my work process to explore new stocks. While I didn't buy the stocks on Robinhood's foundation (I utilized Schwab's application) I utilized Robinhood's apparatuses and records to start my examination into new companies.

I made these speculations with a little piece of my capital in a different record. I will watch these stocks and look into the organizations now that I own them. Robinhood ignited all of this experimentation.

PART V

INVESTING INSPIRATION: TOOLS AND IDEAS

24

IDEAS FROM GREAT INVESTORS

"Through possibilities different, through all changes, we make our way."

- AENEID

I believe there are some ways of thinking about investing that help an investor stay on track. You can call it an "investing mindset," and in my opinion, it's mainly about having the right temperament. You can't get too hot-headed or emotional. You need to be patient for long periods of time, especially when people are losing their minds and going to cash. And at other times you need to be decisive and buy big with the courage of your convictions.

I figure contributing can be simple, however it assists with realizing the reason why you're getting it done. Assuming you are simply doing it for no particular reason, or in light of the fact that you like seeing the diagrams on your cell phone application go up and to one side, then you could get occupied or forget about why you're putting resources into the first place.

The solution to the inquiries "For what reason do you contribute?" is presumably unique for every individual, except as I would see it, "to bring in cash" doesn't go sufficiently far. I ought to explain that by saying that generally incredible financial backers I have known have some motor inside them that observes something invigorating about the process.

I began in my mid 20s essentially in light of the fact that I needed to continue to handbag my photography vocation, and there was a ton of vulnerability to me about whether I would bring in sufficient cash, and what might occur assuming I had a drought and no one employed me. Thus, contributing just turned into a method for saving some cash for the future and allow it an opportunity to return in excess of a bank investment account or CD.

I was another financial backer and had no clue about what sort of return I'd get, whether it would be 7% or 15% or some place in the middle. Additionally, this was the point at which the Internet was simply taking off and there were no cell phone applications to make contributing speedy and simple. You actually needed to contribute through a specialist and data about stocks was difficult to get to on the web. Indeed, this would change soon enough, however right off the bat the thought was to purchase common asset offers or stocks and hold them forever.

But the speed of purchasing or it was not essential to sell stocks or assets. I was really giving all of my energy to improving as a picture taker and fulfilling clients with their photographs, and contributing was simply something I did month to month (I sent in an actually look immediately a month to purchase common asset shares for quite a long time) to fabricate a solid groundwork so I could go on with photography. Generally, I contribute in light of the fact that it gives me independence.

I frequently notice the ideal holding time for a stock is perpetually, however I understand that doesn't check out. After we bite the dust, when we're in the grave, or blowing around in the breeze, what befalls the products of all that examination and learning? Indeed, in the event that you're contributing for having the cash and things it can get, helping you's not going. Perhaps your beneficiaries, in the event that you have them, can spend the cash for you.

The eternity attitude is a superior method for pondering venture than the "hot potato" where you simply purchase something now and perceive how it work, realizing you can sell it in a couple of swipes in the event that it doesn't. But I'm not saying you have to hold on to your stocks and not enjoy the fruits of your hard work as an investor. Possessing stocks allows us to carry on with full and useful lives where, amusingly, cash isn't vital to our existence.

What's the final plan of contributing, the significant reason for this? To beat expansion? To have an immense retirement savings? Simply finding out about stocks and contributing for fun?

Your own solution to "why contribute?" might be completely unique. What is your contributing final plan, the reason for perusing and finding out about stocks? Would you like to beat expansion? Have a major lump of cash when you resign so you can make a trip to Chiang Mai and ride elephants the entire day, and eat your body weight in cushion see ew? Perhaps you need to venture out to Colombia and go for comfortable walks through the greenhouses in Medellin, the city of everlasting spring. Maybe you lean toward a languorous way of life and really like to sit poolside on

a Caribbean journey boat and drink your body weight in piña coladas while absorbing the West Indian sun.

Indeed, *everlastingly doesn't exist for people*. I figure you ought to contribute on the grounds that it gives you choices for your future. Assuming that you rearrange the thought, and inquire “what occurs in the event that I don’t contribute?” you come by various potential results. In the event that you’re lucky to carry on with a long life, the you have saved could lose buying power because of expansion. In the event that you have vehicle inconveniences you probably won’t have to the point of fixing your vehicle or get another one. You probably won’t have sufficient cash for everyday costs like food, or lease, or taxes.

Maybe you need to go in your 30s or 40s or 50s or past, yet possibly you don’t save so it’s anything but a choice, or you don’t contribute and the expense to zoom around and remain in unfamiliar terrains is too expensive.

I think reversing things is much of the time a simple method for pondering important choices, and when we flip things plainly getting ready for the future by contributing appears to be legit. *The amount you contribute*, and how hard you need to function now to take care of sufficient future cash is a decision that is well defined for each person.

I have companions who by and by, assuming they pass on with a lot of stocks in their Robinhood account, they view that as cash squandered. “Cool, I got these wiped out returns, however all that cash is as yet restricted in stocks and presently I’m dead and cold in the ground having done nothing with the profits I procured from contributing for the beyond 50 years… “[1]

One thing that is clear is that there are nobody size-fits-all arrangements. I’d say toward one side of the range you sock away a silly measure of cash in your speculation account, enough that you would never spend everything assuming you challenge Methuselah’s record.[2] On the opposite finish of the range, another person could like to spend their lifetime burning through cash appreciating travel or different encounters throughout everyday life, and crushing the last drops of juice from their venture accounts on their last day.

This is the subject of the grasshopper and the insect, and every one of us needs to sort out our own surplus of work and play.

Why Invest?

1. To have the screen to leave a place of employment you don’t like
2. To support you while you start another independent gig
3. To have a huge piece of cash to venture to every part of the world
4. To have the means to purchase decent vehicles or a pleasant home to enjoy
5. To realize you can bear to pay for medical services if necessary
6. To take care of yourself and not rely upon the generosity of strangers

7. To give cash to youngsters and future generations

While I believe it's a liberal mentality to leave a legacy for your kids, those individuals I realize who were given large chunk of change and didn't need to work for it have been the least happy.

If you give your children an early advantage in life they may never sort out the difficult work it takes to procure their direction on the planet. In some cases having less while you're beginning in life drives you to get innovative and face challenges you'd never take assuming that everything were given to you. I bring this up in light of the fact that the last point above appears to be in principle like something insightful for a parent to do, yet by and by I've never seen it help. Guardians who assist with their children schooling give a supportive beginning throughout everyday life, except sooner or later the preparation wheels need to fall off. Buffett's said to describe his own kids that he needed to leave them "enough cash so they would feel they could do anything, however not such a lot of that they could do nothing."3

From my viewpoint, putting resources into stocks gives you freedom due to the you decisions you can make now and further down the road. Purchase and-hold contributing is a definitive type of deferred satisfaction. You're putting off utilization today for the opportunity to consume more, or experience more, from here on out. I realize that certain individuals truly prefer to have things now, and they will offer up different things as a trade off. For instance, they need to possess the Tesla now, or the Chanel clothing, or the costly house, the new iPhone or MacBook or iPad. They purchase the most current things regardless of whether they as of now have completely great stuff since they need better. However they could detest their work, or perhaps they need to leave their place of employment, yet they'll simply need to work 10 additional years at a specific employment they hate in light of the fact that the home loan installment is so high.

If you contribute well, rather than purchasing all the stuff recorded over, your cash is in resources that produce more cash. That is the very straightforward rundown of resources: they put cash in your pocket. The liabilities of life are generally those different things: vehicles, houses, PCs, cell phones - they remove cash from your pockets. The financial backer is stacking up on resources currently in return for freedom.

If you do your best, you get to appreciate opportunity now. You should not

delay opportunity until you're too old to even consider getting a charge out of it; that looks bad to me. Individuals get malignant growth, coronary illness, or they can get hit by a transport. Assuming that looks bad to defer things you appreciate now since you desire to have more opportunity to destroy them the future.

I like to contribute in light of the fact that the cycle is loads of tomfoolery. It's a method for being imaginative and gain some significant experience every day, and I can in any case fill in as a photographic artist. I have no supervisor instructing me, it's not possible for anyone to fire me, and I can get away at whatever point I need. I like having clear days on my calendar.

"contribute" decends from Latin, yet it entered English through Italian in the mid seventeenth century. In Italian, *investire fostered a unique sense created from the idea of "clothing" cash in another structure*. That utilization was joined to the English word contribute, which ultimately came to allude to a responsibility of cash to procure a return. This monetary feeling of put is validated in the mid 1600s regarding exchanging by the East India Company.

> Havinge left with us in products and monies to honey bee put resources into wares fit for Englande … to the vallew of 4000 li.
>
> - T. ALDWORTH, LETTER TO E. INDIA CO., 1613

One valid justification to contribute is to travel. There might be places you have without exception needed to visit, yet your work or family make a drawn out excursion inconceivable. With enough contributed, you could really get some much needed rest work, or quit your place of employment completely. Or on the other hand perhaps you need to begin your own independent business, yet it will require a year to get everything set up. Your ventures could give you the autonomy from a normal everyday employment sufficiently long to begin your independent vocation.

There is no right response, nobody size fits all answer for why you ought to contribute. I believe it's worth the effort to contemplate your purposes behind contributing, in light of the fact that I think they'll assist you with concentrating, make things charming, and you'll realize the reason why you're investing the effort and energy assuming there is a main impetus, motivation to invest.

A questioner once asked Warren Buffett, "What engaged you about being rich?" "Indeed, I like to be autonomous," Buffett said. "I need to have the option to would what I like to do consistently. What's more, cash allows you to do that."4

A questioner requested that Carol Loomis portray Buffett's greatest strength: "Indeed, his greatest strength, definitely, is his soundness that he brings to business and contributing," Loomis said. "And this is a trait— rationality— that you would think many investors would bring to their work, but the fact is, most of them are swept up by emotions most of the time at some crucial time—and he never does that."5

The other mental idea that assisted me with contributing during the securities exchange breakdown that occurred during the Coronavirus Pandemic was to not fear the present moment. I lifted my eyes based on the thing was occurring on the ground before me, and I lifted my look to the skyline. I considered something that Buffett said about investing:

> *"American business will be worth more after some time. That is the very thing that you're purchasing is a business - you're not accepting a stock, you're purchasing a piece of an entire pack of organizations. Are those organizations going to be worth more 10 or 20 or 30 or 40 years from now? Obviously they are."*
>
> - WARREN BUFFETT

The statement above catches the drawn out vision important to be an effective financial backer. Assuming that you purchase stock in incredible organizations, you don't need to stress over selling it. Assuming you do your exploration and purchase astutely, you can simply pause for a minute and hold your stocks however long you like. Over the long run they will increment in esteem, and considering your justification for contributing you'll have a fulfillment realizing your speculations will in all actuality do fine and dandy without you tending to them.

This eases the heat off of you since you don't need to stress over the news, about the thing the market's doing today or this week or this year. You simply purchase the organization and disregard the market.

Now I'm not recommending you stick your head in the sand like an ostrich. Obviously, you will focus on the news and your portfolio, however you don't need to do anything.

Instead of an ostrich, I figure a financial backer ought to be "sloth-like," described by inaction. I know that in my own contributing life my own outcomes have been driven by a couple of good choices, and afterward not doing stupid

things like selling those organizations in an attack of frenzy or dread on the grounds that the sky was falling. Many individuals however it was, coincidentally, during the dotcom crash, the monetary emergency, and the Covid pandemic. I didn't sell during any of these occasions, I just held on during the dotcom calamity and was a purchaser of stocks during the others. It's not difficult to prevail by having the right disposition and not representing the purpose of activity. Recollect the sloth.

Stocks will compound in incentive for 10, 20, 30 years and then some. You are contributing for yourself, yet assuming you do things right, you're contributing for your youngsters and future generations.

It will assist you with keeping up with the drawn out view in the event that you can have the right demeanor. As Buffett said at the 2020 Berkshire Hathaway yearly gathering, "Dread is the most infectious illness you can imagine."6 So one of your fundamental errands as a financial backer is to protect yourself from dread and different feelings that will disrupt your endeavors. You need to keep cool and just respond to the degree that you can exploit financial exchange falls to purchase stocks when they get cheap.

25

THE MAGIC BOX

"Einstein is credited with saying accumulate interest is the most remarkable power known to man. The thought of taking care of cash is generally essential to the companion that least gets it: youthful people."

- SCOTT GALLOWAY

The magic box

Compound revenue is the way to contributing. Charlie Munger said, "Understanding both the influence of accumulating funds and the trouble of getting it is the essence of understanding a great deal of things."

"Begin taking care of cash, early and frequently. Consider it sorcery. Put

$1,000 into an enchanted box and in 40 years - BOOM! - it's $10,000 to $25,000. On the off chance that you could have this enchanted box, how much cash would you put in it?"1

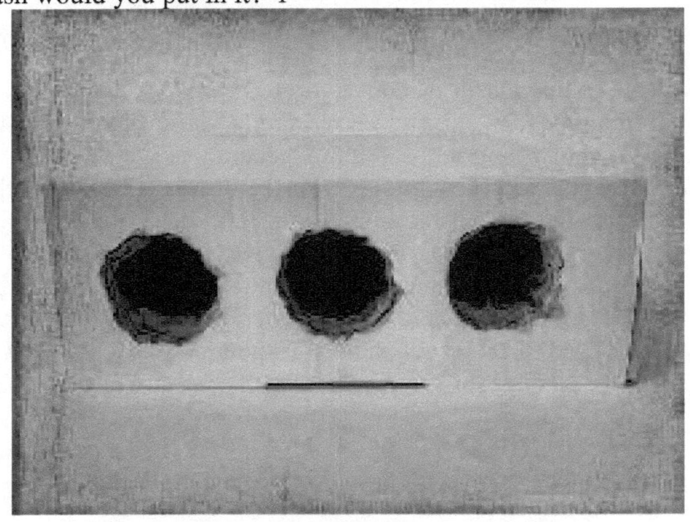

If you had this enchanted box and put $1,000 into it so that in 40 years it's $10,000 to $25,000, how much cash would you put in it?
Photo © Jeff Luke

The idea of a magic box into which you put money is that the value of your shareholder equity—your ownership of the business through stocks—will increase if the company can successfully compound shareholder equity at an attractive rate over the long term. The development of your piece of investor value (reflected in the cost of your stock) after some time is called compound interest.

You ought to try to put resources into organizations with incredible possibilities to develop over the course of the years on the grounds that your venture returns won't be vastly different from the profits on the organizations' profits on capital. On the off chance that they are simply fulfilling existing clients yet not augmenting their canal or spreading out into new regions, in the drawn out the business will not develop. You need to put resources into organizations with dynamic pioneers that track down better approaches to develop, address client needs, create loads of money, and contribute it insightfully (or spend it on acquisitions that add esteem). I'm discussing Google procuring tons from individuals tapping on their promotions and utilizing a portion of that cash to purchase YouTube, or Facebook gaining Instagram. Amazon made a few intense trials to develop past their internet based retail business by imagining the Kindle, Alexa, and Amazon Web Services, and Microsoft created Xbox and Azure. These are dynamic organizations that continually track down better approaches to develop their contributions to enchant customers.

"Over the long haul, it's difficult for a stock to procure a vastly improved return than the business which underlies it acquires," Charlie Munger said.[2] "Assuming the business acquires 6% on capital north of 40 years and you hold it for that 40 years, you won't make entirely different from a 6% return-regardless of whether you initially get it at a tremendous markdown. On the other hand, assuming a business acquires 18% on capital more than 20 or 30 years, regardless of whether you follow through on a costly looking cost, you'll wind up with a fine result."

Compound Interest

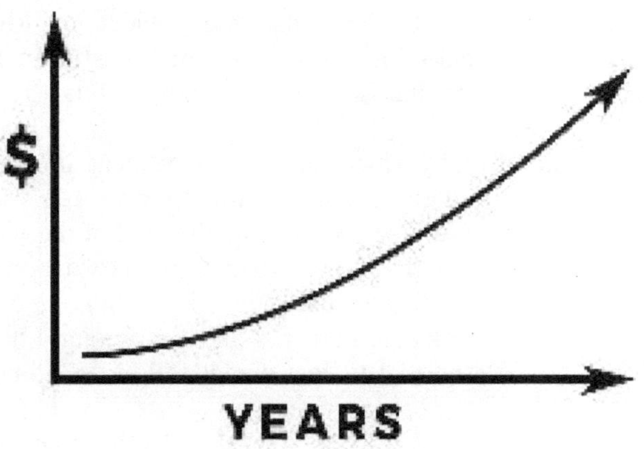

Ben Franklin once stated, "Recall that cash is of a productive creating nature. Cash can bring forth cash, and its posterity can sire more, thus on."

Some individuals are more understanding than others and are brought into the world with a personality that is appropriate for venture. Persistence followed by definitiveness on a couple of events in life is a decent formula for progress. Regardless of whether you are not normally a patient individual, or you need conclusiveness you can foster these characteristics over the long haul to improve as an investor.

It's protected to say, in any case, that not all individuals show restraint financial backers; the

human mind isn't wired to show restraint. People advanced on the grounds that our huge cerebrums enabled us to settle on speedy choices in light of survival. We respond to dangers in our environmental factors as an issue of endurance, yet there is little prize in nature for tolerance. The nature to do things is permanently set up for us. *We are not worked to lounge around and do nothing.*

Yet, feeling based believing is our most terrible adversary with regards to contributing. We really want to go with less choices since inaction allows your speculations to compound over time.

During the 2020 pandemic, I invested some energy watching recordings by a YouTuber whose channel is classified "Beat the Bush3. He had put resources into stocks including Tesla, and these speculations had done above and beyond time. He tried to avoid panicking during the financial exchange crash in March, and shockingly he stayed patient and didn't sell his stocks, however he committed seemingly a genuine error: soon after the financial exchange started to recuperate, he transferred a video on May 11, 2020 named "I Sold All My Stocks." In this video, which is still on YouTube, he introduced his purposes behind speculation stocks would keep on going down.

While I think it is really smart that an assortment of viewpoints are accessible on YouTube, I in all actuality do think individuals watching these recordings could endure assuming they follow the lead of the video maker. I have contributed for a long time, and when I observe a portion of these recordings I need to concede that occasionally I keep thinking about whether individuals selling their stocks are correct - and I'm wrongly holding stocks during the pandemic. It's normal to feel dread; following up on it can hurt your results

Two days after the "I Sold All My Stocks" video, he transferred another video on May 13, 2020 named, "Don't Invest in These Markets." Then, after seven days, on May 20, 2020 he transferred another video named "The amount I Lost Timing the Market." I provide him with a great deal of credit for his trustworthiness in understanding that his momentary view and enthusiastic responses might have constrained him to sell each of his stocks in May of 2020. The aggregate sum he lost timing the market is likely difficult to work out, on the grounds that as business sectors move over the long haul the missed stock increases proceed to grow.

Let me bring up the issue with all that watchers checked whether they focused on those recordings (and many did as anybody can see by perusing the remarks beneath the recordings). Beat the Bush was making expectations on the bearing of the securities exchange. As I have referenced before in this book, financial backers center around their stocks or other investible resources, and brokers center on

attempting to anticipate the market. Beat the Bush said that he felt the post-pandemic market had recuperated excessively fast and would almost certainly crash once more. At the point when the market didn't slump once more, he turned into a securities exchange Cassandra and made a one more video, "Approaching Stock Market Reckoning" in which he recorded many reasons that the securities exchange was going accident further in light of approaching joblessness because of the pandemic lockdown. He refers to numerous reports to help his theory. He said, "I'm searching for a base here, I'm searching for the values to be to some degree safe and I won't see a sensational misfortune soon." The issue is the base had been arrived at 90 days sooner in March 2020.

At the beginning of that video, Beat the Bush declares that the video is supported by WeBull, and he says, "Before I start, this video is supported by WeBull" and he proposes that watchers to pursue a free record to begin exchanging." One watcher posted beneath the video, "the economy will crash and we will lose all our cash. BTW truly do pursue a WeBull record to put aside an installment and begin exchanging :)"

Be careful when you watch recordings of moderators anticipating what will occur in the financial exchange; these forecasts are very difficult to make and no one can outfox the market with any consistency.

The spring of 2020 was a troublesome time for some financial backers since there was a dread that everything was going to heck, and it was typical for individuals to search externally for replies. It was sincerely difficult to just hold your stocks and "sit idle," and certain individuals couldn't deal with their feelings of dread and sold their stocks. Selling in view of feeling has become simpler than any time in recent memory with free exchanging accessible on such countless stages. At one at once to pay an expense to exchange, and frequently needed to call an intermediary to give guidelines. With these obstructions eliminated there could be as of now not any hindrances to visit trading.

He sold his stocks and went to cash after the market had recuperated around 10%, yet the market kept on climbing 30% more in the following two months. Assuming he had sat idle, his speculations would have become another 30% in two months.

The other issue he has is that now the business sectors have recuperated to approach untouched highs, and stocks are more costly than any time in recent memory. To get once again into the market, he should repurchase in at a lot higher cost.

His passionate choice to sell stocks made him "sell low" and to contribute once more, he might need to "purchase high." His choice to time the market presents a mystery: he can address expanded costs to reinvest now that stocks are more costly or remain uninvolved as the market moves from now on. It's a hopeless scenario. One occasion in support of himself would be a financial exchange crash, yet what sort of life is it to simply sit around idly trusting the market declines. Charlie Munger introduced the model he called "Sit on your butt investing" at the 2000 Berkshire Hathaway yearly gathering. Munger said, "You should simply pick a truly incredible organization when it is appealingly estimated, and afterward sit on your butt. The extraordinary benefit being that it just requires one decision."

To contribute wisely, your objective ought to be to allow accumulate interest to happen and never hinder it pointlessly. There are many ways to interrupt it, such as selling stock or fund shares or switching (unnecessarily) from one investment to another. You can likewise purchase a stock, for instance, that loses a great deal of its value.

In 2018, Facebook stock exchanged above $215 right off the bat in the year and afterward dipped under $125 later that very year. Also, Nvidia exchanged above $290 just to fall underneath $125 later in the year. Individuals purchasing these stocks were reasonable simply trusting the costs would continue onward up, which is betting. In the event that they had been patient and not responded to the stock costs going ever more elevated, they might have paused and purchased similar offers a lot less expensive after the costs declined.

Overpaying for stocks is a certain method for obliterating the impacts of progressive accrual. Assuming you address a sufficiently high cost for a stock, it might never recuperate to the cost you paid, or it could take such a long time just to equal the initial investment that each of the years you stand by are squandered in light of the fact that the cash isn't compounding over time.

The critical action item from this part is to make a couple of wise speculations it very well may be one, two, three stocks in the event that you are simply beginning. Advance however much you can, purchase your stocks, and don't feel you really want to make a move for following through with something. Simply plan to purchase a couple of good stocks and allowed your cash to compound in esteem over time.

Charlie Munger put it best: "The entire thought of not accomplishing something exceptional is one all financial backers ought to regard, yet it is not difficult to neglect, especially in distressing circumstances." Munger frequently says that financial backers don't need to do anything remarkable.

One of the most significant examples Munger offers to us to decrease your gamble of drawback misfortune: "It is amazing how much long haul advantage individuals like us have persuaded by attempting to be reliably not dumb, rather than attempting to be very intelligent."

26

FOCUS IS KEY

Great investors focus well. Learning about companies and waiting for the right stock price takes patience. As you become a more experienced investor you'll learn to focus by reading, learning, and following the progress of a company over time. It doesn't have to be a boring or tedious process; it tends to be exciting!

When Bill Gates initially met Warren Buffett, their host at supper, Gates' mom, asked everybody around the table to recognize what they accepted was the absolute most significant component in their prosperity through life. Entryways and Buffett gave a similar single word reply: "Focus."1

You will find it simple to concentrate once you start it you're over the top going to explore organizations that. Notice I didn't say "organizations that interest you" or "organizations that you like." You must be a devotee. You need to like picking up, digging, and getting clarification on some things. I would say, the best financial backers look like insightful correspondents continuously posing inquiries to realize more.

What assuming the organization you're thinking about for speculation makes an item that conflicts with your ethics or morals? I'd say "to contribute or not to contribute" is an individual choice. I like to keep away from stocks that eliminate wellbeing or satisfaction from the world. I realize that smoking is an individual decision, however I'd prefer not to possess tobacco stocks despite the fact that the organizations create steady incomes due to the habit-forming nature of their products.

If you dig deep enough, I think you can find something unsavory about many companies, but my own northern star has guided me away from owning stocks of companies that make guns, nuclear weapons, etc., just as I would not personally endorse these products. I would never tell someone else what they ought to do and regard other financial backers' choices.

Many of the largest channels in business include items that are staggeringly tacky with the eventual result of being habit-forming. Assuming we just required cell phones and PCs to call, email or message we could make due with basic gadgets. However anybody who is fixed on what sorts of applications are most famous in the Apple Store or Google Play realizes that games are amazingly well known, and the equivalent goes for PlayStation, Twitch, or Xbox, which can be very addictive.

So, I think we as a whole need to simply go with our own solace level to the extent that which gadgets offset pleasure with the potential for long haul hurt, and for me supporting computer games is a lot simpler call than a few other expected ventures. I observe too much YouTube recordings and the powerful urge to watch "only one more" is an ideal illustration of the tenacity of web based services.

What you definitely know gives you an edge. Turn into a fan and concentration to limit your field of view. You can't be a specialist in all things, however you can turn into a specialist in a couple of things and focus on them. You should have the option to dedicate consideration regarding learning, keep away from interruptions, and become a specialist in an organization before you at any point contribute. A long capacity to focus will help you in this pursuit.

As we referenced before, Todd Combs, who Warren Buffett recruited to work at Berkshire as a venture administrator, peruses for 12 hours every day. That is the stuff to get a venture record so great that Buffett sees you. I'm not saying that you need to go through each waking hour finding out about organizations, however notice the association between the time spent perusing and success.

Your capacity to zero in on what you comprehend and finishing some genuine perusing will help you colossally. You need to turn into a specialist and jump truly profound. Whenever you comprehend an organization better than most others, that will be an indication that you're getting some place. When you become a specialist in that organization you should be ready to act conclusively when costs get cheap.

One incredible method for guaranteeing you're arranged is to constantly have a money hold in the bank prepared to contribute. As Charlie Munger makes sense of, it can have a significant effect. "Being ready on a couple of events in a lifetime, to act speedily in scale, in doing some straightforward and sensible thing, will frequently decisively work on the monetary aftereffects of that lifetime."2

Focus on learning

Buffett was once posed the inquiry, "What is your best guidance for new investors?"3

> *"For another financial backer, well I would do a ton of perusing before I contributed, I would plan for it. I wouldn't simply bounce in the water 'till I thought I realized I could swim. So I did a great deal of perusing - I read each book that the Omaha public library had about contributing when I was 11. You have a lot of time, you're youthful, to contribute, so why not go in ready as opposed to advancing as you come. You will advance as you come - that accompanies contributing, however it's better assuming you've done some mulling over everything, kind of take as much time as necessary getting into it. But you're not too young to start preparing for it at all."*
>
> \- WARREN BUFFETT

Buffett's methodology generally inclines in the direction of learning, arrangement, and understanding. These practices are enormously helped along by doing a lot of perusing and watching talks and meetings on YouTube and other video stages. You would be stunned by the quality and amount of recordings by extraordinary financial backers, and furthermore by the heads of a significant number of the organizations you may be thinking about for investment.

The time you spend perusing and learning is important for the center expected to succeed as a financial backer.

27

A GOOD CHECKLIST

"No shrewd pilot, regardless of how incredible his ability and experience, neglects to utilize his checklist."

- CHARLIE MUNGER

Once you start using the PALMS filtering system essentially an investing checklist you'll develop ninja-like speed and quickness when it comes to picking promising companies and weeding out the others. You won't even need to check a printout out. Simply take a gander at the palm of your hand.

As I referenced before, before you even beginning the PALMS approach, ensure you comprehend the organization you're considering.

This book gives you the agenda, however it depends on you to analyze an organization and answer every thing yourself.

In his book The Checklist Manifesto,1 Atul Gawande composed that great checklists:

- *... are precise. They are efficient, to the point, and easy to use even in the most difficult situations.*
- *They do not try to spell out everything - a checklist cannot fly a plane.*
- *They provide reminders of only the most critical and important steps - the ones that even the highly skilled professionals using them could miss.*
- *Good checklists are, above all, practical."*

Pilots use agendas since they essentially wipe out slip-ups and oversights. Photograph © Jeff Luke

Professionals use agendas at whatever point lives are in question, whether working in the working room or flying a plane. “Pilots use agendas since they essentially dispose of missteps and oversights. Notwithstanding mechanical agendas mounted in the cockpit, we counsel plasticized and electronic agendas showed on PC screens, and agendas for errands like de-icing.”2

Similarly, the PALMS sifting framework gives a basic framework to assist you with killing missteps and choose if a stock checks out. It’s reasonable and simple to utilize, and you can constantly track down the agenda by looking at the palm of your hand.

You can utilize PALMS to ensure you’re not disregarding any significant speculation factors. In any case, I need to be clear with you that this is anything but a stock-picking equation since one doesn’t exist. You should take as much time as necessary and do your examination; simply believe that since it requires difficult work being a chore’s going. I’m continuously learning new things when I read about companies
—new technologies, inventions, people, etc., and this process always makes me want to learn more.

I accept a structure is superior to an overall recipe, which won’t work for everybody. How could the individual who fostered the recipe share it with others in the event that they could stay quiet? There are books about contributing that give “enchantment recipes,” yet might we at any point sensibly expect that each individual who purchases the book will make progress? In the event that everybody could utilize the equation it would get utilized so frequently that the benefit would disappear.

No, I think a contributing structure checks out. It shows you the contributing elements and allows you to track down your direction. Not a guide to speculation will show you the best way to live to progress in light of the fact that such a guide is unadulterated dream. You will find stocks that seem OK in light of your remarkable comprehension of the world.

The PALMS agenda is intended to keep you on target and posing the right inquiries. It ought to likewise keep you from making mistakes.

Just say ‘No’

Just express no to a ton of awful speculation thoughts. Assuming that the organization has never

made money, simply say no. In the event that you got a hot tip from somebody and you don’t know anything about the organization, simply say no. Why for heaven’s sake do you have the right to get rich putting resources into things that you don’t know anything about? Saying “no” keeps things basic and guarantees that when you say OK you will mean it.

The more you use PALMS the more it will become intuitive, and it will constantly show up for you.

28

EYE ON ETERNITY

"You should take a gander at things in the part of eternity."

- BARUCH SPINOZA

Think about owning shares of a company for decades. With this timeframe, even if you don't get the absolute lowest price when you buy a stock, the company will grow with time and your investment will have a good return even if the purchase price is a little expensive. You will seldom regret paying a fair cost while purchasing the supply of a magnificent company.

Stock costs will generally follow organization benefits. From the start, you might not have any desire to purchase the stock assuming the cost appears to be high; it very well may be difficult to be focused and patient when you need to purchase a stock. I was chatting with a companion as of late, and she let me know that she considered purchasing Amazon stock when it cost $200 an offer. She didn't buy it then, but she did buy it years later when it cost $800 a share. She expressed that at $200 Amazon was a book shop that did another things, yet at $800 clearly Amazon was executing effectively in a wide range of industries.

One of the keys to canny contributing is the capacity to detect organizations like Amazon at $200 and having the option to get a handle on the organization's strong vision for what's to come. Many organizations have large dreams for future achievement yet can't execute on them. When you observe an organization like that, remember that there will be a few extremely tough situations of unfortunate stock execution and times when the market slumps and the stock decreases in esteem. During these times, in the event that the organization is as yet unblemished and run well, you want to

keep the long-
term viewpoint and oppose selling simply on the grounds that the cost becomes modest; this is unequivocally the time you should purchase more stock!

If you return and take a gander at Amazon's 1997 yearly report you can see a plan for what they would before long accomplish. Despite the fact that numerous relaxed eyewitnesses saw a web-based book shop, Jeff Bezos explained his arrangements to the people who read this letter.

"To our shareholders:

Amazon.com passed a large number in 1997: by year-end, we had served more than 1.5 million clients, yielding 838% income development to $147.8 million, and broadened our market initiative in spite of forceful serious section. But this is Day 1 for the Internet and, if we execute well, for Amazon.com. Today, online business sets aside clients cash and valuable time. Tomorrow, through personalization, online business will speed up the actual course of revelation. Amazon.com involves the Internet to make genuine incentive for its clients and, thusly, desires to make a getting through establishment, even in laid out and enormous business sectors... "

- 1997 AMAZON SHAREHOLDER LETTER BY JEFF BEZOS

We can see that Amazon completed its drawn out vision effectively for over 20 years. A financial backer who perceived the indications of progress almost immediately and purchased stock would get extraordinary returns. You don't have to possess many stocks like Amazon to make a fantastic contributing career.

We have previously taken a gander at how to analyze a 10-K to learn about the organization's crown gem and it's development motor. The short section I'm showing you above is only the sort of data that ought to make your eyes lump and jump off of your mind in an animation like way. Assuming you are a starting financial backer, and you can see that another organization has served more the $1.5 million clients, and yielded 838% income development in only one year, you should peruse on.

It might appear glaringly evident now that Amazon would turn into an enormous achievement, however when that Amazon investor letter was distributed in 1997 achievement was not ensured. There were still a many individuals who didn't figure Amazon would prevail as a book shop,

significantly less the retailing and technology
stalwart it has become.

It is evident that clients were finding and purchasing from Amazon in 1997 and the organization was developing quick. As a financial backer who is searching for the following extraordinary organization, search for any signs that a great deal of new clients are purchasing from an organization and that incomes are expanding quickly. The Management Discussion and Analysis (MD&A) we talked about in the prior part, "How to Read a 10-K," will definitely examine and dissect the development of another organization. I would most likely prescribe that as an area to zero in on for significant experiences on a developing company.

One quality that separates Amazon from different organizations is that it has never been excessively worried about assuaging transient investor requests. Many organizations attempt to intrigue financial backers by amplifying quarterly outcomes no matter what or delivering out a predictable profit. They are centered around momentary execution that frequently gooses the CEO and chief group's bonuses.

Bezos and his group have zeroed in first on their clients, and afterward on Amazon's way of life of advancement and making an incentive as long as possible. Subsequently, the organization has drawn in the sorts of investors who stayed close by in years before the organization had such gigantic achievement since they could see the engineer's outline becoming fully awake before their eyes.

Two of Amazon's authority standards are to think long haul and develop in the interest of clients, and the organization underlines those standards regardless of whether that implies they show a benefit immediately. When confronted with showing a benefit or reinvesting cash in the business they pick the last option. It takes discipline to reinvest in the organization when such countless financial backers are centered around momentary benefits. Thusly, thinking long haul serves Amazon well, but on the other hand it's a decent adage for the organization's investors too.

However, intelligent investors can see progress before it's widely apparent to everyone else. For example, I've been a customer of Amazon's, buying many products other than books—cameras, lenses, furniture, etc., and while it's true I never invested in the company when it was not yet turning a profit, it hit a point a few years back when it became profitable. That was still an excellent time to invest in Amazon. The company was growing and profiting at the same time, and the early years of investment without profits were a thing of the past.

Bezos realizes that it is vital for think long haul. Later in the 1997

Amazon investor letter, he stated, “We accept that a principal proportion of our prosperity will be the investor esteem we make over the long *term. This worth will be an immediate consequence of our capacity to broaden and set our ongoing business sector administrative role. The more grounded our market authority, the more remarkable our financial model.”*

Amazon's future is depicted with incredible clearness: Bezos had a dream for Amazon to turn into the market chief. It was recorded in 1997 and the organization has based upon it consistently since.

So, how might being familiar with this influence you as a financial backer? Indeed, you need to search for this sort of vision in any likely organizer or CEO of an organization in which you contribute. You will not be guaranteed to observe a pioneer precisely like Jeff Bezos, yet assuming that you are fortunate you will observe different authors or CEOs who give something their clients need and are headed to continue improving and enhancing for these clients over the long term.

For instance, I did a great deal of examination into little organizations for a book I wrote in 20191, the year prior to the Coronavirus pandemic. I found a little open organization called Zoom Video Communications (ZM) and read a great deal about its author and CEO, Eric Yuan.

I watched a few meetings with him on YouTube-they're all still there - and the more recordings I watched the more intrigued I became with his ability and uprightness. He zeroed in on making his clients blissful and making Zoom an incredible spot to work.

While Eric Yuan and Jeff Bezos lead various organizations, there is a hard thing to measure however exceptionally strong in their presence. When you see that special spotlight on clients and vision for the future it simply leaps out at you.

The very long haul imagining that drives business helps a financial backer too. A financial backer necessities to look past momentary commotion and look not too far off, quite far while envisioning how a business could look past the following 3, 5, or 10 years. Ben Graham urged his understudies to think long haul toward the beginning of his contributing class at Columbia. Marshall Weinberg was an understudy of Graham's at Columbia, and said that something Graham said on the principal day of class right away gotten his attention.[2]

> *“Ben Graham opened the course by saying, ‘to bring in cash on Wall Street you should have the appropriate mental disposition. Nobody communicates it better than Spinoza the savant. Spinoza said, ‘You should check out at things in the part of forever.’ “*

- MARSHALL WEINBERG

Let's say you need to contribute as long as possible and you're not extremely certain assuming you ought to purchase the stock. For some explanation, you could falter and put off contributing. It's normal to need to try not to commit an error and here and there this will keep you from making that underlying investment.

One method for getting energy to put resources into another organization is to purchase few offers to begin. You don't need to go "all in" toward the start. You can simply get one offer, or 10 offers or anyway many offers seem OK to you.

Once you've laid out a little position you can evaluate the organization's advancement and choose if you have any desire to purchase more offers. This way you can essentially get everything rolling contributing with an eye toward time everlasting. Over the long haul, you'll sort out whether or not you pursued a decent choice. Assuming all works out positively, you can continuously purchase more offers later.

29

WE'RE ALL INDEXERS

Picking stocks using the filtering system in this book is not for everyone. Some people don't want to spend the time learning about companies who would be better off investing with low-cost index funds.

Many starting financial backers would be in an ideal situation purchasing a minimal expense record reserve as opposed to attempting to pick stocks themselves. What I'm expounding on in this book is guided toward individuals who need to carry greater power to the game, not that I'm saying it's easy.

I trust at this point perusers will comprehend that it is very hard to beat the market. It takes expertise, karma, the right personality, and a readiness to find out about new organizations ceaselessly. It additionally requires an attitude where you understand you will make a few missteps and lose cash, however you can't be stopped by your mix-ups; as a matter of fact, you'll view at each slip-up as a potential chance to pick disappointment's pocket and gain something from each mistake.

Let's investigate file contributing. Whenever you purchase portions of a record reserve you are purchasing a little piece of various organizations. It's a straightforward method for possessing the whole universe of stocks-or any subset of the market
- in one basic investment.

Now, remember that assuming you own a singular stock, another person is selling it; it's a shut universe. In that sense, we are largely indexers since we're exchanging similar universe of stocks with one another.

Jack Bogle outlined the absurdity of attempting to outfox different financial backers. "Check the complete securities exchange: that is the very thing we as a whole own," he said out. "Presently cut about 33% of that out, and those are indexers who know the worth of ordering, so they own a record reserve, and with no exchanging. Then look at the other two-thirds: those people own the market index, by definition, those stockholders, but they're not satisfied with that. They need to wager against one another, and consequently they lose to the record by how much exchange costs they have."

This outline shows the whole universe of stocks. We as a whole own that. You can cut 33% of that out you can see that those financial backers know the benefit of ordering. The valuable example is that dynamic financial backers and record financial backers are on the whole fishing from a similar stock universe.

One straightforward truth about contributing is that we are for the most part putting resources into similar universe of organizations. On the off chance that you simply take a gander at the universe of organizations in the United States, there are around 4,300 public companies.[1]

When you choose to purchase a stock, at that equivalent second another person chooses to sell. It's difficult to be aware at that point assuming you've gone with the ideal choice, yet there are two costs you'll need to pay without a doubt: exchanging commissions and expenses. These frictional expenses destroy from your speculation returns.

Invest with your eyes totally open. Understand that you are purchasing stocks in a similar universe as every other person. It's difficult to beat the normal financial backer, particularly when you think about the frictional expenses of exchanging charges and taxes.

30

MY INVESTING MISTAKES

I've made my share of investing mistakes, and I felt horrible about them all. I have owned two stocks that sucked like an airplane toilet, and the sinking feeling of owning them lasted until the day I finally sold them. It wasn't a fun experience, however it was instructive.

I depict them in this section since you ought to know that even the writer of a contributing book commits errors. There are additionally a couple of key examples that you can advance right now that could keep you from making something very similar (or comparable) mistakes.

The illustrations that stick are much of the time learned through experimentation. You tell yourself "I won't ever commit this error from now onward!" and realizing this way will make things stick in your memory. It's smarter to commit your errors when you're youthful and have less cash to lose than when you're more seasoned and your misfortunes are bigger. Obviously, it's smarter to gain from others' missteps, however in reality, it is unavoidable that you will make your own. I trust that they are not many, and the measures of any misfortunes are small.

All the books and articles you read about contributing can Sadly give you a limited amount a lot of shrewdness. Unfortunately, the examples that stick must be learned through direct insight. So in the event that you can simply learn not to overreact, not to get bothered, and try to avoid panicking you'll be fine. Considering botches a method for learning is an extraordinary methodology. The significant thing is to really record what you gain from each slip-up. On the off chance that you fail to remember them and rehash them, you will be in a difficult situation. But if you can pick the pocket of each mistake you make then you'll do well.

I composed this part since I need to show you that even an experienced financial backer commits errors. This isn't something that I have an extraordinary outlook on sharing, however that's what I feel assuming I compose a book about how to contribute yet don't examine the missteps I've made, you could think I just use sound judgment, which isn't true. And more importantly, you will not realize how much you can actually learn from the market's feedback.

You will end up being a specialist in distinguishing deplorable ventures and staying away from them. Not messing yourself up is a large portion of the fight! Thusly, you need to stay away from specific exercises altogether and figure out how to manage blunders in judgment expeditiously at whatever point they arise.

The pieces of truth in this part are that all fruitful financial backers, assuming they've been busy sufficiently long, have committed errors. This part is just focusing a light on a couple of I've made to show you that you can commit a few idiotic errors yet get by. You will gain from these mix-ups (essentially that ought to be your objective) and what you realize will make you a surprisingly better, more grounded, and more smart investor.

You can likewise see a portion of the missteps I made in light of the fact that I didn't have a framework. I didn't understand the significance of any of the parts of the PALMS framework when I began, so all that I shared before in this book was not given to me toward the beginning. Through not seeing enough about organizations and not posing an adequate number of inquiries, I ended up committing a few excruciating errors. I've figured things out and continued on with my contributing (allowed to commit considerably greater and more awful errors!) and I realize you can profit from finding out about my terrible choices and not rehashing them yourself.

The primary gamble I confronted while beginning was not realizing a thing about contributing! I was around 25 years of age and simply beginning as a photographic artist in Seattle. I realized I needed to contribute however didn't have numerous instances of fruitful financial backers. I had an optometrist who made a duplicate of a magazine article for me to peruse (it was extremely useful beginning), however you need to understand that this was the mid-1990s and the Internet was fresh out of the box new. There was no such thing as google and Youtube at this point, and it was absolutely impossible to find out about contributing online.

The first common asset I put resources into quite a while run by an accomplished worth financial backer, Michael Price. I picked the asset since it put resources into stocks that were offering inexpensively comparative with their worth. It ended up being an extraordinary first asset since I began putting resources into the years paving the way to the website crash in 2000. The shared asset didn't take an interest in the speculative way of behaving and subsequently, it did very well.

After a couple of years, I likewise began putting resources into the Dodge and Cox Stock asset, a safely overseen stock asset, and that reserve additionally stayed away from the speculative overabundances of the time. You need to understand that the majority of the hot cash was filling tech subsidizes like those run by the Janus Fund family, and those investors endured wretchedly during the accident.

So you might be asking, who cares, where's the mix-up? Indeed, I hadn't committed any enormous errors yet. I chose to begin putting resources into the Vanguard 500 list. I accept this was on the grounds that it was generally known as a minimal expense shared asset, and it appeared to be an incredible method for getting openness to "development" stocks (on the grounds that my other common assets were both "esteem" reserves. The choice to purchase portions of this asset was fantastic; my mix-up was that I chose to ultimately sell my portions in the S&P 500 asset (which puts resources into the 500 biggest US organizations) and utilize the returns to buy only two stocks.

If I had just held my portions of the file store I would have accumulated my contributing dollars at a lot quicker rate. However I was positive about my choice and it appeared to be shrewd at that point. I was quite sure the two stocks would do to some degree as well as, and presumably much better, than the list store. That ended up being a terrible mistake.

Here's the thing: while you're contributing accurately, it ought to exhaust. At the point when I chose to sell my list asset and purchase stocks I was presumptuous from my prosperity picking common assets and figured this capacity would mean stock picking: it didn't. One truth I took in the most difficult manner was that in my initial years I was greater at picking shared assets than putting resources into stocks.

Now, 15 years later, I can explain what happened.

1. My common assets were moving along, compounding in worth, and I got exhausted. I wanted to get a few stocks and "hit it enormous" with a couple wins.
2. My common assets were doing extraordinary, and I accepted my great asset choices would mean exceptional stock selections.
3. I thought I comprehended the stocks I was purchasing, yet in all actuality, I had close to zero insight into the basic organizations or their leaders.

Let me give you foundation about two or three terrible choices I made and what I've gained from them.

It was 2004, and for the beyond couple of years, I'd been purchasing portions of the Vanguard S&P 500 record store. I had been contributing $200 consistently and it intensified pleasantly in esteem. Rather than being content with my file subsidizes' prosperity, which required next to no work on my part, I chose to enhance the completely good 10.4% return of the Vanguard S&P 500 record reserve that year. Rather than staying with file reserves, I figured I'd take a shot at picking stocks and beat the exhausting S&P 500 list fund.

So, toward the year's end I sold all of my Vanguard record store shares and utilized the returns to purchase two stocks.[1] Yes, you read that accurately. I chose to place every one of my eggs in just two bushels. I went from 500 organizations in the record asset to possessing only two stocks.

Here are the two stocks that I bought:

Stock 1: Leucadia National Corporation

I took a risk on this organization basically on the grounds that I comprehended close to nothing about what this organization did. I figured you could be "Adequately close" in getting a stock. I knew that generally the stock had performed well, and I had heard that the CEO, Ian Cumming, was an all around regarded dealmaker.

Leucadia National Corporation had as often as possible been alluded to as a "Child Berkshire Hathaway" and it was controlled by two experienced financial backers, Cumming and Joseph Steinberg. Everything considered, the correlation with Berkshire Hathaway was a stretch since Berkshire Hathaway purchases quality organizations with solid serious "channels," and Leucadia's supervisors purchased modest, rumpled, undesirable organizations and breast fed them back to wellbeing to sell at a major benefit. In land speech, they were great at "flipping" companies.

Shortly after I purchased the stock their prosperity changed. They encountered a few little disappointments, one achievement (an interest in an Australian mining organization called Fortescue), and afterward the organization spun out of control after the monetary emergency. Leucadia has not taken an interest in the financial exchange recuperation beginning around 2009. Leucadia National stock has failed to meet expectations the S&P 500 record eight of a long time from 2010-2020, following the file by as much as - 32.86% in 2014.[2]

Leucadia put resources into a biotech fire up considered Sangart that explored a manufactured blood substitute that could be utilized in injury circumstances, for example, car

mishaps or in battle where patients need blood right away and human blood isn't accessible for bondings. Sangart fostered a substance called Hemospan (otherwise called MP4OX). This substance was a polyethylene glycol-formed human hemoglobin. This blood substitute took part in clinical preliminaries in the US and Europe. In creature models, Hemospan was demonstrated to be powerful in instances of hemorrhagic shock.[3]

There was a ton of trust that Hemospan would be a blockbuster red platelet substitute as it was fit for moving a lot of oxygen. Sangart declared positive outcomes from a stage II review for this item in November 2005.

Over numerous years, Leucadia put countless dollars in Sangart, and at last possessed the whole organization. In the event that Hemospan had been a blockbuster the bet would have paid off, however eventually, the blood substitute was not supported by the FDA and Sangart promptly shut down its business. The Hemospan dream passed on and all in all nothing remained to be displayed for the investment.

Though it was only one of Leucadia's numerous speculations, I feel Sangart encapsulated Leucadia's destruction. In its initial days the ball bobbed in support of themselves, yet when things begin turning sour the disappointments speed up, and Sangart was the good to beat all of terrible investments.

But Leucadia wasn't done at this point. The organization's last hurrah was the acquisition of 78.95% of National Beef Packing Company for $867.9 million. Not long after purchasing a larger part interest in that business, the hamburger business hit tough situations. The dairy cattle crowd in the United States started to diminish and the cost of hamburger declined, which diminished incomes in the meat handling industry.

Leucadia CEO Ian Cumming and Chairman Joseph Steinberg concluded the time had come to resign from Leucadia, so they designed an arrangement in which they consolidated Leucadia with a venture bank called Jefferies Group, which was controlled by CEO Richard Handler, whom they appreciated and had worked with on many arrangements previously. The joined organization would hold the Leucadia name. In proposing the arrangement to investors, the heads of the two organizations talked about collaborations in the arrangement where Jefferies (a venture bank) would furnish Leucadia with exceptional speculation amazing open doors, and money rich Leucadia would give Jefferies the money rich post of an accounting report that Jefferies frantically needed.

The cooperative energies examined before the consolidation won't ever emerge. I held the stock for a considerable length of time after the consolidation, meanwhile trusting the joined element would live up to up to the assumptions set by the pioneers who designed the merger.

After claiming Leucadia stock for over 10 years, I sold my portions at a similar cost $23 an offer that I had gotten them for 10 years sooner. While I didn't lose cash in my Leucadia speculation, I would have fared better had I recently left the cash in the Vanguard S&P 500 file store, which returned 74% during a similar time frame.

As a commentary to this catastrophe, however I sold my situation in 2014, I saw that Jefferies Group CEO Richard Handler (Leucadia National changed its name to Jefferies) was profiled in the Wall Street Journal as the most generously compensated banking and monetary CEO in 2018 procuring a sum of $44,674,231.

Handler got this high remuneration notwithstanding his organization slacking the S&P 500 by - 13.19% over the past decade.[4] An article named, "Money Street Chiefs' Pay Doesn't Sync With Returns" depicts this very error between the CEO's compensation and stock returns.[5]

Lessons learned: Just in light of the fact that you read that an organization is like a "Child Berkshire Hathaway" doesn't mean it's valid. Regardless of whether apparently shrewd shared store directors own the stock, that doesn't mean it's smart. I really want to show up at a comprehension all alone, and not simply believe that the organization's racers will keep on dominating their races, regardless of how shrewd they appear. At the point when an organization faces an endless flow of frustrations, it's smart to get over whatever might already be lost and continue on. There are better purposes of time and cash than trusting and hanging tight for more brilliant days.

Stock 2: White Mountains Insurance Group

White Mountains Insurance had a magnificent history under its author, Jack Byrne, who was a legend in the protection world. I purchased this stock fundamentally in light of the fact that I had heard the amount Warren Buffett respected Jack Byrne (they had cooperated before, during when Byrne saved GEICO from insolvency) and talked unquestionably exceptionally of Byrne's capacities. So when I put resources into White Mountains I thought I was turning into an investor in a moderately run organization with an incredible CEO.

Three years after I turned into a financial backer in White Mountains, Jack Byrne ventured down as CEO and was supplanted with a replacement. I can't tell you much about what occurred with the organization after Byrne left, yet like numerous insurance agency, White Mountains Insurance appeared to be an exhausting business. That will be normal since insurance agency are not so invigorating as the Wimbledon finals. Safety net providers gather expenses (called "float") and get to clutch that cash and contribute it before they at last need to pay claims, which might be a long time from here on out. Insurance agency can equal the initial investment on guaranteeing, yet at the same time create gains by contributing the float. The genuinely extraordinary safety net providers create a gain on endorsing and by contributing the float.

I couldn't actually say whether this specific insurance agency was very much run since I didn't comprehend the computations important to assess their business. It requires investment to find out about the various sections of the protection business (protection, reinsurance, guaranteeing, contributing) and I cared very little about turning into a specialist on insurance.

Investing in an insurance agency could seem OK for a financial backer who previously had insight in this industry. Over the long haul I could see that the stock cost of White Mountains Insurance Group was not staying aware of the S&P 500 file, and following a couple of years I chose to sell the stock since I couldn't say whether the terrible relative presentation was connected with the board, an awful environment for back up plans, or something else.

Lessons learned: Because I didn't comprehend White Mountains Insurance or the protection business by and large, I shouldn't have put resources into the organization. Whenever Jack Byrne, who worked really hard running the organization, chose to resign I ought to have sold the stock. Proceeding to hold the stock when the pioneer who assembled the incredible record leaves can be a mistake.

What were my stock returns?

Though I was certain I could pick extraordinary stocks, I was not yet great at picking stocks and my fair returns demonstrated it: Leucadia's 10-year normal yearly returns6 were - 5.66%. White Mountain Insurance Group's 10-year returns were 7.77%. The normal annualized joined return for the two organizations during the past 10-year time frame was 1.06%. Presently, I like a positive return as much as anybody, yet that is not the very thing I call a major move.

I didn't lose cash, yet I missed out on the potential chance to have that cash put resources into different organizations I understood.

I get a sense of ownership with those profits. I picked the stocks when I got them, and assuming things had turned out contrastingly and their costs shot up to the moon I would have thought myself pretty brilliant. As it turned out, the returns were mediocre at best and I have no one to blame but myself. That is the main way I can gain from the circumstance. Obviously, I could pin the crummy outcomes on misfortune, however I wouldn't get to learn anything.

Even however I didn't lose cash it was a quite terrible speculation considering I faced the challenge of claiming stocks and deteriorated returns than cash in the bank. To show you the open door cost of my choices, during a similar 10-year time frame the Vanguard S&P 500 file reserve returned 10.37%.[7]

The open door cost of my terrible choice was 10 years' deficiency of self multiplying dividends. The cash would have developed at a fabulous rate on the off chance that I'd quite recently left it in the file reserve. All things considered, by selling my record reserve shares (1) I needed to make good on capital additions charges and (2) for over 10 years I had acknowledged stock-like gamble in return for currency market returns. The arrival of 1% didn't stay up with expansion, so my dollars lost buying power.

I intruded on the strong impacts of self multiplying dividends. It resembled sticking a stick in my spokes while riding a bicycle. I incurred superfluous damage when I might have done nothing.

My "take-home" lessons

The S&P 500 list reserve is a brilliant vehicle for intensifying cash over the long haul, and my choice to sell my file store offers to purchase individual stocks was an impractical notion at the time since I had hardly any familiarity with the organizations I chose to purchase. I expected to get those two stocks on a lot further level. I had not done what's needed examination, and it was what I didn't have the foggiest idea about that truly harmed my returns.

Warren Buffett says, "Chance comes from not realizing what you're doing" and furthermore "The most effective way to limit risk is to think." I thought I had a decent comprehension of those two stocks, yet here we are. I knew around 5% of what I had to be aware. I had an essential layout of the organization subsequent to perusing the yearly report, yet that wasn't enough.

I believe it's vital to reexamine your explanations behind purchasing a stock assuming the organization's CEO changes, or on the other hand in the event that the organization converges with another organization. In the event that the withdrawing pioneer directed the organization's previous achievement, you might need to sell when they leave. Assuming you stand by too lengthy you could wish you had sold sooner.

> *"Would it be a good idea for you end up in a constantly spilling boat, energy committed to changing vessels is probably going to be more useful than energy dedicated to fixing leaks."*
>
> - WARREN BUFFETT

Pay no regard for any CEO articulations about how they intend to make something happen from now on. Numerous pioneers talk a decent game, yet guarantees of a more promising time to come are in many cases in view of idealism, not reality.

I'll provide you with an illustration of why I accept it's vital to focus on the rider running the organization. Starbucks had an extraordinary run when its organizer, Howard Schultz, drove the organization as CEO.

Schultz originally resigned in 2000, and not long after he left, Starbucks lost its. Same-store deals deteriorated and the stock cost went no place for a very long time. The impression of Starbucks as a top of the line bistro melted away and it appeared to be the brand had become exhausting; the characteristics that made the bistros exceptional had disappeared. Things got so terrible for Starbucks that Shultz emerged from retirement and took over as CEO in 2008 following an eight-year break. He stayed at the organization for a very long time and gotten Starbucks back on track.

When Schultz ventured down again in 2016 he was supplanted by Kevin Johnson, and the organization appears to have recuperated. Starbucks is an illustration of an organization that is reliant upon a pioneer for progress. It isn't enough for Starbucks to sell espresso just. The brand is subject to a pioneer to assemble the way of life and impression of the brand as a unique objective. Obviously Starbucks won't prevail under any pioneer it needs somebody who keeps on giving a very good quality client experience and impression of connoisseur coffee.

A wise financial backer should keep on top of initiative changes at any organization they claim or are thinking about for speculation, and think about selling the stock-or if nothing else screen what is happening cautiously when another CEO replaces the organization's founder.

Why did Starbucks run into some bad luck? Some portion of the explanation could be owing to the originator's flight, yet another clarification could be that the organization developed quickly for a long time, and at last that development eased back. Individuals in the long run maximize on how much espresso they drink in a day, so the store has needed to fan out into selling new food things and juice, smoothies, and different things, yet the development of the past has not returned.

Starbucks has spread out and begun opening stores in Brazil, China, and numerous nations all over the planet. However development in these nations brings new expenses and dangers. Starbucks stock has moped during this time span, shutting at $54.24 on July second, 2015 and after three years, on July second, 2018 the stock shut at $49.06. A Starbucks investor who claimed the stock during that time period saw the stock cost declined -10.2%, while the S&P 500, which could be possessed reasonably through a list reserve, returned
+31.2%. There has been an incredible open door cost of claiming Starbucks stock during that time frame.

The organization is certifiably not a terrible venture in light of the fact that the stock cost has declined. In the event that the organization stays strong and the stock cost declines, its engaging quality as a venture rises. This doesn't imply that any organization turns out to be more important when its stock cost declines, however taking everything into account, the edge of security and potential returns ascend as the cost declines.

So, the resolve of the story here is to ensure you comprehend the business and ensure the CEO answerable for an organization's drawn out progress stays at the organization as CEO. Assuming they resign, regardless of whether they hand-pick their replacement, you ought to have one or two misgivings of the organization's future in light of the fact that the organization might change decisively after their flight. For verification, look no farther than General Electric after Jack Welch left and Jeff Immelt became CEO.

That is the illustration I learned with Leucadia National and White Mountains Insurance. I will continuously consider the flight of the CEO as motivation to watch out for the organization under the new leader.

An exercise you can use

If you've invested in a company and either the company or its stock has not performed as you'd hoped (and in most cases, let's face it, that just means it hasn't gone up!) then what should you do? The quick and easy answer might seem that you should just sell it, but in these situations you should be careful not to be a knee-jerk seller or buyer. Eliminate your feelings from any choice and focus your endeavors on retesting the suspicions hidden your thesis.

Here's the activity: utilize a "spotless piece of paper" system to decide if the organization's benefit has changed. To utilize the Starbucks model, assuming that you read through the organization's yearly report (which you should

read consistently assuming you're a financial backer) you will observe a segment dedicated to the organization's financials. Inside that part search for the line stamped "total compensation," which is a different way to say benefits. Ensure the organization ceaselessly increments benefits. Contrast the latest benefits and earlier years, and ensure the number is growing.

If you see that the company is increasing profits and its fundamentals are good, yet the stock price (the valuation) has stagnated or declined, then it's not necessarily a good idea to sell the stock. That stock may be a decent worth at a low cost, particularly assuming the organization is growing.

Read however much you can to find out about the worries confronting the organization and its industry. Inquire as to whether the organization is in as cutthroat a situation as when you initially purchased the stock. Anything that you choose to do, ensure it depends on insightful thought and not a speedy choice in light of your frustration.

Short-term difficulties shouldn't eclipse a solid fundamental organization. Assuming that the organization is strong and essentially confronting a troublesome economy or transient disagreeability, it very well may be definitely justified to endure the hardship. If you have been watching the situation closely, however, and you have noticed a fundamental change in the company, its leadership, or a diminution of its competitive advantage, then it might be time to sell.

The Boiling Frog

The bubbling frog is a tale it being gradually bubbled alive to depict a frog. The premise is that if a frog is suddenly put into a pot of boiling water, it will jump out, but if the frog is put in tepid water which is then brought to a boil slowly, it will not perceive the danger and will be cooked to death. The story is much of the time utilized as an illustration for the failure or reluctance of individuals to respond to or know about evil dangers that emerge continuously instead of suddenly.[8]

It would appear as per present day researcher, the reason is bogus, and a frog that is steadily warmed will change its area as a feature of its essential endurance instinct.

With contributing, nonetheless, I think there is a propensity to stay with holding stock in a that has a gradually declining stock cost since organization basics are breaking down. The bubbling frog analogy applies somewhat in light of the fact that you will hold the stock significantly longer than was "healthy."

As financial backers, we get connected to the possibility that our underlying justification for it be great to purchase the stock should in any case. We need to be correct, and we get appended to that unique contributing reason regardless of whether things are gradually getting worse.

Put another way, things don't change for the time being at an organization. There is no "signal" that out of nowhere you ought to sell your stock. All things being equal, things gradually deteriorate, and keeping in mind that at first you could feel like you're showing restraint, in the end you could detect you're being obstinate. It's a hard call to make, on the grounds that as a rule a touch of persistence is all that is needed.

In my circumstance, particularly as it connects with Leucadia National, I ought to stand out enough to be noticed to what was truly occurring at the organization, and not what I trusted could happen soon. The initiative was disintegrating throughout the long term, yet the corporate remuneration was increasing.

Instead of running for the ways out, I held my portions, not having any desire to "sell low." I'm sure that I was energized by the new CEO, Richard Handler, who communicated idealism that the post-consolidation future looked splendid. Numerous CEOs, it ends up, are excessively hopeful about their capacities to change companies.

Believing the circle back story, combined with my trusting Leucadia would make something happen, around, made me hold the stock significantly longer than I ought to have. Gain from my experience in the event that you would be able, and when an organization faces difficult situations whether because of unfortunate authority or a changing business climate you might need to consider selling the stock.

I am in good company in this outlook either; Warren Buffett has frequently spoken about how he sunk truckload of cash into the perishing material that was once Berkshire Hathaway. The material business was crumbling, but instead than shutting the material factories Buffett kept on attempting to save a perishing business. Buffett said, "So at first, it was generally material resources that weren't any benefit. And afterward, slowly, we assembled more things on to it. But always, we were carrying this anchor. And for 20 years, I fought the textile business before I gave up. Rather than placing that cash into the material business initially, [had] we just began with the insurance agency, Berkshire would be worth two times however much it is now."9

In the 1985 Berkshire Hathaway letter to investors, Buffett stated, "In this way, we confronted a hopeless decision: tremendous capital speculation would have assisted with keeping our material business alive, yet would have left us with horrible profits from always developing measures of capital. After the speculation, besides, the unfamiliar rivalry would in any case have held a significant, continuing

advantage in labor costs. A refusal to contribute, notwithstanding, would make us progressively non-cutthroat, even estimated against homegrown material manufacturers."

I partake in Buffett's capacity to observe humor even in predicaments. I generally thought myself in the position portrayed by Woody Allen in one of his movies:

> 'More than some other time ever, humanity faces a junction. One way prompts despair and sheer terribleness, the other to add up to eradication. Allow us to supplicate we have the insight to pick correctly.'"
>
> \- WOODY ALLEN

This shows that even the best business personalities once in a while get into hard business circumstances where there is no basic arrangement, and the best arrangement is simply to quit placing cash into an awful business. I feel the very applies to holding the supply of an organization that is enduring and trusting things will change.

Why do I help myself to remember some stock contributing misstep I made over 10 quite a while back? It's unpleasant, and I can't change the past, so why? I figure the response might be found in an old Russian adage that Jack Byrne shared this his White Mountains Insurance Group's investor letter: *"Choose not to move on and you'll lose an eye; fail to remember the past and you'll lose both eyes."*

Our errors are fight scars that remind us we made due past difficulty. Here and there the conflicts endured quite a long while, and pondering the difficult stretches keeps us humble and reminds us to be thankful for the things that work out. Charlie Munger addresses the benefit of recalling your screw-ups when he said, "I realize I'll perform better assuming I shame me with my mix-ups. This is a superb stunt to learn."

Buffett summarizes contributing along these lines: "On the off chance that you played golf and you hit an opening in one on each opening, no one would play golf, it's unpleasant," Buffet told FT. "You must hit a couple in the unpleasant and afterward escape the rough.... That makes it interesting.[10]"

31

EQUANIMITY

Equanimity is the key to investing success. It's characterized by your ability to keep cool under pressure. If you can control your temperament you will greatly improve your chances of success.

You ought to plan to purchase stock in incredible organizations and hold them for quite a long time. Different ways to deal with purported "contributing," to be specific day exchanging, guessing on investment opportunities, or attempting to anticipate future value developments are for the most part types of betting. You ought to permit your cash to compound after some time with not many interruptions.

Warren Buffett and Charlie Munger accept that the progression of time is the companion of the financial backer or money manager, with anxiety being their adversary. Whenever got some information about a major drop in the worth of Berkshire Hathaway's stock, Munger said succinctly:

> *"This is the third time Warren and I have seen our property in Berkshire Hathaway go down, top tick to base tick, by half. I believe it's in the idea of long haul shareholding of the typical changes of*

common results of business sectors that the drawn out holder has his cited worth of his stocks go somewhere near say 50%.

"as a matter of fact, you can argue that if you're not willing to react with equanimity to a market price decline of 50% two or three times a century you're not fit to be a common shareholder and you deserve the mediocre result you're going to get compared to the people who do have the temperament, who can be more philosophical about these market fluctuations."

- CHARLIE MUNGER

Aim to keep cool-headed notwithstanding financial exchange storms. Since the market is climbing or dropping doesn't mean you want to do anything. A ton of others will feel these desires, however in light of the fact that they're dumbfounded doesn't mean you need to be. The advantage of a declining market is that you can exploit low costs in stocks that you need to purchase. Serenity will assist you with keeping your head when everybody around you is losing theirs.

In the 2017 Berkshire Hathaway Annual Report, Buffett composed that it's a horrible idea to utilize acquired cash to claim stocks. "There is essentially no telling how far stocks can fall in a brief period," he said. "Regardless of whether your borrowings are little and your positions aren't quickly undermined by the plunging market, your psyche might very much become shaken by frightening features and winded critique. And an unsettled mind will not make good decisions," Buffett said.

Speaking of the unpredictability of business sectors, and the significance of keeping up with composure, Buffett said:

"In the following 53 years, our portions (and others) will encounter declines… No one can let you know when these will occur. The light can whenever go from green to red without passing at yellow," Buffett said. "Whenever significant downfalls happen, in any case, they offer exceptional open doors to the individuals who are not crippled by obligation. That is an ideal opportunity to regard these lines from Kipling's If:"

> If you can keep your head when about you are losing
> theirs…
> If you can stand by and not be drained by pausing …
> If you can think - and not make considerations your
> point … If you can trust yourself when all men
> question you … Yours is the Earth and all that is in it.

I don't question that assuming you contribute for more than a few years you will encounter market declines or some likeness thereof. Regardless of the situation, consistently mean to stay harsh and systematic. Pay attention and pursue choices with a quiet mind.

32

THREE USEFUL ATTRIBUTES

This chapter contains three investing factors that you may find useful in your own investment operations. The first is to not be active for the sake of doing things, the second is knowing when to sell stock, and the third addresses the sort of missteps a financial backer is probably going to commit.

Sometimes do nothing

Once you own stocks, the best arrangement is generally to sit idle. Inaction is the best arrangement since when you act, particularly founded on feeling, you're normally wrong.

Warren Buffett contrasted his organization's venture style with a sloth in an investor letter.[1]

> *"Dormancy verging on sloth stays the foundation of our speculation style. This year we neither purchased nor sold a portion of five of our six significant holdings."*
>
> - WARREN BUFFETT

Sometimes it is a decent decision to sit idle. It isn't generally a great opportunity to purchase stocks. Whenever costs appear to be pricey, and an air pocket may be framing, you can be greatly improved holding on until costs become more sensible.

There are times when stocks are famous, costly, and everyone and their cousin are getting them. Since others are doing dumb things doesn't mean you need to take part. Purchasing when every other person is following the group is never really smart since stocks are many times evaluated excessively high. It's smarter to hold on until after a market decline, of something like 10% or more.

Nobody will hold you back from purchasing, yet your future returns will lower in the event that you purchase stocks when they are costly. Taking everything into account, assuming that you purchase stocks economically you have a superior opportunity of better yields. So remember the benefit of being patient when others are blowing a gasket. Attempt to think in opposition to the group and understand that behaving like a sloth, moving gradually when everyone is going around like insane, is in many cases the best path.

Remain patient while you learn, read, and plan to act when you accumulate sufficient data to settle on a decent choice, and in the end, the market will transform (it generally does) and you'll be all the more clear about the stock you need to purchase at a reasonable price.

When to sell a stock

There are times when tolerance isn't compensated. In his book Common Stocks and Uncommon Profits,2 Philip Fisher frames his three principles for selling a stock:

1. Wrong Facts: There are times after a financial backer buys a stock that they understand that the realities don't uphold their unique reason. In the event that the buy postulation was at first based on an unstable establishment, the offers ought to be sold.
2. Changing Facts: Current realities of the first buy might have been considered right, yet realities can change adversely over the long run. The board decay as well as the fatigue of learning experiences are a couple of motivations behind why a stock ought to be sold by Fisher.
3. Scarcity of Cash: If there is a deficiency of money accessible, and in the event that an interesting open door introduces itself, Fisher educates the deal concerning different protections to subsidize the purchase.

Sometimes it's hard to sell a stock in light of the fact that in some way or another it powers you

to concede that you committed an error when you got it. You should keep in mind that when you bought, your decision was probably a good decision based on everything you knew then. Maybe now you have new data about the organization, or the administration or business has changed. Whatever the explanation, assuming you got the realities wrong when you contributed, or they changed, or you want the money, these are largely substantial motivations to sell.

In many areas of contributing your understanding will be compensated, yet I have observed that with regards to offering acting early in view of one of the over items' ideal. Pausing and trusting that things will change is seldom an effective technique, in some measure as far as I can tell, and at last, when you sell your stock you'll ask yourself, "For what reason didn't I do this sooner?" At least that is my experience; I wish I had pursued the choice before for each stock I've sold.

Errors of commission and omission

The two mix-ups you're probably going to make are either:

- *Errors of commission* in which you do something by mistake that doesn't work out. This includes buying a stock when you don't understand the company well, or when you buy stock and the economy changes dramatically and the company's prospects deteriorate. For example, buying airline, cruise, or hotel stocks right before the Coronavirus pandemic.
- *Errors of omission* in which you don't act when you should. This includes understanding a company but waiting or never buying the stock because it seemed too expensive at the time, etc. This happens when you learn a lot about a company through reading, watching videos, or through your work, and you suck your thumb instead of backing up the truck and loading up on the stock.

Most individuals who have contributed for some time know the sensation of accomplishing something moronic, and these are not difficult to excuse yourself for in light of the fact that every individual who contributes for any timeframe will make some mistakes.

The blunders of exclusion can get you since you were ready however didn't act; when you know to the point of settling on a strong choice, yet you simply lounge around and sit tight at a superior cost that never arrives.

So, the fix to staying away from mistakes of oversight is to hold on until you feel sure about how you might interpret an organization, and afterward go with a choice when you feel prepared. You might not have any desire to hold on until you know 100 percent about a circumstance since that won't ever occur. When you have around 70% of the data you want it very well may be an ideal opportunity to ponder purchasing the stock.

I could have invested sooner

My mix-up - assuming I'm straightforward in evaluating my contributing record over the beyond 10-15 years-is that I purchased no stock in three organizations I belittle most: Adobe, Amazon, and Apple. As an expert photographic artist, I've utilized Photoshop pretty much consistently beginning around 2003. Adobe is the best picture altering programming around, yet I've never purchased Adobe Systems stock. Huge mistake.

I've claimed just iPhones and MacBook Pro PCs since I began purchasing Apple items in 2008 and I've won't ever think back. Each telephone or PC I've purchased since is made by Apple, and the equivalent could be said to describe a significant number of my companions. However I've never purchased Apple Stock.

Finally, I've been an Amazon Prime part and an ordinary client of Amazon's starting around 2006, yet I never purchased Amazon stock. This is presumably the greatest non-choice I've made. I've seen the many advantages of purchasing things from Amazon throughout the long term, and I've been a faithful client. I've purchased practically every one of my cameras, focal points, and business gear from Amazon throughout the most recent 15 years, yet I never purchased Amazon stock.

Learn from my error: If you center your examination around organizations that you see well-particularly through your immediate experience as a client you will enjoy a benefit. Additionally, check out you; you might see that a ton of others are disparaging similar organizations and are exceptionally content with the items and services.

Once you have made a rundown of organizations you know well, you'll then be totally ready to plunge profound and pose the inquiries I'll show you in forthcoming chapters.

33

DECISIVENESS

If you're just getting started with investing you will be better prepared by spending time learning and not being too active. Warren Buffett said, "You only have to do a very few things right in your life so long as you don't do an excessive number of things wrong."

Charlie Munger expresses that as opposed to being continually moving, it's ideal to invest energy planning for opportunity.

> Experience will in general affirm a long-held thought that being ready, on a couple of events in a lifetime, to act immediately in scale, in doing some basic and coherent thing, will frequently emphatically work on the monetary consequences of that lifetime. A couple of significant open doors, obviously conspicuous accordingly, will normally come to one who constantly searches and pauses, with an inquisitive psyche that loves finding including numerous factors. And afterward everything necessary is an eagerness to wager vigorously when the chances are incredibly ideal, utilizing assets accessible because of judiciousness and tolerance in the past.
>
> - CHARLIE MUNGER

My most prominent individual contributing mix-ups have been mistakes of exclusion of not making a quality, high-speed choice on a stock like Adobe or Amazon that I saw well. I've discovered that I ought to embrace a superior dynamic cycle. Before, rather than purchasing Adobe and Amazon, for instance, I purchased the stocks in three different organizations I knew less well,

chiefly in light of the fact that I saw them as "great stocks to put resources into" however they weren't organizations I understood.

Adobe and Amazon have developed at a shocking rate, and I ought to have perceived their cutthroat situations in their separate business sectors since I purchase from Amazon consistently and I use Adobe Photoshop pretty much every in my photography business. It was a blunder of oversight not to purchase both of these stocks years ago.

The other mix-up I have made on no less than three events is overall too definitive about stocks I didn't totally have the foggiest idea. I was putting more with the expectation that the stock cost would go up, and my certainty depended on the supervisors running these organizations. It was to some degree like wagering on the rider as opposed to the pony. These organizations had remarkable chronicles, yet the CEOs answerable for these records would resign not long after I purchased the stock. This has been my experience two times - first, when Jack Byrne resigned from White Mountains Insurance Group, and afterward when Ian Cumming resigned from Leucadia National Corporation. I ought to have sold the two stocks the moment each ventured down.

You will possibly lament being definitive when you purchase battling organizations or those you don't have any idea. I might have worked on my outcomes by putting resources into organizations I comprehend as a client - organizations like and comprehend. The rundown of organizations I comprehend incorporates Adobe, Amazon, Apple, Berkshire Hathaway, Google, and Starbucks in addition to a couple of others. I utilize their items and administrations and my comprehension depends on direct insight. You will have your rundown of organizations, and when you have the cash and the cost is reasonable, definitive activity will serve you well.

34

ZERO-BASED THINKING

Once you start investing you may notice one of your stocks is not performing well. For some reason, the story changed from when you bought it. The company may not be earning much money, or the leadership is not innovating fast enough. Maybe the business is losing out to new competition. There are so many reasons that stock prices decline. Your task as an investor is to be like an investigative reporter and find out why the company is failing, as well as determine if the problem is temporary and will likely pass or on the other hand in the event that it's foundational and it's the ideal opportunity for you to sell the stock.

It's not simply you. You might feel alone and caught experiencing the same thing, yet numerous different financial backers have confronted comparable problems. It's not simply you, it's the truth of being a section proprietor of a business that occasionally you need to take a decent, hard, objective gander at what's happening and conclude whether you ought to hold on or conclude that now is the right time to go with a choice and sell the stock.

In my view, the most obviously awful thing you can do is stay baffled and need to sell don't however do anything all things being equal. In the event that you think feeling these feelings and not settling on choices with clearness is simply something you're doing, let me advise you that you are in good company. Many individuals would prefer to continue to drive off course as opposed to recognizing that they've made an off-base turn. Even great investors hold onto stocks long after the company has changed for the worse. At the point when you perceive this has occurred, you can simply endure things and trust what is happening improves, or you can sell the stock and move on.

I have possessed stocks too lengthy time and again. I can review five stocks that I figured I would claim perpetually, and my longing to stay with them

everlastingly blurred my practical insight and held me back from selling when I ought to have. At the point when an organization has inconvenience for a little while in succession, you might be in an ideal situation selling it as opposed to trusting things will improve.

It appears to be that when organizations begin to battle for some explanation (the business crumbles, the administration is awkward, or both) you are lucky to be simply selling. The most terrible choices I've made were the point at which I had an awful really strong inclination about an organization that I ignored.

I think the brain research behind this conduct is that when you purchased the stock, you thought the organization was smart (clearly, or you could never have gotten it!). Then the company performs worse than you hoped it would, so you either have to sell it (which means admitting to making a bad decision) or stick with a bad stock hoping things get better, which they rarely do. It's the victory of trust over experience.

Individuals in awful connections commit a similar kind of error. There is an inclination that you've proactively contributed such a lot of significant investment, so there is a reluctance to separate. This' referred to in financial matters as a sunk cost,[1] which is an expense that has previously been caused and can't be recuperated. Sunk expenses can be differentiated future costs that might be stayed away from assuming activity is taken.

People participate in what's known as a sunk expense paradox when they proceed with a way of behaving or try because of recently contributed time, cash or effort.[2]

The financial expert Richard Thaler delineates the hypothesis with an illustration of individuals who could arrange an excessive amount of food and afterward over-eat just to "get a fair shake". Likewise, an individual might have a $20 pass to a show and afterward drive for quite a long time through a snowstorm, since they believe they need to go to due to having paid for the ticket.

If the expenses offset the advantages, the additional expenses caused (burden, time or even cash) are held in an unexpected mental record in comparison to the one related with the ticket transaction.

With contributing, the time you've previously spent calmly holding up as the organization has gone no place (or more awful, declined) can cloud a financial backer's choices about what they ought to do now. Obviously, managing what is happening is a lot more grounded than connecting oneself to the past, yet people will generally stick to sentiments or recollections, or on account of contributing, give a lot of weight to a mistake of interest in the past.

If a business is monetarily enduring it is a lot harder to fix things and continue on. With fellowships and connections, it is much of the time simple enough to

resolve a misconception and continue on, however organizations that get downright ugly are like The Titanic; they move too leisurely to course-right and end up sinking. There are a bigger number of purposes behind business disappointment than I can rundown, and when terrible things begin happening it's exceptionally difficult to fix problems.

As invigorated as you might have been the point at which the journey started, you should be practical about any progressions to the organization or how the ongoing business environment might have weakened the business and be prepared to escape in the event that you believe it's sinking.

Try not to be enthusiastic about your speculations, albeit this is very troublesome in light of human inclination. Be as apathetic as possible, " "try to avoid panicking, and look cautiously to check whether there's a simple fix in sight and in the event that administration is finding a way reasonable ways to right the wrongs. If not, you might be in for a long and costly example that will ultimately show you something new the hard way.

What would you do now?

Here is the inquiry to ask:

"Assuming I were beginning once again today: what is the best choice to make right now?"

It's a great question, because if you own stock and the company or its industry changes, you can feel emotionally stuck. You ponder the past and the time and cash you squandered and may never get back. You begin agonizing over what to do. You need to understand that the past is a distant memory. Any slip-ups in contributing are two-way roads. Assuming you purchased something in the past you can sell it today and settle your problem.

What is zero-based thinking?

Zero-based believing is the contrary way to deal with utilizing a sunk-cost paradox. At the point when you utilize zero-based thinking, you pursue a choice today founded on all that you know the present moment; no significance is given to past choices. Harping on errors and sucking your thumb when you ought to act will waste your time. Assuming you imagine that you're beginning new right now you pursue better choices for what's to come. Zero-based thinking3 is a dynamic interaction in view of envisioning yourself back at the point before

specific choices were made, and allowed to pursue those choices with the information that you have now about their outcome.

Here's a truly straightforward method for utilizing zero-based thinking, and I gained it from Brian Tracy, who proposes that you ask this questions:4

"Is there anything that I am doing today that, knowing what I currently know, I wouldn't get into today assuming I needed to do it over?"

Tracy considers this a "KWINK" investigation - "Knowing What I Now Know," and he expresses that in the midst of quick change, there are generally regions in your own and business life you wouldn't get into today in the event that you needed to do them over. He says your ability to ask and truly answer this inquiry is the way to staying adaptable and sharp witted in the midst of turbulence.

One part of contributing that I appreciate is that it urges you to think carefully in new ways. We are simply used to carrying on with life settling on choices in numerous everyday issues where it's difficult to evaluate choices, and you can go on it be OK to feel a ton regardless. But with investing, or any situation where the financial stakes are high, you need to keep your wits about you and not get swept up in emotion.

For instance, one thing I've seen in my own contributing, and furthermore the ventures of others, is that whenever you've possessed portions of an organization for quite a while, you might feel nostalgic for it. It's like pulling for a games group; the group could be horrendous, yet you're as yet faithful to the group since you realize it well and you've pull for it for such a long time.

Are you currently great at eliminating your feelings from the dynamic cycle, or is this hard for you? On the off chance that you simply stay with realities then you as of now enjoy a benefit, yet many individuals feel somewhat unsure and wistfulness that can disrupt the general flow. As people, we are normally going to go with choices in light of our "hunches" or on the grounds that we need something, however understand that we as a whole offer these tendencies.

You can figure out how to recognize when your feelings are adversely affecting your capacity to pursue judicious choices, and eliminate them from the situation. Proficient poker players are a genuine illustration of this. To win reliably at poker you must have the option to ascertain the chances and utilize that data to choose when to hold them or crease them, however even the best poker players are weak following winning or losing a major hand.

Similar circumstances exist in maintaining a business. We can pursue misfortunes or spend tons of cash on projects that we ought to drop, yet we falter and trust things could make something happen in the future in spite of signs to the contrary.

The benefits of zero-based thinking

Zero-based speculation eliminates everything from a choice with the exception of your unmistakable perspective on what has proactively occurred before, and it assists you with settling on hard decisions. Despite the fact that it sounds complex, how about we investigate a way that you can give it something to do simply.

Let's say you purchased a stock quite a while back and the organization hasn't been becoming very well of late. The administration isn't doing anything astounding, yet they're not bombing pitiably by the same token. You've been trusting they would make something happen, however it just hasn't as yet worked out. You're trusting it bobs back.

Now envision that at nightfall today you need to sell this stock and afterward rebuy it with no expense at all. No business charge and no issue. Could you repurchase the stock? In the event that you would, no issue, you're good to go and you genuinely trust in the company.

But, assuming you'd delay with regards to purchasing that stock after you had to sell it, then you have new data. You presumably don't have any desire to claim that stock. You're clutching it for some unacceptable explanation. You are hesitant to concede you committed an error, you're being nostalgic, or you're trusting things will change from here on out. These are for the most part entanglements in light of feeling, and they're issues that zero-based speculation can help you avoid.

If you've been contributing for some time, then these thoughts will likely sound good to you. If you haven't invested in stocks yet or do not have much experience with them yet, then you're in a good position to learn a lot now. Remember the idea of zero-based thinking and you will find it tremendously supportive with venture as well as in numerous different aspects of your life. Simply ask yourself, "Knowing all that I know currently, would I do this again?"

Time spent investigating a stock previously, similarly as purchasing the stock and following the organization's promising and less promising times over numerous years is additionally a sunk expense. Any misstep you made is history; gain from it, and choose if you would purchase a stock today assuming that you had it to do over once more. In the event that the response is "yes," stay with it. In the event that the response is "no," why for heaven's sake are you actually holding the stock?

The social piece of contributing is captivating in light of the fact that it manages expectations and dreams, with acquiring and losing. Understanding how brain science functions and being aware of what we do when we commit errors and how we course-right is helpful. It's additionally useful to note on the off chance that we have a past filled with not course-adjusting when we ought to. I have had a few instances of holding stocks I ought to have sold before, and holding up when I ought to have recently purchased. I attempt to gain from however many missteps as I can.

Sometimes you simply need to acknowledge you committed an error and begin once again. It resembles when you'd make a drawing or painting and you detested it, so you fold it up and begin once again. I think as we age, and particularly submit cash to a venture, there's an inclination that we need to rescue everything, that assuming we put time and cash into something we want to separate everything and make everything valuable. I believe there's an insight to perceiving the "sunk costs" of life when you recently messed something up and now is the ideal time to begin once again. Salad in the refrigerator offers you the hint that now is the ideal time to prepare it when it shrinks. Milk begins to smell. That bread with the blue-green shape motions to you that now is the ideal time to toss it.

Stock speculations don't give you a viewable signal that they never again seem OK and now is the ideal time to sell them. It's different for each financial backer, however that's what i'd say assuming the organization you've put resources into has changed altogether, or its industry has changed and the organization is as of now not cutthroat, then now is the right time to rethink your situation. You need to focus on the organizations you own. I think the best test is in the event that you have a superior open door in another stock, simply sell your ongoing stock and reinvest it in something with better prospects.

If the company you have invested in is growing at about 6% a year, and you can't see any way that will improve, and you see another company that looks like it could grow at 10% a year, then to me there is an opportunity cost to staying the course. Assuming the new stock passes the PALMS separating framework, it's a good idea to seek after another potential chance to accumulate your cash at a higher pace of return.

In a nutshell

One thing we can gain from our own slip-ups, or those of others, is that assuming that you're pursuing a misfortune on your ventures, that misfortune is bringing down future additions. Consistently you're stuck possessing stock in a weak or mediocre organization you are prior gains.

Ask yourself: "On the off chance that I was not experiencing the same thing, knowing what I currently know, would I get into it today?"

It's astonishing the number of individuals will remain experiencing the same thing or go on with an awful strategy, due to their reluctance or powerlessness to concede that they committed an error or that they weren't right in the past.

Remember that when you pursued the choice it was presumably a decent choice in light of the circumstance around then, yet presently the circumstance has changed. Presently you need to assess what is going on in view of the current reality.

We can't change the choices we have made before, however we can utilize all that we've learned in the past to go with shrewd choices right since will emphatically affect our future.

35

A CALM CAPTAIN

Think of yourself as the captain of a ship in a storm. As an investor, you will find some days are sunny and warm, and others are stormy and cold.

You want to be like a calm captain. Steer the ship through the waves, winds, and the torrential rain. Keep your eyes focused on where you're going and don't be distracted by the strong gusts and the ocean's salt spray across your face.

Many individuals get scared when markets decline. They alarm when costs begin to decline, and markets fall unexpectedly surrounding them. This group conduct to get unfortunate pervades markets bringing about additional selling and cost declines. Which starts like little waves before long transforms into torrents of fear. The exceptional financial backer can keep even-tempered under pressure.

There is an explanation that Sully Sullenberger handled his US Airways trip on the Hudson River in 2009. He was ready after the plane was incapacitated by striking a group of Canada Geese following departure; each of the 155 individuals on board survived.[1]

He was intellectually pre-arranged that day and set down the plane smoothly. Remember his quiet presence as a financial backer and you'll get along nicely. The key is to put resources into incredible organizations and hold them through various challenges. You can definitely relax if the business sectors decline.

Shortly after departure, after the plane struck the herd of geese, it lost power in the two motors. Sullenberger immediately resolved he would not be able to arrive at any air terminal, so he steered the plane to a water arrival on the Hudson River. All on board were safeguarded by neighboring boats.

Sullenberger, portrayed by companions as "modest and hesitant," was noted for his balance and quiet during the emergency; the city chairman of New York, Michael Bloomberg, named him "Chief Cool." Despite the exterior of quiet, Sullenberger endured side effects of post-horrendous pressure issue in the resulting weeks, including restlessness and flashbacks. He said that the minutes prior to the dumping were "the most terrible nauseating, pit-of-your-stomach, failing to work out the-floor feeling" that he had at any point experienced. He additionally said, "One perspective on may be that for a long time, I've been making little, ordinary stores in this bank of involvement, schooling, and preparing. And on January 15, the balance was sufficient so that I could make a very large withdrawal."

As a financial backer, you won't ever experience the thoughtful genuine decisive experience that Captain Sullenberger experienced. You won't have 155 lives in your grasp, nor the obligation of setting down a gigantic plane on water. Be that as it may, you can figure out how to deal with the unforeseen with composure. Regardless of how awful things appear to be in contributing (or any part of life) you will in all actuality do best when you resist the urge to panic and just deal with the things that are inside your control.

Every contributing climate is unique, yet you ought to be not interested in the clamor around you. I'm not proposing that you disregard recent developments, market news, for sure's happening on the planet. In actuality, you ought to be also educated as could be expected. However the propensity for the vast majority is to want to act, and they as a rule do some unacceptable thing at exactly some unacceptable time. This means purchasing when every other person is insatiable and costs are high, and selling when everyone is unfortunate and costs are low. That is on the grounds that the vast majority adjust to the way of behaving of the group; reasonable a developmental way of behaving generally serves populaces well.

The ongoing circumstance isn't steady. Recall that and be ready for change. For instance, as I compose this book the market is in the 10th back to back year of a positively trending market in stocks. Numerous new financial backers have just seen stocks go up in esteem, and their loved ones become more affluent as time passes, week, month, and year. So the human cerebrum sort of activities this example to proceed forever.

As you read this you might be amidst a similar positively trending business sector, and you may not know how you will respond when markets decline. The smartest idea is as a rule to sit idle. Assuming you have been smart in your choice interaction and own extraordinary organizations, then you don't have to do anything on the grounds that the market drops.

It is additionally conceivable that the positively trending market in stocks has changed since this book was composed, and the it is unique: stock costs have declined for days, weeks, months, or even a very long time to contribute scene. Assuming that is the situation, there is still compelling reason need to change your stock property as long as the singular organizations behind those stocks remain solid.

You can in any case utilize the equivalent separating framework to pick stocks, and you might even see that as assuming business sectors have declined extensively a large number of the stocks you comprehend are selling at low costs. This is frequently on the grounds that different financial backers are unfortunate of purchasing stocks, and fear the securities exchange overall. To possess long haul, a bear market frequently gives the low costs that make for incredibly effective long haul investments.

The best methodology is to try to avoid panicking, hold stocks in extraordinary organizations, and even consider adding to your situations insofar as nothing has crumbled monetarily with the organizations that premium you. Stay away from unexpected portfolio developments, prize sloth-like inaction, and understand that when individuals act genuinely they ordinarily make terrible decisions.

Keep as a primary concern the picture of the quiet skipper, whether on a boat adrift or flying a plane, with your hand solidly on the haggle eyes not too far off in spite of the disarray whirling around you.

36

THE ANTIFRAGILE INVESTOR

Antifragility is past flexibility or power. The versatile opposes shocks and stays something similar; the antifragile gets better.

- NASSIM NICHOLAS TALEB

There is a word for things that benefit when they are exposed to shocks. They get stronger when they encounter stressors, volatility, or randomness. I believe every investor should have a vision when they buy stocks to get ready for unavoidable market crashes.

The point isn't only to endure the market declines when they occur, however to exploit the arbitrariness and turmoil so you can purchase stocks that are modest and will rise out of the bedlam more grounded than when it arrives.

In his book Antifragile,[1] Nassim Nicholas Taleb presents the hypothesis of antifragility along these lines: "A few things benefit from shocks; they flourish and develop when presented to unpredictability, haphazardness, confusion, and stressors and love experience, chance, and vulnerability. However, in spite of the universality of the peculiarity, there is no word for the specific inverse of delicate. Allow us to call it antifragile. Antifragility is past versatility or heartiness. The strong opposes shocks and stays something similar; the antifragile gets better."

There is a colossal chance for any financial backer who utilizes an antifragile approach and puts away money at advantageous times. As Buffett says, "Anticipating precipitation doesn't count. Building arks does." You need to be prepared when the tempest hits.

Nobody can instruct you precisely to become antifragile. The actual idea of arbitrary occasions implies you can't get ready for them.

Below are a couple of thoughts that you could see as helpful. Consider them you track down ways of working on your own investing.

Barbells: Keeping things separate

First comes the idea of "an antifragile balance," the possibility of two limits kept separate with nothing in the middle.

The hand weight methodology is an antifragile system where you play it exceptionally protected in certain areas and face challenges in different regions. However you abstain from being "in the middle."

This goes against the customary way of thinking that says you ought to have a very much expanded arrangement of stocks, bonds, cash, and so forth. A few financial backers truly like bonds, and I can see the benefits. Stocks don't generally go up, in spite of prevalent thinking and late market conduct in the ten years from 2010-2020. There have been broadened timeframes when stocks went sideways or down, and I comprehend the reason why a few financial backers like the enhanced methodology of claiming a tad bit of everything.

My own contributing has left from that expansion model to speculations that are more thought. I actually own a portion of the common subsidizes that I set up over 10 years prior, and I own some file asset and ETF offers, and those records are expanded. My point is that despite the fact that I am substantially more packed in my stock contributing now, it took a long time before I was certain enough in my way to deal with put the greater part of my cash into individual stocks.

Another way of discussing Taleb's "barbell strategy" is to call it "asset allocation" where you divide your investments into two kinds of "buckets" some very safe with cash or bond-like returns and others with more potential volatility but the chances for outsized gains.

The monetary exhorting calling recipes that are frequently promoted as "one-size-fits-all" equations that they prescribe to their clients. Since the thought is taken care of to you doesn't mean you need to eat it! One recipe proposes you ought to deduct your age from 100 and that is the percent you ought to put resources into stocks (for instance, assuming you're 30 years of age, you would put 100-30 = 70% in stocks and the rest in bonds. As you progress in years your stock allotment decreases).

I don't believe that general guidelines apply to everybody. To choose your resource designation, then, at that point, following an

venture equation may be smart. Notwithstanding, I think indiscriminately following any venture measuring stick helps a counsel who can involve it as a defense from moving you from one resource class to another.

I concur with the view that a financial backer ought to constantly have a hold reserve put away for crises. It generally makes sense to have cash that is not contributed that you can get your hands on assuming you at any point need it.

Only after you've made a save store for crises does it appear to be legit to put resources into stocks. In my own contributing, I like to have 90% put resources into stocks for the long haul instead of possessing a great deal of "safe" bonds whose profits are practically 100% not to match those of stocks over the long haul. I for one think securities are an awful long haul speculation, yet for certain financial backers (particularly the people who are worried about losing cash) securities can make sense.

One method for utilizing the antifragile hand weight approach is to placed a huge piece of cash in a protected venture like money, a transient depository reserve, or a currency market record, and make more forceful wagers on stocks with a modest quantity of your investible assets.

For instance, you could put 90% of your total assets in a currency market record, and utilize the other 10% for less secure ventures. On the off chance that you contribute this way you can never lose over 10% of your total assets, yet you are presented to a possibly gigantic upside.

I found out about this methodology by learning about Taleb's idea of antifragility. I don't consider it's the best qualified for each financial backer, however it merits pondering and I like to consider the free weight approach as an option in contrast to stacking up on resources "in the middle."

While Taleb likes the methodology of having the most cash in safe speculations and a limited quantity in incredibly forceful and dangerous ventures, Buffett has given the contrary directions to cash conveyed to a legal administrator for his significant other's advantage. Rather than apportioning the vast majority of the cash in sans risk ventures and placing a modest quantity in stocks, he's flipped it.

Buffett's directions are for 10% in momentary government bonds and 90% in the S&P 500 file. I observe it interesting to take note of that both Taleb and Buffett utilize the hand weight approach, despite the fact that they contribute diversely at each end. Buffett's directions are made sense of as continues in his will:

"One endowment gives that money be conveyed to a legal administrator for my better half's advantage... My recommendation to the legal administrator couldn't be more basic: Put 10% of the money in momentary government securities and 90% in an extremely minimal expense S&P 500 file reserve. (I recommend Vanguard's.) I accept the trust's drawn out outcomes from this approach will be better than those accomplished by most investors."

Warren Buffett

In your reasoning, know about ways that you can safeguard your ventures through being exceptionally protected with a part of your cash, and permit yourself to win big time with more hazardous wagers that could pay off spectacularly.

Examples of antifragility

It's helpful to take a gander at different instances of antifragility to set up the psyche for amazing open doors. The following are a couple of instances of ways that individuals can leave the entryway open to profit from unforeseen events.

A comedian driving Uber

One illustration of antifragility is a joke artist who drives for Uber as a normal everyday employment while doing stand-up gigs to additional his vocation on evenings and ends of the week. Another is a specialized essayist for a product organization who composes fiction during her extra time holding back nothing. These dangers of turning into a joke artist or writer might be remote chance wagers and they are hazardous, yet the expenses to partake are low; essentially the time spent seeking after the endeavors.

A snowboarder or surfer

A snowboarder who is acquainted with falling at high velocity might turn out to be great at falling. In like manner, a surfer might become skilled at dealing with sea conditions that would probably suffocate a customary person.

The really learning you do, and the more you practice, the better you will be at exploring the slants and rushes of the consistently changing securities exchange. You don't need to exchange frequently, yet you really want to increase your training. Work on acting rapidly and making little investigations with your stock buys so you can get into a groove.

You need to think like a competitor who gets a ton of training, who has a ton of redundancies added to their repertoire. This will assist you with fostering an instinct about contributing; it will turn out to be natural. Similarly as a snowboarder can endure shocks, you can in much the same way "accept circumstances for what they are" when things get choppy.

Play

Children with the opportunity to play gain insight of things like injustice, vulnerability, and disappointment that set them up for genuine circumstances. In the event that grown-ups consistently step in to address every injustice between kids, seize each misstep, and implement inordinate principles, a youngster may not create to their full potential.

Damocles, phoenix, and hydra

In his book, Taleb utilizes antiquated guides to make sense of the set of three of delicate, strong, and antifragile. Damocles, who eats with a sword hanging over his head, is delicate. A little pressure to the string holding the sword will kill him. Damocles resembles the financial backer who purchases stock on edge utilizing influence, or purchases choices they don't have any idea, or YOLOs a stock they know nothing about.2 These delicate circumstances leave you defenseless against calamity assuming the market betrays you.

The Phoenix, which bites the dust and is reawakened from the cinders, is vigorous. It generally gets back to a similar state while experiencing an enormous stressor.

But the Hydra exhibits antifragility. Whenever one head is cut off, two bounce back. There are stocks that advantage from turmoil. Amazon is one company that grew stronger and prospered during the Coronavirus pandemic; Zoom is another company that became more robust amidst the crisis for its ability to bring society together when social distance pulled them apart. Both of these organizations demonstrate how antifragile ventures develop further during seasons of crisis.

Nature

Nature is a common show of antifragility. Whenever you lift loads, your body adjusts to lift heavier loads sometime later. With contributing, you might pick a few terrible stocks from the beginning that cause a few transitory misfortunes. You will look into when to hold stocks and when to sell them through stock "exercise," and you will end up being a more grounded and more versatile investor.

Fragile and antifragile jobs

To act as an illustration of an antifragile work, for a top rated writer like Taleb, there is little he can do that will lessen the offer of his books.

However, assuming you're a midlevel bank laborer and you finish off an irritating savored a bar you'll presumably get terminated, get captured, and have your work possibilities become seriously restricted. You're very fragile.

A cabbie has more opportunity since they are not so subject to their standing. Taleb likewise takes note of that individuals who don't appear to mind how they dress or look are hearty, or antifragile. Individuals who need to wear formal outfits and stress over a terrible standing are fragile.

Buridan's ass

Buridan's butt is a delineation of a mystery in way of thinking in the origination of unrestrained choice. It alludes to a theoretical circumstance where a

jackass that is similarly eager and parched is put unequivocally halfway between a pile of feed and a bucket of water. Since the oddity expects the ass will generally go to whichever is nearer, it passes on from both appetite and thirst since it can't choose which to consume first.[3]

An irregular push in one course or the other will take care of the issue for this unfortunate jackass! Irregularity assists with independent direction and becoming unstuck. If you try to remove random events then the beneficial stresAlong these linesr disappears. So, it's great to have capricious occasions since they push us in new and surprising headings. Ponder the times in your day to day existence when a surprising crisis or emergency made you more grounded. Discussing Microsoft's development during the pandemic, CEO Satya Nadella said, "We've seen two years of computerized change in two months."4 Antifragile organizations get more grounded through openness to valuable stressors.

Stoicism

Taleb frequently discusses indifferent standards as approaches to dealing with irregularity and becoming antifragile. For instance, achievement can make you delicate, in light of the fact that once you are fruitful you have substantially more to lose than you did previously. You're anxious about becoming poor. There is a method called "rehearsing neediness" that decreases your delicacy. Basically, you dispose of the relative multitude of overabundance things, attire, and accessories of life as an approach to keeping yourself from fearing losing your wealth.

Develop an antifragile vision

Prepare for the unforeseen. Since we don't have any idea what will occur, attempt to stay away from the outlook of "how much might I at any point win with this venture?" to one where you inquire, "how much could I at any point be hurt assuming that things turn out badly?" when you contribute. Simply consider stressors a certainty and be ready for the fallout.

A strong beginning to fostering an antifragile vision starts with having cash saved and prepared to send at the right second. This implies you really want quick admittance to cash so you can purchase something at awesome costs when the time introduces itself-and you might have just a question of hours.

[Image: image26.jpeg
] Sage advice.

The antifragile vision doesn't need your everyday consideration. It ought to keep you inspired and keep you alarm to irregularity, however a large portion of your time ought to be gone through living your time on earth and taking care of your responsibilities as usual.

Build antifragility into your life and your putting framework so it's continuously running behind the scenes and open at whatever point required. You become antifragile by being aware of what could occur early and getting ready for the inescapable shocks.

If you're completely contributed at the highest point of the market, you'll not have anything to contribute at the base. Individuals who are "in with no reservations" at the market top have the money to purchase at deal costs later. Warren Buffett's perception sounds valid when he said, "Just when the tide goes out do you find who's been swimming exposed." All stock financial backers look splendid in a buyer market. Put resources into quality supplies of organizations you get it and keep cash accessible to plan for when the tide goes out.

An antifragile portfolio

If you maintain that your outcomes should withdraw from the group, you should do things differently.

Keep your eyes on as not many as five stocks or 20 and no more. It is improbable you will foster a profound comprehension of in excess of 20 organizations, yet you are responsible for your speculations, and if you need to claim that many stocks that approach checks out. Simply try to remain inside your "circle of capability" by possibly putting resources into the organizations you understand.

Get definitive when one or a couple of those stocks get modest. Take a risk putting resources into a stock you comprehend, regardless of whether you're not 100 percent sure about it. Assuming you're 70% certain that the organization is brilliant and the stock is selling for a fair (or modest) cost you likely as of now have sufficient data to choose to purchase. You won't ever have ideal information about anything, so it is a waste of time to hold on until you're 100 percent sure.

Have cash

The other significant part of antifragility that money infuses into your portfolio is that if (and when) financial exchanges decline you have the liquidity of money to exploit instability. You will actually want to benefit and be avaricious when others are unfortunate, and in doing so you will actually want to face challenges during securities exchange pressure and your portfolio will be more powerful and strong on account of it.

In the last section, you'll review a companion of mine let me know he realized the securities exchange would fall the day after Trump's official triumph in 2016 and would have contributed after the Dow Jones Industrial Average fell

800 focuses IF he had some money available.

The issue was an absence of readiness and unequivocal activity. It is an illustration of an extraordinary thought and unfortunate execution. You would rather not be an astute individual who realizes the securities exchange will crash yet sits idle. Knowing yet not acting is useless.

My companion said he would have put away assuming he had cash. The vulnerability and probability of "IF" is installed in "antiFragile."

Having cash available, setting yourself up by realizing which stocks you would purchase assuming business sectors crashed, and having the option to convey cash by purchasing stocks when conditions introduce themselves will empower you to become more grounded and more vigorous when the inescapable instability strikes.

37

THREE WAYS TO SUCCEED

There are three ways to succeed as an investor. You can succeed intellectually, physically, or emotionally; a fact I have learned through personal experience, observing other investors, and reading a lot (and I mean a ton) about investing.

Intellectually

The scholarly way is the way we as a whole fantasy about contributing. It's overall so gifted you simply realize which stocks to purchase and when. The scholarly way requires bits of knowledge into organizations and the future.

One exemplary illustration of the scholarly stock financial backer is Warren Buffett. Individuals like him appear just a single time in a drawn-out period of time, and copying their success' very troublesome. It resembles adoring ball and attempting to be the following Michael Jordan; it's a commendable objective, however for a great many people it's not in the cards.

Physically

The second method for succeeding is the actual method for working harder. You get up really early and filled by espresso or Red Bull you start first thing in the morning and toil away till 12 PM. You are continually stuck to screens and read records of phone calls. You're watching the flickering red and green images and quest for divine signs from the stock graphs like you're perusing tea leaves. Then you return home and read more, and you work throughout the end of the week as well. This is

what the investigators on Wall Street do; no less than everybody attempts it and cases it works. It should work for some of them-however I can't say without a doubt. I live in Seattle and I'm a long way from the hustle of Wall Street, however I notice a great deal of financial backers and I see that a significant number of them can't beat the midpoints… since they are the midpoints. However they should think it works or they wouldn't continue to attempt so hard.

Emotionally

The third method for prevailing as a financial backer is troublesome. At the point when the market begins to tank, you should give no consideration to it, regardless. Assuming that it drops 10%, you don't fear. Assuming it drops 20% or 25% and the features are requiring the death of the economy as far as we might be concerned, you don't worry.

Ellis says that the enthusiastic method for contributing is the main dependable technique he knows to prevail as an investor.

"I'm not adequately shrewd to succeed the scholarly way, and I can't do what is necessary succeed the actual way. But the emotionally difficult way takes very little time and makes no intellectual or physical demands on you at all. Genuinely, based on how general society contributes, a great many people could do without the sincerely troublesome way. Of course, an ever increasing number of individuals are attempting it; how much cash in list subsidizes has been rising many years. The enthusiastic way is the main solid way that I am aware of to succeed."

- CHARLIE ELLIS

I understand what a remote chance it is to succeed mentally, yet I partake in the test. It never irritates me that it's actually requesting to invest energy perusing and learning promptly in the first part of the day. I don't think of it as a task; I think of it as loads of tomfoolery. The enthusiastic way appears to be the most straightforward method for succeeding in light of the fact that it doesn't need scholarly brightness or 70-hour long weeks of work. You simply need to try not to do dumb things.

The passionate way is one of three important ways of succeeding. I urge you to keep a composed attitude when every other person is losing theirs. You'll track down the best blend of scholarly, physical, and enthusiastic ways of succeeding. I think it's

supportive that you're mindful of them, and at last you'll sort out the methodology that fits you best.

PART VI

THOUGHT INTO ACTION: PUTTING IT ALL TOGETHER

38

THOUGHT INTO ACTION

Writing this book has changed the way I invest. It forced me to ask myself why I had been too passive and not decisive enough when it came to buying stock in Amazon, a company I know well as a customer. I have thought about buying stock in Amazon many times over the past few years, yet it generally appeared expensive.

I as of late heard a meeting with Berkshire Hathaway administrator and CEO Warren Buffett making sense of, "It's a little hard when you take a gander at something at x and it sells at 10x to get it," he expressed, concurring with a questioner's idea that the "train has left the station as of now" for anybody hoping to purchase Amazon stock.[1]

I've been a long-lasting Amazon client and as a Seattle inhabitant, I've seen the organization develop before my eyes. It wasn't generally clear that Amazon would turn into the corporate stalwart that it is today, not to mention productive. Nor had anybody accepted that it would be so predominant in both retailing and distributed computing. Whenever obviously Amazon would rule retail and have gigantic accomplishment with Amazon Web Services (AWS), the stock cost had previously move to crazy statures - $500, then

$700, then, at that point, $1,000. The stock generally appeared expensive.

By focusing on late stock costs I was accomplishing something many refer to as "anchoring,"2 a mental peculiarity that Daniel Kahneman portrays in his book Thinking Fast and Slow.3 Anchoring happens when we see a number (like a stock cost) before we think about the worth ourselves. The number that has been displayed to us influences our gauge, which will constantly be moderately near that first number, which is known as the anchor.

Because I saw Amazon selling before at a low value, all resulting costs appeared to be costly. It's the very inclination that Buffett alludes to when he said, "It's a little hard when you take a gander at something at x and it sells at 10x to purchase it."4

A conduct predisposition can hamper clear independent direction if you don't watch out. Allow me to make sense of why I accept this is so: Amazon stock cost has climbed pretty much in a state of harmony with the organization's development. The inquiry we really want to pose is whether the expansion in cost precisely mirrors the organization's worth, or on the other hand assuming that the cost has climbed excessively high contrasted with what the organization is worth.

39

DECISIVE ON AMAZON

"Go through every day attempting to be somewhat savvier than you were the point at which you woke up."

- CHARLIE MUNGER

I have encouraged readers throughout this book to only invest in companies they're capable of understanding. It makes sense to buy great companies early on when their growth is just beginning because you can often get a low cost, and you have more long stretches of compounding to enjoy.

Amazon is one organization I see well, yet on the grounds that the cost generally appeared to be high I have never purchased stock in the company.

I began to treat Amazon in a serious way as a potential speculation when it became imbued in my buy examples and those of individuals around me. Right away, I just purchased a couple of things on Amazon, a present here and a book there. However at that point I began to purchase things like cameras, and focal points, and PC shows that I used to purchase elsewhere.

I saw that I wasn't the only one drawn to this comfort. I was chipping away at my PC in a Starbucks around the time I was considering putting resources into Amazon my companions were saying, "why not simply get it on Amazon?" in discussion. It went from being a web-based book shop to the store with everything in a short time.

A similar model is the iPhone: in 2006 no one had known about an iPhone. It was presented in 2007, and inside a couple of years they were all over the place. Also, Amazon was none chiefly as a web-based book shop, and

in a matter of seconds they were the place where the entire world looked for cameras, clothing, hardware, furniture, food, music, real time video, and everything in between.

Looking back, it was not generally clear that Amazon and Bezos would execute their arrangement with much achievement, however presently the organization has demonstrated its solidarity in Internet retail and distributed computing. Considering that, I chose to put Amazon to the PALMS separating test.

PALMS FILTERING SYSTEM FOR AMAZON

- **P**rofitable: Yes.
- **A**dapting to Technology: Yes.
- **L**oyal: Yes. Loyal customers keep buying.
- **M**oat: Yes. A huge, ever-widening moat.
- **S**ensible: Yes. Stock sells for a sensible price.

Reasonable cost is the main component I have not been totally sure about. Each time I take a gander at the cost it appears to be costly. However I think the cost isn't that costly when you understand it mirrors the organization's brilliant future. Amazon is developing at such a high speed that the stock cost appears to be high and continually going higher. That is my explanation that I never purchased; my former perspective was to purchase stocks when they are "modest," and Amazon stock has never been modest. But even if the stock has never been cheap, the question remains: "Is it sensibly priced?"

Though I can't say without any hesitation, I'm 70% certain the cost is reasonable, yet assuming I hold on until I'm 100 percent sure I may never really possess this stock.

Even however I have been proposing that perusers be adaptable while deciding a reasonable value, I have been acting extremely moderately. I have respected Amazon however never purchased the stock since "it appeared to be costly" contrasted with the value I'd seen a few a long time back. I was secured to a past value as opposed to opening my eyes toward the future.

All of these "old" approaches to assessing the stock kept me from getting it for some years.

But then, while writing this book, I kept reminding myself how important it is to be flexible on price. I reviewed Buffett saying how he passed up a major opportunity by not accepting Amazon stock. At the point when gotten some information about it in a meeting, he said, “It’s one I missed large time.”

Spinoza’s words reverberated to me: “You should take a gander at things under the part of eternity. ”

I had chosen to put resources into Amazon before the year’s over, which was December 29th, 2017, the last exchanging day of 2017. And if I was going to act on my decision and buy Amazon stock, I only had a few hours of the trading day left to buy the stock. I didn’t be aware unhesitatingly assuming the cost was reasonable, however I’d felt as such for quite a long time, and I never purchased on the grounds that I was unable to say without any hesitation that the cost was reasonable; it appeared to be costly 100% of the time. My aversion kept me uninvolved, continuously watching and pausing, however never pursuing the choice. As I sat tight at a lower share cost it kept on climbing year after year.

On that last exchanging day of the year, I had around 70% of the data I wished I had about Amazon. I knew to the point of making the excellent, high-speed decision1 to purchase the stock.

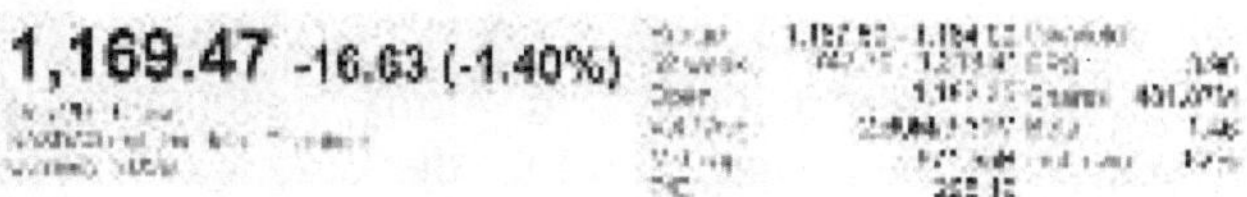

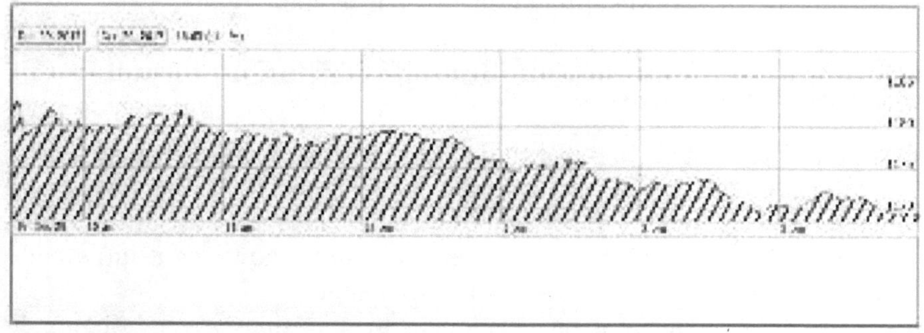

Amazon stock on the day I at long last chosen to invest.

At market open on December 29, 2017, Amazon was selling at about $1,180 an offer. I saw the cost declining somewhat, a pattern that continued over the course of the day. As I arranged to purchase shares, the stock cost continued to get less expensive. Since I had previously concluded I would purchase shares before the day's over, I held on to find out how low the stock cost would turn out. In the day's last minutes, I put a purchase limit order2 at $1,169.50. Minutes before the market shut, the cost declined and my request was filled. Following quite a while of appreciating the organization and being an unwavering client, I had at long last turned into an Amazon investor. It was a wonderful inclination, and fairly difficult to depict. I had delayed on the grounds that I thought the stock was excessively costly for a really long time. However at this point my sifting framework gave a bit by bit technique on the most proficient method to make a decision.

Time will tell how well the PALMS framework functioned. Whatever occurs in the present moment is impossible to say, however over the course of the following three to five years (and then some) I accept Amazon will proceed to develop, and assuming it keeps on prevailing in its central goal, Amazon's portion cost ought to mirror the organization's success.

While composing this book, I took in the significance of being adaptable on cost up to an organization meets other significant venture standards, and I needed to heed this guidance myself. I needed to limit any lament of not accepting Amazon; I would rather not think back when I'm eighty and say, "For what reason didn't I get it? Amazon was a phenomenal organization. I missed it huge time!"

I purchased this stock for the long haul since I accept that Amazon will turn into a much more creative and tremendously noteworthy organization in the following 5, 10, 20 years and then some, and that their stock cost will follow. A decent result of the buy is that perusers presently have a "reality" illustration of the PALMS sifting framework in action.

What sets Amazon apart

One thing I've seen about Amazon that held me back from contributing for a long time is that they never appeared to be productive, and I generally involved that as a measure of whether an organization checked out as a venture. I actually think benefit matters colossally, however it turns out I essentially wasn't seeing what Amazon was doing.

First, Amazon focused on developing their business over bringing in cash. The organization focused on developing deals and wasn't stressed over the main concern as it kept on putting vigorously in its numerous organizations. The early speculations to develop the organization were harming benefits, yet they put Amazon

in a good position in the long term.[3]

Amazon kept on putting resources into areas of development to the detriment of productivity, something most different retailers can't bear to do. Amazon had the option to purchase deals to the detriment of the reality and the organization could support this position both in light of the fact that Amazon was producing a ton of money and was not losing money.[4] For instance, now and again Amazon's portion cost would fall in the wake of missing investigators' income gauges, yet the organization was not worried about not creating a gain that quarter since it was building the organization to grow three years into the future.[5]

Instead of worrying about momentary benefits, Amazon zeroed in on carrying out its own private-name brands in home merchandise, staple and style, obtaining and further developing its Whole Foods procurement, and exploring different avenues regarding various actual store designs like Amazon's book shops to sell books and its devices.

Amazon's CFO Brian Olsavsky likewise said that Amazon keeps on putting resources into satisfaction limit and strategies administrations, Amazon Prime Video, Prime Now, AmazonFresh and Prime benefits.[6]

Forsaking transient benefit to fabricate high-development region of the business separates Amazon. Contenders like Walmart, for instance, may have their emphasis on benefits this quarter or next, yet Amazon has shown it is less worried about momentary benefits and more centered around building the organization by stressing development in the long-term.

I never contemplated Amazon that way, as an organization that can muscle others out of the game. That is on the grounds that I zeroed in less on Amazon's opposition and more on the thing they were improving for their customers.

I could see an ever increasing number of individuals going to Amazon first to look for things they expected to purchase. Amazon was turning into a web crawler like Google that assisted individuals with tracking down a wide assortment of items in a single spot. I additionally heard the organization's name spring up in ordinary discussion: "How about you simply get it on Amazon?" or somebody shouting in amuse, "I got it on Amazon and it showed up the following day." People were purchasing Alexa-empowered Echo gadgets left and right and in a split second joining them into their day to day routines at home to play music, set clocks while cooking, make shopping records, and pay attention to jokes. Notwithstanding all of that, I could see Amazon Web Services (AWS) beginning to overwhelm distributed computing while at the same time turning into Amazon's most productive subsidiary.

There were such countless positive things blossoming at Amazon in view of the exploratory seeds they had planted numerous years earlier.

Final thoughts on thumb-sucking

I lounged around during the most recent couple of years respecting Amazon and simply sucking my thumb when I ought to have purchased the stock.

It's memorable's great that not a single one of us are conceived savvy. We can't hope to constantly pursue extraordinary choices, however we can further develop our decision-production process.

Reflecting on Munger's recommendation to "go through every day attempting to be somewhat smarter than you were the point at which you woke up,"7 I feel that composing this book has constrained me to figure out how to utilize new instruments, and I accept perusers can do likewise.

40

AMAZON, ONE YEAR LATER

"To imagine you need to try, and assuming you know ahead of time that it will work, it's anything but an experiment."

- JEFF BEZOS

When I wrote this book a year ago, I had no idea how applying the PALMS filtering system to buying Amazon stock would work. I was a bit fearful about writing a book teaching other people my approach to contributing just on the grounds that I had no clue on the off chance that it would work.

I trusted my methodology would work. I invested a great deal of energy exploring and expounding on it, yet in the end I realized that even my smartest thoughts could fizzle. How is it that I could keep up with my validity with perusers assuming they saw I screwed up?

As you'll review from the last section, I put resources into Amazon at $1,169.50 on the last exchanging day of 2017. I decided to apply my filtering system in real life and put it in writing for future readers of this book as a case study in applying my investing method.

I'm happy I purchased the stock when I accomplished for two primary reasons. The first is that the organization has developed and the stock cost has move since my buy. The cost could without much of a stretch have gone down and I would have attempted to make sense of how one year is too short an opportunity to pass judgment on any venture. In certain regards, most would agree that Lady Luck had been my ally, to some degree in the short term.

The subsequent explanation I'm happy I purchased Amazon stock will be educational to this book's perusers. I pushed through my apprehension about purchasing Amazon stock even

however I wasn't 100 percent sure it would be smart. Some of the time you might feel you need more data to be unequivocal. I'm happy I chosen to purchase the stock and it worked out in light of the fact that it supports a courageous mentality of going into all out attack mode and taking risks instead of being defensive.

The book begun with that statement by Picasso, "I'm continuously doing things I can't do. That is the manner by which I get to do them." That statement implies a great deal to me since it reminds me to continuously attempt new things and examination. In some cases the situation work out the manner in which I need, however I generally pick disappointment's pocket and attempt to discover some new information along the way.

One year after my PALMS analyze started, I am presently seeing the outcomes and can say with full certainty that it works since I had accomplishment through my own direct experience.

NOTES

2. Accelerate Your Learning

1 Charlie Munger Talks Investment Filters. https://youtu.be/WlC40B9qZ20

2 Charlie Munger said, "The professional can't justify their existence if that's all they have to say; it's so obvious and so simple, what would they have to do with the rest of the semester?" https://youtu.be/WlC40B9qZ20

3. What Do You Understand?

1 A circle of capability is the branch of knowledge which matches an individual's abilities or mastery. The psychological model was created by Warren Buffett and Charlie Munger to portray restricting one's monetary interests in regions where an individual might have restricted understanding or experience, moving in regions where one has the best commonality, and to underline the significance of adjusting an abstract appraisal of one own's ability with genuine capability. Source: Wikipedia - https://en.wikipedia.org/wiki/Circle_of_competence

2 Berkshire Hathaway's 1996 Letter to Shareholders — Source: Berkshire Hathaway website https://www.berkshirehathaway.com/letters/1996.html

3 An Euler graph is a diagrammatic method for addressing sets and their connections. They are especially valuable for making sense of mind boggling orders and covering definitions. They are like one more set graphing method, Venn outlines. Not at all like Venn charts, which show all potential relations between various sets, the Euler outline shows just significant connections. Source: Wikipedia https://en.wikipedia.org/wiki/Euler_diagram

4 Source: Business Wire https://www.businesswire.com/news/home/20200617005786/en/Waters-Corporation-Announces-CEO-Succession-Plan

5 Morningstar gives monetary examination of common assets and stocks. This data is given in asset or stock examiner reports that financial backers can access through a membership administration or participation with a library framework that buys into Morningstar's administration. While these investigator reports are not the last word in stock examination, they give respectable synopses and I observe they are valuable contributing assets. Morningstar Reports and Value Line Surveys will be talked about later in this book.

6 The Man Who Saved Floundering Geico, by Stephen Miller. Source: The Wall Street Journal https://www.wsj.com/articles/SB10001424127887324096404578354660595121902

7 Jack Byrne GEICO joke – Source: https://www.sec.gov/Archives/edgar/vprr/1300/13002521.pdf

8 Better Buy: Veeva vs. Zendesk by Leo Sun, Source: Motley Fool https://www.fool.com/investing/2020/12/23/better-buy-veeva-systems-vs-zendesk/

9 For the unenlightened, WallStreetBets is a subreddit, or message board, committed to making huge wagers on stocks, which the banners habitually allude to as "stonks." Many of the post and remarks advance the conviction that one should have the YOLO mentality ("You Only Live Once") and put all of your cash into ludicrously remote chances. As the name proposes, the normal demeanor is one of making wagers, as

preposterous and silly as they appear. One captivating part of the way of life is that they celebrate monstrous misfortunes as an identification of fortitude. Individuals much of the time post screen captures or recordings of exchanges that swung off course and cleared out their whole Robinhood account. Then again, there are barely an adequate number of individuals who make YOLO wagers and win all the tendies (shoptalk for chicken strips) despite everything, a considerable lot of whom become tycoons on a solitary exchange. These triumphs appear to energize others and further sustain the conviction that "stonks just go up."

10 Will there at any point be another Charlie Munger? Source: 25iq https://25iq.com/2015/11/27/will-there-ever-be-another-charlie-munger/

5. P For Profitable

1 Source: 2018 Berkshire Hathaway Annual Letter

2 WallStreetBets is a message board on Reddit.com and has turned into the spot for the individuals who invest heavily in making large wagers, or like to YOLO (You Only Live Once) on stocks with at least some expectations of enormous gains.

7. L For Loyal

1 Brand Keys Loyalty Leaders List 2017 http://brandkeys.com/wp-content/transfers/2017/10/Press-Release-2017-Loyalty-Leaders.pdf

2 Full revelation: my vehicle is guaranteed by GEICO

3 Satya Nadella — Source: Wikipedia https://en.wikipedia.org/wiki/Satya_Nadella

8. M For Moat

1 Warren Buffett depicted the best canal in a video with his companion Jorge Paulo Lemann. Source: Youtube: https://www.youtube.com/watch?v=Co3GFCqQInw&t=666s

2 Microsoft Working on In-House Chip to Replace Intel Processors on Surface Laptops - Source: Gadgets 360 https://gadgets.ndtv.com/PCs/news/microsoft-in-house-chips-surface-PCs 2-in-one-server-PCs intel-substitution 2340884

3 Google Developing Own Processors for Smartphones & Chromebooks - Source: Tom's Hardware https://www.tomshardware.com/news/google-creating own-processors-for-cell phones and-chromebooks

4 Chip Giants Intel and Nvidia Face New Threats From Amazon to Google to Apple - Source: Wall Street Journal https://www.wsj.com/articles/chip-goliaths intel-and-nvidia-face-new-dangers from-amazon-to-research to-Macintosh 11608460201

9. S For Sensible

1 1 Amazon Web Services (AWS) is an auxiliary of Amazon that gives on-request distributed computing stages and APIs to people, organizations, and states on a metered pay-as-you-go

premise. Source: Wikipedia https://en.wikipedia.org/wiki/Amazon_Web_Services

2 Disney bought 21st Century Fox on March 20, 2019. "Obtaining of 21st Century Fox by Disney." Source: Wikipedia https://en.wikipedia.org/wiki/Acquisition_of_21st_Century_Fox_by_Disney

3 This process requires reading about and understanding on your part. You can start with the company's annual report and also read the company's financial reports. Watch YouTube videos about the company, talk to friends, go to stores, converse with individuals, do whatever it takes to get to know what the entire company would be worth if valued in its entirety.

4 For more information about the concept of margin of safety please see Chapter 20 of Benjamin Graham's book, "The Intelligent Investor," published by Harper & Brothers, 1949.

5 3 Reasons Costco is a Great Company – Source: Investopedia In fiscal 2019, Costco sold $152.7 billion worth of merchandise. Its gross margin, excluding membership fees, was around 11%, as it has been since at least 2014.

6 3 Reasons Costco is a Great Company – Source: Investopedia https://www.investopedia.com/stock-analysis/040915/3-reasons-costco-great-company-cost.aspx

7 The Costco stock price of $367.00 was the statement at market close on December 18, 2020.

8 Seth Klarman means buying something at a high price, and afterward the cost falling suddenly, and then having to wait for years for the price to reach the original purchase price. Source: Novel Investor https://novelinvestor.com/seth-klarman-conjecturing modesty cycles/

9 Timeless and Time-Tested Warren Buffett Watch Predictions. Source: CNBC https://www.cnbc.com/id/34206949

11. A New Way

1

12. How to Invest Today

1 “The Intelligent Investor” by Benjamin Graham and David Dodd, “Margin of Safety” by Seth Klarman, “Common Stocks for Uncommon Profits” by Phillip Fisher, and One Up on Wall Street by Peter Lynch.

2 2 “The Intelligent Investor” by Benjamin Graham, Harper and Brothers 1949.

3 A circle of competence is a term that Buffett uses to describe the areas in which an investor has a deep understanding. The circle doesn’t need to incorporate various things. The most important aspect is that one must know the edges of their competency.

4 “Missing his chance to invest in Google” section of article: “Warren Buffett’s Failures: 15 investing mistakes he regrets” https://www.cnbc.com/2017/12/15/warren-buffetts-failures-15-investing-mistakes-he-regrets.html

5 Letter to Shareholders by Jeff Bezos, Chairman and CEO of Amazon.com. Reprint of 1997 Annual Report on page 4 of 2016 Annual Report. https://www.annualreports.com/HostedData/AnnualReportArchive/a/NASDAQ_AMZN_2016.pdf

6 CNBC Excerpts: Billionaire Investor Warren Buffett Speaks with CNBC’S Becky Quick on “Squawk Box” Today https://edit.nbcumv.com/news/cnbc-passages extremely rich person financial backer warren-buffett-talks

cnbc%E2%80%99s-becky-fast cackle box-today

7 Letter to Shareholders by Jeff Bezos, Chairman and CEO of Amazon.com. Reproduce of 1997 Annual Report on page 4 of 2016 Annual Report. https://www.annualreports.com/HostedData/AnnualReportArchive/a/NASDAQ_AMZN_2016.pdf

13. What is a Stock?

1 Warren Buffett’s investor letter in the 2017 Berkshire Hathaway Annual Report

14. Find Your Edge

1 Forbes Magazine: “Understanding Circle of Competence and Knowing the Edge of Your Competency” https://www.forbes.com/locales/gurufocus/2015/01/02/getting circle-of-ability and-knowing-the-edge-of-your-capability/#430dcd1645a7

2 Forbes Magazine Jan 2, 2015 https://www.forbes.com/destinations/gurufocus/2015/01/02/getting circle-of-skill and-knowing-the-edge-of-your-ability/#5125e66145a7

15. Buffett on Edge

1 Becoming Warren Buffett (2017) TV-PG | 1h 30min | Documentary | 30 January 2017 (USA) Director Peter W. Kunhardt and Writer Chris Chuang

16. A Reliable System

1 Billionaire peers Gates and Druckenmiller warned Buffett he'd be wrong on IBM - Source: Yahoo! News https://www.yahoo.com/news/very rich person peers-doors druckenmiller-cautioned 140646560.html

18. How to Read a 10-K

1 Proxy Statement – Source: Investopedia https://www.investopedia.com/terms/p/proxystatement.asp

2 Proxy explanation - Source: Wikipedia https://en.wikipedia.org/wiki/Proxy_statement

3 Form 10-K - Source: Wikipedia https://en.wikipedia.org/wiki/Form_10-K

4 What is a 10-K? Source: Investopedia https://www.investopedia.com/terms/1/10-k.asp 5

Marc Benioff – Source: Wikipedia https://en.wikipedia.org/wiki/Marc_Benioff

6 Salesforce Information - Source: Morningstar.com Investment Research Center - Dan Romanoff, Equity Analyst

7 How to Read a 10-K - Source: sec.gov https://www.sec.gov/quick responses/answersreada10khtm.html

8 Source: Investopedia – Noncurrent liability https://www.investopedia.com/terms/n/noncurrent-liabilities.asp

9 In Tennessee Williams' 1947 Pulitzer Prize-winning play "A Streetcar Named Desire," the fictitious person Blanche DuBois says, "Whoever you are, I have generally relied upon the graciousness of outsiders," she implies that she hopes to be treated with deference and honor since she is a Southern, privileged White lady. Notwithstanding, the statement additionally shows that she has disassociated from the real world. Source: Wikipedia https://en.wikipedia.org/wiki/Blanche_DuBois#References

10 Closing offer value as of December 15, 2020.

11 Fiscal Year 2019 Financial Highlights - Source: Adobe.com

12 Is Salesforce Paying Too Much for Slack? By Matthew Frankel, Source: The Motley Fool https://www.fool.com/contributing/2020/12/15/is-salesforce-paying-a lot for-slack/

13 Amazon CEO Jeff Bezos and sibling Mark give an interesting meeting about growing up and little-known techniques. https://youtu.be/Hq89wYzOjfs

14 Eric Yuan discussing Zoom. Source: YouTube video https://youtu.be/MTCq9bjAPi4

15 In 2019 I distributed "No Bullsh*t Investing," and section 7 zeroed in on loads of little organizations. I zeroed in on Twilio, mongoDB, and Zoom. Of those three, Zoom was my number one - however my math proposed that the stock was too costly to even think about purchasing at the time.

19. Why Invest with Robinhood?

1 Robinhood is the principal free stock exchanging application I experienced. It isn't the main stock application, and not really awesome. Apparently, be that as it may, they were the first application to furnish clients with "commission free" exchanging, and in this manner they began an upset in the retail financier industry. Robinhood - Source: Wikipedia https://en.wikipedia.org/wiki/Robinhood_(company)

2 Robinhood Revenue and Usage Statistics – Source: Business of Apps https://www.businessofapps.com/information/robinhood-insights/

3 Robinhood - Source: Wikipedia https://en.wikipedia.org/wiki/Robinhood_(company)

4 Robinhood Revenue and Usage Statistics – Source: Business of Apps

https://www.businessofapps.com/information/robinhood-measurements/

5 Edwin Schloss, speaking of Ben Graham in YouTube video, "Legacy of Benjamin Graham" Source: YouTube https://youtu.be/m1WLoNEqkV4

6 "What is UX design" by Caroline White, Source: Career Foundry https://careerfoundry.com/en/blog/ux-plan/what-does-a-ux-originator really do/

7 UX creators will quite often fill in as a feature of a more extensive item group, and overcome any barrier between the client, the advancement group, and business pioneers. As a UX originator, it's your work as a matter of first importance to advocate for the end client or customer."What does a UX planner do?" via Caroline White, Source: Career Foundry https://careerfoundry.com/en/blog/ux-plan/what-does-a-ux-architect really do/#2-what-does-a-ux-fashioner do

20. Shade thrown on Robinhood

1 Robinhood consents to pay a $65 million fine for beguiling clients - Source: CNN Business Robinhood consents to pay a $65 million fine for misdirecting clients

2 Robinhood Financial fined $65 million by SEC for deluding clients. Source: CBS News https://www.cbsnews.com/news/robinhood-sec-fine-65-million/

3 Robinhood Financial fined $65 million by SEC for deceiving clients. Source: CBS News https://www.cbsnews.com/news/robinhood-sec-fine-65-million/

4 Robinhood consents to pay a $65 million fine for deluding clients - Source: CNN Business Robinhood consents to pay a $65 million fine for misdirecting clients

5 Robinhood Financial fined $65 million by SEC for deceiving clients. – Source: CBS News https://www.cbsnews.com/news/robinhood-sec-fine-65-million/

6 Robinhood Is Not Gamifying Markets, It's Democratizing Them, by Adam Brown – Source – Bloomberg Opinion https://www.bloomberg.com/assessment/articles/2020-12-17/robinhood-is-democratizing-markets-not-production them-a-game

7 Robinhood Is Not Gamifying Markets, It's Democratizing Them, by Adam Brown – Source – Bloomberg Opinion https://www.bloomberg.com/opinion/articles/2020-12-17/robinhood-is-democratizing-markets-not-making-them-a-game

8 Robinhood Financial LLC Complaint – Source: Massachusetts SEC https://www.sec.state.ma.us/sct/current/sctrobinhood/MSD-Robinhood-Financial-LLC-Complaint-E- 2020-0047.pdf

9 SEC fines Robinhood $65 million for misleading users – Source: engadget https://www.engadget.com/robinhood-extortion examination 65-million-dollar-fine-172019441.html

10 Here's how Robinhood is raking in record cash on customer trades — despite making it free – Source: CNBC https://www.cnbc.com/2020/08/13/how-robinhood-makes-money-on-customer-trades-despite-making-it-free.html

11 SEC charges Robinhood with misleading customers about how it makes money – Source: CNBC https://www.cnbc.com/2020/12/17/sec-charges-robinhood-with-misleading-customers-about-how-it-makes-money.html

12 Massachusetts Securities Division complaint vs. Robinhood - Source: sec.state.ma https://www.sec.state.ma.us/sct/current/sctrobinhood/MSD-Robinhood-Financial-LLC-Complaint-E-2020-0047.pdf

13 Robinhood Is Not Gamifying Markets: It's Democratizing Them – Adam Brown – Source: Bloomberg Opinion https://www.bloomberg.com/opinion/articles/2020-12-17/robinhood-is-democratizing-markets-not-making-them-a-game

23. Robinhood Dreams

1 Zoomer is an epithet alluding to individuals from Generation Z, those brought into the world in the last part of the 90s and mid 2000s. Its utilization is especially well known as a differentiation to person born after WW2 or boomer, however before Gen Z was laid out, zoomer was utilized to allude to particularly dynamic children of post war America. "Words We're Watching: 'Zoomer'" Source: Merriam Webster https://www.merriam-webster.com/words-at-play/words-were-watching-zoomer-gen-z

2 Beginner's psyche is an idea from the Zen Buddhism signifying "amateur's brain." The Buddhist term "Shoshin" refers to having an attitude of openness, eagerness, and lack of preconceptions when studying a subject, even when studying at an advanced level, just as a beginner would. The term is especially used in the study of Zen Buddhism and Japanese martial arts.[1].

3 Benjamin Graham was the creator of "The Intelligent Investor" and was Warren Buffett's teacher at Columbia University and guide. Buffett worked for Graham's organization, "Graham-Newman Corporation" after graduating from Columbia. https://www.investopedia.com/articles/07/ben_graham.asp

4 Edwin Schloss — Source: YouTube: Legacy of Benjamin Graham https://youtu.be/m1WLoNEqkV4

5 Robinhood Revenue and Usage Statistics (2020) – Source: Business of Apps https://www.businessofapps.com/information/robinhood-measurements/

6 Source: CoStar Group Announces Acquisition of Houses.com URL

https://www.businesswire.com/news/home/20201218005096/en/CoStar-Group-Announces-Acquisition-of-Houses.com-URL

7 Pick-and-Shovel Play – Source: Investopedia https://www.investopedia.com/terms/p/pick-and- shovel-play.asp

24. Ideas from Great Investors

1 A genuine statement from this book's manager, Eric Wyman. He squeezes me to give point of view and connect with my crowd why they ought to invest.

2 Warren Buffett once said, "I love running Berkshire, and in the event that appreciating life advances life span, Methuselah's record is in risk." Methuselah passed on at 969 years old, having experienced the longest of all figures referenced in the Bible. Source: Wikipedia https://en.wikipedia.org/wiki/Methuselah

3 Warren Buffet Quotes — Source: Wikipedia https://en.wikipedia.org/wiki/Warren_Buffett

4 "Just a Regular Billionaire" - Source: Youtube https://www.youtube.com/watch?v=P9YTKb5PgR0

5 Carol Loomis is a previous Fortune Magazine writer, writer, and a long-term companion of Warren Buffett. Source: Wikipedia https://en.wikipedia.org/wiki/Carol_Loomis

6 2020 Berkshire Hathaway Annual Meeting transcript. Source: Rev https://www.rev.com/blog/transcripts/warren-buffett-berkshire-hathaway-annual-meeting-transcript-2020

25. The Magic Box

1 Scott Galloway, "The Algebra of Happiness" Source: Youtube https://www.youtube.com/watch?v=qMW6xgPgY4s

2 Charlie Munger asset page - Source: Valuewalk https://www.valuewalk.com/charlie-munger-page/

3 Beat the Bush is a YouTube channel, and assuming you look for it there are no spaces between words. It is recorded as BeatTheBush. As of December 18, 2020 the channel had 337,000 subscribers.

26. Focus is Key

1 The Snowball: Warren Buffett and the Business of Life by Alice Schroeder 2009 Bantam

2 "Poor Charlie's Almanac - The Wit and Wisdom of Charles T. Munger, altered by Peter D. Kaufman - The Donning Company, Publisher

3 Warren Buffett Gives Advice to Girl Scouts at Dairy Queen - Youtube Video https://www.youtube.com/watch?v=4BJfEI3o0rY

27. A Good Checklist

1 The Checklist Manifesto: How to Get Things Right - Picador - 2011

2 When do pilots use checklists? http://enroute.aircanada.com/en/articles/when-do-pilots-use-checklists

28. Eye on Eternity

1 Smart Stocks: The Insightful Book for Intelligent Investors, 2019, Kindle Direct Printing

2 Marshall Weinberg said he has experience with theory, and the way that Ben Graham had some awareness of Spinoza and cited him right away sold him on Graham. Source: YouTube — "Legacy of Ben Graham" https://youtu.be/m1WLoNEqkV4

29. We're All Indexers

1 Number of US Publicly Traded Companies falls by 50% — Source: https://www.valuewalk.com/2018/07/number-of-us-public-organizations fall-50/

30. My Investing Mistakes

1 1 While this was a reckless choice, it was a carefully weighed out course of action. I kept my interests in two other shared reserves I referenced before. I likewise had some money in the bank. I wasn't putting my whole wagered on only one twist of the roulette wheel, yet I made an adequately large venture that the mix-up is vital. I discovered that I didn't know anywhere near enough about one or the other organization to take such a striking action. I thought I knew a ton since I read their yearly reports, however I ought to have put resources into organizations I saw better, or just stayed with the file fund.

2 Source of Leucadia National chronicled stock returns: Morningstar Resource Center. For those searching for historical information about Leucadia National, please note that the company changed its name to Jefferies Financial Group on May 23, 2018. Source: Businesswire.

3 What are the next-generation blood substitutes? Source: Medscape https://www.medscape.com/replies/207801-168636/what-are-the-cutting edge blood-substitutes

4 As of Jul 07, 2020 | Source: Morningstar

5 Wall Street Chiefs' Pay Doesn't Sync With Returns — Source: Wall Street Journal

https://www.wsj.com/articles/divider road bosses pay-doesnt-sync-with-returns-11562580018

6 Leucadia National Corporation (LUK) was renamed Jefferies Financial Group (JEF) in 2018. For those investigating Leucadia National Corporation, that organization's records have been converged with those of Jefferies Financial Group. The 10-year returns for Leucadia National Corporation and White Mountain Insurance Group gave were as of July 23, 2018

7 I might want to call attention to those perusers who are keen on monetary subtleties that in spite of the fact that I claimed both Leucadia and White Mountains stock, the 10-year time span finishing July 23, 2018 isn't my precise holding period. My acknowledged returns are comparative, nonetheless: the two stocks found the middle value of a compound normal return of 1% over the 10-year time frame, during which the S&P 500 returned around 10%.

8 While some nineteenth century tests recommended that the fundamental reason is valid assuming the warming is adequately steady, as per contemporary scholars the reason is bogus: a frog that is bit by bit warmed will leap out. Without a doubt, thermoregulation by changing area is an essentially important step by step process for surviving for frogs and different ectotherms. Source: Wikipedia, The Boiling Frog

9 Warren Buffett: Buying Berkshire Was $200 Billion Blunder - Source: CNBC https://www.cnbc.com/id/39710609

10 Warren Buffett on making mistakes: That makes it interesting – Source: CNBC https://www.cnbc.com/2019/04/29/warren-buffett-on-production botches that-makes-it-interesting.html

32. Three Useful Attributes

1 Source: Berkshire Hathaway Corporation 1990 Annual Report

2 Common Stocks and Uncommon Profits by Philip Fisher, Wiley, 1957

34. Zero-Based Thinking

1 Sunk cost - Source: Wikipedia https://en.wikipedia.org/wiki/Sunk_cost

2 Sunk cost fallacy – Source: https://www.behavioraleconomics.com/resources/mini-encyclopedia-of-be/sunk-cost-fallacy/

3 1 What is Zero-Based Thinking? http://whatis.techtarget.com/definition/zero-based-thinking-ZBT

4 Brian Tracy: Zero-Based Thinking - Source: Youtube https://www.youtube.com/watch?v=2s2at9o9yYg

35. A Calm Captain

1 Source: Chelsey Sullenberger Wikipedia: https://en.wikipedia.org/wiki/Chesley_Sullenberger

36. The Antifragile Investor

1 Antifragile: Things that Gain From Disorder by Nassim Nicholas Taleb. Arbitrary House, 2014.

2 For those readers who haven't spent copious amounts of time on the Wall Street Bets subreddit (an Internet message board) YOLO is an acronym for "You Only Live Once" and represents the practice of putting all of your money into an all or nothing bet in hopes of winning big. These huge wagers appear to end in disastrous misfortunes more frequently than stunning victories.

3 Burdian's butt - Source: Wikipedia https://en.wikipedia.org/wiki/Buridan%27s_ass

4 Two Years of Digital Transformation in Two Months – Satya Nadella – Source: Microsoft https://www.microsoft.com/en-us/microsoft-365/blog/2020/04/30/2-years-digital-transformation-2-months/

38. Thought into Action

1 "Why Buffett Still Isn't Sure If He'd Buy Amazon, Alphabet Stock Now" — Source: https://www.investors.com/news/berkshires-buffett-owns up to-additional tech-botches amazon-letter set/

2 Anchoring "is a mental predisposition which happens when we think about a specific worth of an obscure amount prior to assessing such amount. The worth we have thought of or that have been displayed to us previously, unequivocally decides the gauge we will make, which will continuously be generally near that past worth, which is known as the anchor." - Source: Facile Things https://facilethings.com/blog/en/mooring effect

3 "Thinking Fast and Slow" by Daniel Kahneman, 2011 Farrar, Straus and Giroux

4 Warren Buffett on CNBC's "Squawk Box" on Monday, May 1, 2017 https://www.cnbc.com/2017/05/06/warren-buffett-concedes he-committed a-error on-google.html

39. Decisive on Amazon

1 2 In the Amazon 2016 Letter to Shareholders, CEO Jeff Bezos examined the characteristics that separate an organization with the "Day 1" fire up mindset from those organizations that settle on choices gradually - what Bezos alludes to as "Day 2" organizations. Bezos said, "To keep the energy and dynamism of Day 1, you need to some way or another make superior grade, high-speed choices." I trust that to put reSources into organizations like Amazon one necessities to embrace a similar mentality to make top caliber, high-speed choices. In the event that you sit around idly always and never purchase stock, that could end up being a costly mistake. Source: 2106 Amazon Letter to Shareholders https://www.amazon.com/p/include/z6o9g6sysxur57t

2 A purchase limit request is a method for purchasing portions of stock at an assigned cost or lower. It guarantees you don't pay an excessive amount of when you purchase shares. A purchase limit request must be executed at the breaking point cost or lower. For instance, if you need to purchase a portion of stock at $33 per offer and it's as of now selling at $40 an offer, a purchase limit request will possibly execute in the event that the stock value tumbles to $33 an offer or less. It possibly guarantees that your request might execute assuming a pre-decided cost is reached. Limit orders "limit" the value you will pay while trading stock, however they don't ensure your request will be filled. A breaking point request isn't ensured to execute. For more data on limit orders, visit the SEC site. Source: https://www.sec.gov/quick responses/answerslimithtm.html

3 Retailers be warned: Amazon isn't worried about making money right now – Source: CNBC https://www.cnbc.com/2017/07/28/retailers-be-warned-amazon-isnt-worried-about-making-money- right-now.html

4 Retailers be warned: Amazon isn't worried about making money right now – Source: CNBC https://www.cnbc.com/2017/07/28/retailers-be-warned-amazon-isnt-worried-about-making-money- right-now.html

5 Amazon's shares fall after big earnings miss. Source: CNBC https://www.cnbc.com/2017/07/27/amazon-income q2-2017.html

6 Retailers be warned: Amazon isn't worried about making money right now – Source: CNBC https://www.cnbc.com/2017/07/28/retailers-be-warned-amazon-isnt-worried-about-making-money- right-now.html

7 Poor Charlie's Almanac: The Wit and Wisdom of Charles T. Munger

www.ingramcontent.com/pod-product-compliance
Lightning Source LLC
LaVergne TN
LVHW091311150826
845673LV00006B/1610
9798818302973